Genocide

A Normative Account

In this study, Larry May examines the normative and conceptual problems concerning the crime of genocide. Genocide arises out of the worst of horrors. Legally, however, the unique character of genocide is reduced to a technical requirement, that the perpetrator's act manifest an intention to destroy a protected group. From this definition, many puzzles arise. How are groups to be identified and why are only four groups subject to genocide? What is the harm of destroying a group, and why is this harm thought to be independent of killing many people? How can a person in the dock, as an individual, be responsible for a collective crime like genocide? How should we understand the specific crimes associated with genocide, especially instigation, incitement, and complicity? Are criminal trials in the aftermath of genocide the best strategy for achieving reconciliation and the return to the rule of law? Paying special attention to the recent case law concerning the Rwanda genocide, May offers the first philosophical exploration of the crime of genocide in international criminal law.

Larry May is W. Alton Jones Professor of Philosophy and Professor of Law at Vanderbilt University, as well as Professorial Fellow at the Centre for Applied Philosophy and Public Ethics at Charles Sturt and Australian National Universities. He is the author of nine books, most recently, *Crimes Against Humanity: A Normative Account*, *War Crimes and Just War*, and *Aggression and Crimes Against Peace*, which have won six awards in philosophy, law, and international relations.

Genocide

A Normative Account

LARRY MAY
Vanderbilt University

CAMBRIDGE
UNIVERSITY PRESS

CAMBRIDGE UNIVERSITY PRESS
Cambridge, New York, Melbourne, Madrid, Cape Town, Singapore,
São Paulo, Delhi, Dubai, Tokyo

Cambridge University Press
32 Avenue of the Americas, New York, NY 10013-2473, USA

www.cambridge.org
Information on this title: www.cambridge.org/9780521122962

© Larry May 2010

First published 2010

Printed in the United States of America

A catalog record for this publication is available from the British Library.

Library of Congress Cataloging in Publication data

ISBN 978-0-521-19465-5 Hardback
ISBN 978-0-521-12296-2 Paperback

Contents

Contents vii

PART D. RESPONSIBILITY FOR GENOCIDE

Acknowledgments

This volume completes my four-volume "trilogy" on normative and conceptual issues concerning the main substantive crimes that fall under the International Criminal Court's jurisdiction. I began this project while in law school, where I had returned 25 years after first applying to study law (instead I went into philosophy). The work has won awards in political philosophy, international law, and international relations. I have worked on the project for a dozen years now and am happy to bring it to an end. I will next turn my attention to a monograph on procedural justice.

I benefited from the strong support of several institutions in the writing of this book on genocide. A first draft of the book was completed while I was at the Centre for Applied Philosophy and Public Ethics (CAPPE) in Canberra. I am very grateful for the time I had for research, largely provided by generous funding from Charles Sturt University, and enormous stimulation from my colleagues in CAPPE as well as those at the Australian National University's program in Social and Political Theory and at the ANU Law School. In addition, I would like to thank the Philosophy Department at Washington University, which has continued to support my research efforts over the years. In the final stages of the production of this book, I also benefited from support from my new home institution, Vanderbilt University.

I received sage advice from many people over the two years that I have worked on this book. As always, Marilyn Friedman gave of her valuable time and provided the kind of detailed feedback, especially on early drafts, that one cannot but hope for. She commented on the penultimate draft of the manuscript, as did Kit Wellman and Mark Drumbl. In all three cases, my debt is enormous – for they have spared me from making blunders and infelicities of style on countless occasions. I also received unusually frank and helpful feedback from several anonymous reviewers at Cambridge University Press.

Nearly 10 years have passed since William Schabas's wonderful book *Genocide and International Law*. I have learned much from Schabas and from the recent case law on genocide, especially from the International Criminal Tribunal for Rwanda. Indeed, this book came to life as a series of reflections on Schabas's book. I have also learned from the enormous literature on genocide in political philosophy and social psychology, even as I take issue with many of the ideas in these literatures. And most importantly, I have learned from the emerging subtle and sensitive court opinions by the ad hoc tribunals in international criminal law. If it were not for this literature, I could not have written this book.

Various parts of this book are being published as free-standing essays. Chapter 3 was recently published as a chapter of an edited collection, *International Criminal Law and Philosophy*, which Zach Hoskins and I edited for Cambridge University Press's new series in conjunction with the American Society of International Law. A very early version of Chapter 4 appeared in the 2005 issue of the journal *International Legal Theory*, edited by Mortimer Sellers. Chapter 7 will be translated into German and published in a volume edited by Veronique Zanetti for Surkamp Verlag. Chapter 9 will be published in a special issue of the journal *Res Publica*, edited by Jesper Ryberg. An early version of Chapter 13 was published for conference participants as a plenary address at the 2007 International Conference on Philosophy of Law and Social Philosophy (the IVR) in Kraków.

I presented versions of these various chapters at conferences or colloquia in Bielefeld, Canberra, Charleston, the Hague, Kraków, Nashville, Normal, Oslo, Oxford, Philadelphia, Salt Lake City, San Francisco, St. Louis, Sydney, Wagga Wagga, and Washington, DC. I am grateful to the many people at these events who have commented on the individual chapters in this book. I would especially like to thank Christian Barry, Margaret Battin, James Bohman, John Braithwaite, Geoffrey Brennan, Sam Buell, Tom Campbell, Hilary Charlesworth, Phil Clark, Steve Clarke, Antony Duff, Gerald Eisenberg, Leslie Francis, Matthew Gill, Bob Goodin, Virginia Held, Zach Hoskins, Jack Knight, Bruce Landesman, John Lango, Burton Leiser, Ian McMullen, Seumas Miller, Richard Nunan, Mary Ellen O'Connell, Rianna Oelofsen, Max Penske, Thomas Pogge, Andrew Rehfeld, Neil Richards, David Rodin, Brad Roth, Kim Rubenstein, Leila Sadat, David Schweikart, Michael Selgelid, Helen Stacy, Daniel Starr, and Veronique Zanetti.

As always, Cambridge University Press has been extraordinarily supportive of my work, especially Beatrice Rehl, who has been unfailingly helpful as she has shepherded my set of manuscripts into beautifully produced books. I am also grateful to Zach Hoskins for once again supplying a high-quality index.

1

Introduction

Problems of Genocide

Genocide is defined in international law as the intent to destroy one of four protected groups: racial, national, ethnic, or religious. Genocide is considered morally unique as a wrong, and as the most serious of all international crimes. I will critically assess the conceptual and normative underpinnings of this "crime of crimes." My view is that genocide should not be seen as morally unique and significantly worse legally than other serious international crimes. As genocide's status changes, its scope should also be expanded, most especially to allow for cultural genocide and ethnic cleansing to be counted as crimes of genocide. And the list of protected groups should be expanded from the current group to include gender and even political groups. I will defend such a reconceptualization of genocide in international law, and will do so by focusing on actual legal cases of genocide, with special attention to the Rwandan genocide. But even if my modest changes are not accepted, my hope is that this volume will stir debate about how best to think of the crime of genocide. In one of my previous books, *Crimes Against Humanity: A Normative Account*,[1] I included a chapter on genocide. In the current volume I provide the full defense of the view that I had sketched, and I also explain why I think in the end that genocide should be thought of not as the crime of crimes but as one of, if not the most important, crimes against humanity.

This is the fourth volume of my long-term project on the normative, especially moral, foundations of international criminal law. The project was first conceived as a paper-length treatment of the subject, which then grew to a volume-length treatment, and then to a trilogy-length

---

[1] Larry May, *Crimes Against Humanity: A Normative Account*, New York: Cambridge University Press, 2005, ch. 9.

treatment. With the completion of the current volume, I have now provided a book-length treatment of the normative and conceptual issues
that arise in each of the four crimes under the jurisdiction of the main
court to prosecute international crimes today. The first three volumes
concern crimes that were prosecuted in 1946 at Nuremberg: crimes
against humanity, war crimes, and crimes against peace. In addition to
the three Nuremberg crimes, the International Criminal Court's 1998
Rome Statute also lists a fourth crime under its jurisdiction, namely,
genocide, the subject of the current volume.[2]

There has been much written about genocide over the last 60 years
since the 1948 Genocide Convention brought the idea to the attention
of the world community. I cannot possibly do justice to this extensive
literature, but will instead comment on some of what I regard to be
the most important contributions of this literature for the conceptual
and normative issues I identify. My aim is for this genocide volume to
be multidisciplinary, drawing from sources in philosophy, law, political science, sociology, and psychology. But I will probably not satisfy
anyone working in any one of these areas. Instead, my hope is to provide a fresh perspective on the crime of genocide, especially on how
best to think of crimes that involve groups as perpetrators and as
victims.

In many ways, genocide in international law presents some of the
most significant philosophical challenges of all of the areas of international criminal law. This is mainly due to the fact that genocide elicits
some of the most passionate responses from people, and yet legally
what is supposed to make genocide unique is a technical requirement,
that the perpetrator's act manifest an intent to destroy a protected
group. This fact calls into question decidedly nonemotional topics
such as the ontological status and normative value of groups, topics
that philosophers have worried about since at least the late Medieval
period. In addition, even more than other international crimes,
genocide raises significant questions of how to think about individual
culpability because the crime of genocide is both in act and in intent
a collective crime.

Legally, genocide concerns the intent to destroy a group. Groups
are increasingly the focus of international law, especially international

---

[2] The other books that I have published in this area include *Crimes Against Humanity; War
Crimes and Just War*, New York: Cambridge University Press, 2007; and *Aggression and
Crimes Against Peace*, New York: Cambridge University Press, 2008.

criminal law. Yet no one has tried to craft a book-length treatment of the status and importance of groups in international law. One legal scholar devotes one long chapter of his seminal book to this topic.[3] Another author provides important documentation of the major genocides of the twentieth century,[4] but is not focused on the conceptual questions that I wish to answer. Other authors have done important work on conceptual issues in genocide, although not focused on international law.[5]

In this introductory chapter, I will first provide a discussion of the general idea of genocide, focusing on some of the differences between the specialized way that genocide is understood in international law and contrasting it with the way that genocide is often understood in nonlegal contexts, especially contexts of moral appraisal. Second, I will explain what is especially problematic about seeing genocide as primarily a crime that is perpetrated by groups against other groups. Third, I will discuss the various ways that genocide is of concern to the international community. Fourth, I will discuss why it is thought to be significant that individuals are prosecuted for international crimes such as genocide. Fifth, I will discuss in a preliminary way the special problems of intent that characterize the crime of genocide. Finally, I will end this chapter with a summary of the main arguments advanced in the book.

Throughout this introductory chapter, I will try to whet the reader's appetite for thinking critically about a subject that in many ways is the hardest for humans to conceive, that is, where a plan is hatched not only to kill or harm individuals because of their group membership, but also ultimately to destroy the group itself, to wipe it off the face of the map. More than 60 years after the Holocaust, this subject is still hard for people to fathom, and yet it continues to be of the utmost importance today, especially in various corners of Africa, but also relatively recently also in parts of Europe. Even in Australia and the United States, it is arguable that genocide occurred in the not too distant past concerning the way native peoples were treated.

---

[3] William Schabas, *Genocide in International Law,* New York: Cambridge University Press, 2000, 2nd edition 2009.
[4] Samantha Power, *A Problem from Hell,* New York: Harper and Row, 2002.
[5] Berel Lang, *Act and Idea in the Nazi Genocide,* Chicago: University of Chicago Press, 1990; Claudia Card, *The Atrocity Paradigm,* New York: Oxford University Press, 2002.

I. The Idea of Genocide

Raphael Lemkin coined the term "genocide" when he forced together a Greek term for people and a Latin term for killing.[6] In this way genocide was coined to mean the killing of a group. In international law, genocide has a specialized meaning that is not necessarily consonant with that of the public's understanding of genocide, because it includes acts that do not involve mass killing. Article II of the Convention on Genocide says genocide is:

> Any of the following acts committed with intent to destroy, in whole or in part, a national, ethnical, racial or religious group, as such:
> a) Killing members of the group;
> b) Causing serious bodily or mental harm to members of the group;
> c) Deliberately inflicting on the group conditions of life calculated to bring about its physical destruction in whole or in part;
> d) Imposing measures intended to prevent births within the group;
> e) Forcibly transferring children of the group to another group.[7]

Article III of the Convention on Genocide lists five acts punishable by the Convention: "(a) Genocide; (b) Conspiracy to commit genocide; (c) Direct and public incitement to commit genocide; (d) Attempt to commit genocide; (e) Complicity in genocide."[8] I will focus on the legal definition and elements of genocide throughout this book. By focusing on this specialized meaning of genocide I will occasionally say something about the broader idea of genocide, but this will be rare. This is because I think that it is a mistake to let our legal thinking be overly influenced by considerations that properly should be kept separate, at least in part, because they risk emotionalizing an issue that is best understood as involving the treatment of defendants who are on trial for very specific acts, not for more generalized horrors. Many good books have tackled the latter nonlegal topic of genocide, but few look at the legal issues in the appropriately dispassionate manner that the subject requires.

In the nonlegal context, genocide has come to be thought of as the epitome of "evil." And when one considers seemingly the paradigm case of genocide, the Holocaust, such an assessment is hard to dispute.

---

[6] Raphael Lemkin, *Axis Rule in Occupied Europe, Laws of Occupation, Analysis of Government, Proposals for Redress,* Washington, DC: Carnegie Endowment for World Peace, 1944.

[7] Convention on the Prevention and Punishment of Genocide, adopted December 9, 1948; entered into force January 12, 1951, 78 U.N.T.S. 277.

[8] Ibid., Article 6.

Indeed, some authors have argued that we should regard genocide as merely a plain fact[9] that should not be further investigated lest we risk that our explanations and conceptual inquiries will be mistakenly seen as forgiveness for the horror of what genocide is.[10] I do not think that explanation or understanding of the horror of genocide leads to forgiveness or exoneration of the perpetrators. But I am aware that the dispassionate writing style I will adopt might risk insulting those who are the victims, or the family members of the victims, of genocide. So let me begin this book with a heartfelt acknowledgment that we should always keep in mind that the crime of genocide begins with a perpetration of terrible acts. To give the phenomenon its due, I hereby quote from the preliminary accounts of the Rwandan genocide, the first major international trial for genocide to occur since the Holocaust, and the main example that I will refer to in this book.

In the Akayesu case, the decision of the trial chamber of the International Criminal Tribunal for Rwanda recites some salient facts:

> Akayesu, in his capacity as bourgmestre was responsible for maintaining law and public order in the commune of Taba and that he had effective authority over the communal police. ... It has also been proven that a very large number of Tutsis were killed in Taba between 7 April and the end of June 1994, while Akayesu was bourgmestre of the Commune. ... [He] was present during the acts of violence and killings and sometimes even gave orders himself for bodily or mental harm to be caused to certain Tutsi, and endorsed and even ordered the killing of several Tutsi.

> Between 7 April and the end of June 1994, numerous Tutsi who sought refuge at the Taba Bureau communal were frequently beaten by members of the Interahamwe on or near the premises of the Bureau communal. Some of them were killed. Numerous Tutsi women were forced to endure acts of sexual violence, mutilations and rape, often repeatedly, often publicly, and often by more than one assailant. Tutsi women were systematically raped, as one female victim testified to by saying that "each time that you met assailants, they raped you." Numerous incidents of such rape and sexual violence against Tutsi women occurred inside or near the Bureau communal. It has been proven that some communal policemen armed with guns and the accused himself were present while some of these rapes and sexual violence were being committed. Furthermore it is proven that on

---

9 See Warren K. Thompson, "Ethics, Evil, and the Final Solution," in *Echoes from the Holocaust,* edited by Alan Rosenberg and Gerald E. Myers, Philadelphia: Temple University Press, 1988, pp. 181–97.
10 See Arthur G. Miller, Amy M. Buddie, and Jeffrey Kretschmar, "Explaining the Holocaust: Does Social Psychology Exonerate the Perpetrators?" in *Understanding Genocide,* edited by Leonard S. Newman and Ralph Erber, New York: Oxford University Press, 2002, pp. 301–24.

several occasions, by his presence, his attitude, and his utterances, Akayesu encouraged such acts, one particular witness testifying that Akayesu addressed the Interahamwe who were committing the rapes and said that "never ask me again what a Tutsi woman tastes like." In the opinion of the Chamber, this constitutes tacit encouragement to the rapes that were committed.[11]

Although the Trial Chamber's description of the role that Akayesu played in the Rwandan genocide is not emotion laden, it is nonetheless highly effective at conveying the terror involved and in indicating how Akayesu's individual acts connect to the crime of genocide for which he was ultimately found guilty.

Accounts such as the one just conveyed will probably still not satisfy some readers who look only to the victims for their own story of what transpired, and who look also only to the victims to decide what should be done to the perpetrators. Such an approach may seem uncontroversial when dealing with the moral judgment of the perpetrators. But when dealing with legal judgments, unless one supports a "show trial," the judgment must include both the victim's story and the alleged perpetrator's story, all filtered through the lens of an impartial adjudicator. In this way the idea of genocide comes out most clearly, as was true, in my view, of the description above of the way that Akayesu's acts linked him to the Rwandan genocide and supported the charge that he was not only morally responsible for what he did but also legally guilty of the crime of genocide. As we next see, constructing a description of what an individual did and connecting it to the larger collective crime is only the first of several conceptual and normative problems that arise in genocide cases.

II. The Place of "Groups" in the Crime of Genocide

Genocide has popularly come to be seen as the "crime of crimes," largely because of the scope of the harms. But keeping to the legal definition of genocide, it is unclear why it should matter that the acts of killing or harming were directed at the destruction of a group. If genocide is the crime of crimes because genocide is alone in requiring that it be proved that there was an intention to destroy a group, then there must be something especially wrong about aiming at the destruction of a group that

---

[11] *Prosecutor v. Jean-Paul Akayesu*, International Criminal Tribunal for Rwanda, case no. ICTR-96-4-T, Trial Chamber Judgment, 2 September 1998, paras. 704–7.

makes otherwise wrongful acts of killing, torturing, and raping even worse. Conceptually, destroying a group must be different from merely killing the group's members. And normatively, this difference must be significant if genocide is to be the crime of crimes.

On the simplest conceptual level, one could say that individual human persons are the constituents of a group. The immediate question follows: Is there any other constituent of a group, or is a group nothing but its individual human persons as members? Even the phrase "as members" should make us wonder whether a group is nothing but individual human persons. If for no other reason, we should wonder whether every time individual human persons gather together we necessarily also have a group. Are the five people who read this paragraph the "members of" a group? And does the group matter more than the individuals who compose it? Or is there more to a group than merely its members only concerning certain types of groups?

In an earlier work, I argued that groups "exist" when a collection of persons displays either the capacity for joint action or common interest.[12] I then gave a wide reading of common interest to include the capacity to be harmed as a group. In the current book, I wish to explore this topic in much greater depth than I did before. Along the way, my earlier view will have to be revised in various ways, although the core idea just expressed will remain mostly the same. I will confront the topic of groups in the context of one of the newest areas of law, international criminal law, which concerns the prosecution of individuals for what are primarily collective crimes.

The general view I defend in subsequent chapters is that groups do not have value in themselves; the harm to groups is in terms of how individuals are affected. The destruction of a group, where most of the members are also killed, is a truly terrible crime. But this seems to be primarily because of the widespread killing of individuals involved. The destruction of a group, where individuals are not killed, is harder to see as a great crime. Groups are an important resource for sustaining relationships and forming identity of individuals. When a group is destroyed something is lost for the individuals who are its members. In this book I will try to make sense of the harm of genocide by considering how the destruction of groups might harm individual humans who are members. Genocide may not be the worst of crimes, but it is still a

[12] See Larry May, *The Morality of Groups*, Notre Dame, IN: University of Notre Dame Press, 1987.

very serious crime that should be prosecuted in international criminal tribunals, as it was (under a different name) at Nuremberg, as it is in the ad hoc Rwanda tribunal, and as it will be in the International Criminal Court. A theoretical inquiry into the nature of harm to groups will be the centerpiece of this book.

The formulation of genocide in the Genocide Convention provides many puzzles, both conceptual and normative, that will be the focus of this volume. How are groups to be identified, and why are only four groups subject to genocide? What is the harm of destroying a social group, and why is this harm thought to be independent of killing lots of people? What should be the act and intent elements of a mass crime like genocide, and how can an individual person in the dock satisfy these elements and hence, as an individual, be responsible for a collective crime like genocide? How should we understand the specific crimes associated with genocide, especially instigation, incitement, and complicity? And is it the case that holding criminal trials in the aftermath of genocide, instead of truth and reconciliation commissions, is indeed the best strategy for achieving reconciliation and the return to the rule of law?

In discussing each of the above-mentioned issues, in this book I will focus on the case of the Rwandan genocide. I do this because there are especially intriguing conceptual and normative questions here. Concerning the identification of social groups, the Tutsis who were the victims of the genocide did not have their own language or culture, and although people in the villages were by and large able to distinguish Tutsis from Hutus, across the country it required government-issued identity cards to distinguish the two dominant groups from one another. Concerning the harm of genocide, it is undeniable that nearly 1 million people were killed, and the vast majority were Tutsis. Given that the groups in Rwanda had become so intermingled in Rwandan society, what precisely was the harm of targeting Tutsis to the point where the continued existence of Tutsis was threatened?

Concerning the elements of genocide, it is interesting that so many world leaders at the time were reluctant to say that the massacres in Rwanda constituted genocide. Aside from the politics of the matter, there was a serious question of whether there could be a genocide that so failed to resemble that of the seemingly paradigmatic genocide, the Holocaust. In particular, can there be genocide without a government having established a central plan for the elimination of a particular ethnic group? As I argue in Chapter 11, such a central plan seems to have been lacking in Rwanda. Concerning the forms of culpability in the Rwandan genocide, if there was no master plan, should those who incited the genocide be considered the ones who are principally responsible? And how should complicity, a form of secondary responsibility, be understood when it is relatively unclear who the principal agents of the genocide were? Finally, is there reason to think that criminal trials are a better way to achieve reconciliation and security in Rwanda than truth and reconciliation commissions? In this respect, I will be especially concerned with *gacaca*, a unique form of trial occurring across Rwanda.

III. Genocide and International Harm

Although it is not normally recognized, genocide is a security issue, not merely a human rights issue. And although I will address genocide, as is almost always done today, primarily as a human rights issue, perhaps it is worth saying just a few words about the security aspect of genocide before trying to explain why it might be the most important of human rights concerns. The right not to be persecuted or to be subject to genocide is one of the main bastions against infringements on the security of individuals and groups. When NATO decided to send troops into Kosovo it was because of a concern that the ethnic cleansing campaign in the Balkans had already risked spreading into a wider European problem. The current genocide in Sudan, if it is genocide, is not merely a horrific humanitarian crisis for the people who are being starved to death, it is also a major factor destabilizing the region. Genocide can be understood in terms of its effect on security: personal, collective, and national. For this reason, it could be argued that genocide should be taken seriously by the international society for self-interested, not merely for humanitarian, reasons.

In the Universal Declaration of Human Rights, Article 7 declares that "All are equal before the law and are entitled without any discrimination to equal protection of the law." Article 14 declares that "Everyone has the right to seek and enjoy in other countries asylum from persecution." It is clear that genocide harms the international community in that it destabilizes security for many of those who are affected, individuals and States alike. There is the significant risk that this international crime will spread across borders. This can happen either when the genocide itself extends to people who are its object, and who happen to live across the border from where the main genocide is occurring, or it can happen in an ancillary way when large numbers of refugees cross the border to seek asylum from the ravages of a genocidal campaign. Yet this kind of

harm is contingent, for there have been past genocides and certainly
there can be future genocides that do not cross borders or risk doing
so. The harm of genocide seems to be best understood not in this contingent way, if all genocide is to be condemned and condemned in the
strongest of terms.

But there is another way that genocide causes harm to the international community as well, namely, by adversely affecting all of humanity
or by adversely affecting the common identities of the people who are
members of the group. As in the case of other international crimes, and
perhaps even more so in the case of genocide, there is a sense in which
humanity is harmed by each occurrence of international crimes, and
especially in the case of all genocides. What exactly it is that adversely
affects humanity, or enough of humanity to be considered of supreme
importance, will require very careful conceptual and normative analysis.
Ultimately, I will reject this understanding of the harm of genocide.

Claudia Card has argued that the harm of genocide is best understood in terms of the loss of significant aspects of one's identity.[13] I do
not follow Card in thinking that this loss is equivalent to physical death,
but I agree that it is a highly significant loss nonetheless. Loss of significant aspects of one's identity can occur across a wide range of differences depending on how much the individual in question identified
with that aspect of his or her identity. My religion may have been quite
significant to me as a youth and now may have very little importance to
me as a middle-aged adult. On the other hand, my ethnic identity may
have mattered little to me as a youth but may come to have more importance in my life the older I become. The relativity of the importance of
identity means that its loss is not like death, or at least not for everyone
who experiences this loss.

In subsequent chapters I will argue that genocide primarily involves
a "status harm." Status harms are different from biological or even
psychological harms. When a group is destroyed, the members of the
group lose their group-based rights; indeed, vis-à-vis loss of membership they become rightless. And because groups are often the primary
repositories of rights-protections, when a group is destroyed the individual members of the group are significantly harmed. There is a sense in
which these individuals retain other rights, such as their human rights.
But when the group to which they belong is destroyed, the individuals

---

[13] Claudia Card, "Genocide and Social Death," *Hypatia*, vol. 18, no. 1, Winter 2003,
    63–79.

who are now deprived of group membership lose status even in terms of their human rights.

As will become clear in subsequent chapters, I will argue that the harm or wrong of genocide is not morally unique and not necessarily of greater importance than harms involved in certain crimes against humanity or other international crimes. But this by no means is to say that the harm or wrong of genocide is not very important. I will argue that the crime of genocide should indeed be seen as an international crime and that those responsible for genocide should be punished very severely. The near-obsession with genocide in the twentieth and twenty-first centuries, though, is not warranted, in my view. Instead, genocide should be reconceptualized to be an especially serious form of crimes against humanity, only somewhat different in importance than the crime of persecution that is also appropriately listed as a crime against humanity. As an especially important crime against humanity, genocide deserves very careful attention, and this book will give it that attention.

IV. Prosecuting International Crimes

International law has made a significant turn in recent years.[14] Rather than being primarily concerned with the relations of States, one significant branch of international law, namely, international criminal law, now concerns individuals. As with any such change, many questions and problems arise. I have written three volumes on international criminal law, where in each case I ask how we can justify holding individuals responsible for international crimes that are predominantly mass crimes that require coordination and many acts of individuals. I wish to devote this section to rehearsing some of the conclusions from those first three volumes.

I began this multivolume project with what many people believe to be the hardest case, namely, justifying the international prosecution of individuals for crimes against humanity. One of the problems here is that the acts in question, such as murder, rape, and torture, look like garden-variety crimes that domestic courts have traditionally handled. And because the requirement that these crimes be committed during war or armed conflict has been dropped as one of the elements of these

---

[14] For an excellent discussion of this issue see, Steven R. Ratner and Jason S. Abrams, *Accountability for Human Rights Atrocities in International Law*, Oxford: Oxford University Press, 1997.

crimes, they also can be committed wholly within the territory of, by, and against the nationals of, just one State. Not only are there individuals in the dock for those sorts of crime, but they have done things that normally would be prosecuted according to the exclusive prerogative of domestic, not international, criminal courts.

In international law, to get around this problem, crimes against humanity were defined as attacks constituted by otherwise garden-variety domestic crimes, directed against a population in a systematic and widespread manner. Yet here as many questions and problems are raised as are answered. Why are we entitled to put an individual in the international dock for the commission of a mass crime, a coordinated crime against an entire population group, where the individual's *actus reus* is not, and really cannot be, the act of mass violence? We are not helped by seeing the aim of being directed at a population group or the systematicity and widespreadness as elements to be proven, unless there is some clear way to link these elements to what the individual person did. There may be elements of the mass crime that do not have much relation to the *actus reus* or *mens rea* of the individual in the international dock, for instance, because the individual act cannot directly manifest widespreadness.

I argued that we need to take seriously the title of this crime, namely, "crimes against humanity." The crimes that are prosecuted in international courts under this label must be shown to be in some sense assaults against humanity, not merely against the domestic State. I proposed that it is group-based acts, that is, acts committed against individuals because of their membership in groups, that are most clearly harmful to humanity and that should be the type of crimes that are prosecuted under the crimes against humanity rubric in international criminal law. Group-based acts, or group-based crimes, pose a special problem for humanity in that the individuality of the victim is undermined by treating him or her merely as a group member rather than as a unique human being with dignity.[15]

The second volume of my project on international criminal law concerns war crimes. War crimes have been seen as international crimes for quite a long while, dating back at least to Hugo Grotius's magnum opus,

---

[15] I have received much criticism for this strategy, but it still seems to me to be the best on offer. See my most recent defense of this idea in international law, "Humanity, International Crime, and the Rights of Defendants," *Ethics & International Affairs*, vol. 20, no. 3, 2006, pp. 373–82.

De Jure Belli ac Pacis, in the early 17th century and probably much farther back than that. A war crime is the clearest example in the history
of ideas of individuals, as opposed to States, being held responsible for
violations of international law. And the acts for which they are accused
are often more straightforwardly individual, rather than mass acts, such
as torturing a prisoner of war, using a banned weapon, or shooting an
unarmed soldier bathing.[16]
War crimes do not take place outside of the context of war, and so
one of the most obvious questions is how to connect that context to the
individual criminal act of the accused. Although killing and torturing
are domestic crimes in most jurisdictions, for them to be war crimes,
as the name suggests, they must be committed during wartime. And if
we are going to discriminate between justified and unjustified intentional killing during war, we must explain why war matters for ascriptions
of responsibility. The context of war, or armed conflict (the preferred
term today), seems to be a license to kill enemy soldiers, and so why hold
individuals responsible for violations of the so-called rules of war that
often involve seemingly lesser crimes than intentional killing?
In my view, what matters is that soldiers have taken on certain duties
by becoming soldiers. Most importantly, soldiers have taken on steward-
ship or even fiduciary duties to those who have been rendered incapable
of defending themselves, or who lack the means to defend themselves,
in armed conflicts. The context of war changes the domain of responsibility for the individuals who participate in it. In U.S. criminal law it
is considered aggravated murder to incapacitate the victim before taking his or her life. Similarly, in international law, it is an egregious act
that calls for international prosecution when a soldier abuses or tortures
someone who has been incapacitated by virtue of being captured and .
held prisoner. Yet this is not a matter of justice strictly understood, but
rather a matter of mercy and equity, raised to the level of duties by the
context of war or other forms of armed conflict. Because such crimes
often cross State borders, or risk doing so, it is clearer why the international community has an interest in prosecuting them, as has been
understood for quite some time.

---

[16] This is not to deny that there has been significant disagreement about how war crimes
are prosecuted, especially in very recent years. Questions have been raised about why
we should think that killing an enemy soldier is not subject to criminal prosecution,
but torturing him is, and about why we should think that it doesn't matter that the
soldier who is killed is clearly on the side that is acting unjustly.

One of the hardest of the international criminal prosecutions to justify is that of the crime of aggression or the crime against peace. Indeed, today such crimes are not being prosecuted because the international community cannot agree on what constitutes aggression. In my view, the harder question concerns why individuals should ever be held responsible for initiating or sustaining war because individuals normally cannot do either of these things on their own. War is, by definition, a collective enterprise, that can be waged only by the coordinated actions of many individuals. To single out one or two individuals and hold them responsible for initiating or waging a war seems initially to be something of a category mistake. States, or perhaps large non-State actors, wage war, not individuals, and this is also true of initiating war.

If we are to hold individuals responsible for initiating or waging a war, it will have to be based on the roles that these individuals play, for instance, the role of president or commander-of-armed-forces. Yet these roles are assigned by others, and in a democratic government, the citizens of the state are often the ones who authorize their leaders to take them to war. So, it is unclear why those who have been authorized to act in the name of the people of a State should be held individually responsible for initiating war. Indeed, except for someone such as Hitler, who seems to have planned nearly every aspect of Nazi Germany's aggression against its neighbors, it does not seem justified even to prosecute the highest-level political or military leaders who rarely can, or do, act alone.

Yet, if such international prosecutions are justifiably to take place, it does seem that the context surrounding the initiation of war must be an element in the individual crime, and there must be a clear link between what the individual did and the larger collective act of war. We should focus primarily on what the leader did. To see what the individual did as a part of the waging of aggressive war, it is crucial to look at the role played by that individual. The individual should not be held responsible for the role, but for what was accomplished by the individual acting in that role. Indeed, we might want to try to discount the individual's responsibility by what is added by others who have established, or facilitated the performance of, that role. But an individual could indeed be prosecuted for what that individual did, without diminishing the idea that the crime is largely a collective crime, if what the individual did can be significantly linked to the aggressive war. I suggested that the way to make this linkage is by considering the circumstances of that individual's act.

Roger Clark gives an account of how to understand the relation between State and individual acts in various international crimes by reference to the idea of "contextual circumstances":

> a manifest pattern of similar conduct, in the case of genocide; a widespread or systematic attack against a civilian population, in the case of crimes against humanity; and an armed conflict, in the case of war crimes. Perhaps the act of aggression by a State, which . . . is an element of the crime of aggression by an individual, as currently defined in the negotiations, can be classified as a 'contextual circumstance.'[17]

I will follow Clark's suggestion of thinking that the act element must include the larger context of the act, and that the contexts will differ for each type of international crime.

In the case of genocide, it will be conceptually difficult to figure out what is meant by a "pattern of similar conduct." I have written about this type of circumstance in more detail elsewhere.[18] Suffice it here to say that in all four cases – crimes against humanity, war crimes, crimes against peace, and genocide – the act of the individual has to be linked to the mass criminal act by reference to these circumstances, a task not always easy to accomplish. Not the least of the problems is how to understand "similarity" when the types of conduct in genocide are seemingly so different.

V. Problems of Intent in the Rwandan Genocide: Some Examples

In this section I will briefly describe three cases from the Rwanda genocide to illustrate some of the conceptual and normative problems I have been discussing. First, consider the case of Ferdinand Nahimana, a founder, and Hasan Ngeze, the editor, of the newspaper *Kangura*. They were prosecuted for incitement to genocide on the basis of, among other things, publishing the cover of the November 1991 issue of *Kangura* that a trial chamber of the International Criminal Tribunal for Rwanda (ICTR) described as follows:

> In a black box on the left of the cover, the word "SPECIAL." ... Under the picture of President Kayibanda is the text: "How about re-launching

---

[17] Roger S. Clark, "The Crime of Aggression," in Carsten Stahn and Goran Sluiter, editors, *The Emerging Practice of the International Criminal Court*, Leiden: Martinus Nijhoff, 2009, p. 719.

[18] Larry May, "Act and Circumstance in the Crime of Aggression," *Journal of Political Philosophy*, vol. 15, no. 2, 2007, pp. 169–86.

the 1959 Bahutu revolution so that we can conquer the *Inyenzi-Ntutsi*." Just left of the picture of Kayibanda is a black box with vertical text reading: "WHAT WEAPONS SHALL WE USE TO CONQUER THE *INYENZI* ONCE AND FOR ALL?" and just left of this black box is a drawing of a machete. To the right of the picture of Kayibanda is the vertical text "We have found out why Nzirorera has a problem with the Tutsi."[19]

This case raised a number of issues: for example, how to interpret what was said, and what intent to infer from these words. It is, of course, very interesting that the means used in many of the subsequent killings in the Rwandan genocide was a machete. But did these media moguls intend to cause such violence by allowing these images to be published? Does it matter that so much time elapsed – nearly two and a half years – from the time that this issue was published and the start of the genocidal violence? And does it matter that the people on trial did not write or design the cover, but merely allowed it to be published?

Second, consider the case of Jean-Bosco Barayagwiza, who was prosecuted for incitement on the basis of his leadership position at the radio station RTLM. Here is an excerpt from a 1994 broadcast that was one of the main pieces of evidence cited by the ICTR:

> Another man…went to the market disguised in a military uniform and a gun and arrested a young man called Yirirwahandi Eustachwe in the market. … In his Identity Card it is written that he is a Hutu though he acknowledges that his mother is a Tutsi. If you are Inyenzi you must be killed, you cannot change anything. … No one can say that he has captured an Inyenzi and the latter gave him money, as a price for his life. This cannot be accepted. If someone has a false identity card, if he is Inkotanyi, a known accomplice of RPF, don't accept anything in exchange. He must be killed.[20]

In this case the act of incitement happened much more closely in time to the genocidal violence, but it was also mediated by others – Barayagwiza did not broadcast this speech but only allowed it to go over his radio station's airwaves. Is the speech a direct call to violence, or is it more properly interpreted as a more general warning? And does it matter whether there were acts of violence that were directly inspired by this speech, or only that it was highly likely to have that effect?

---

[19] *Prosecutor v. Ferdinand Nahimana, Jean-Bosco Barayagwiza, and Hassan Ngeze,* International Criminal Tribunal for Rwanda, case no. ICTR-99–52-T, Trial Chamber Judgment, 3 December 2003, para. 1055.

[20] Ibid., para. 427.

Third, consider again the case of Jean-Paul Akayesu, bourgmestre of Taba commune, who was prosecuted for incitement, based largely on the following evidence:

> The Morning of April 19, 1994, following the murder of Sylvere Karera, Jean-Paul Akayesu led a meeting in Gishyeshye sector at which he sanctioned the death of Sylvere Karera and urged the population to eliminate accomplices of the RPF, which was understood by those present to mean Tutsis. Over 100 people were present at the meeting. The killing of Tutsis in Taba began shortly thereafter.
>
> At the same meeting in Gishyeshye sector on April 19, 1994, Jean Paul Akayesu named at least three prominent Tutsis, Ephrem Karangwa, Juvenal Rukundakuvuga, and Emanuel Sempabwa – who had to be killed because of their relationships with the RPF. Later that day, Juvenal Rukundakuvuga was killed in Kanyinya. Within the next few days, Emanuel Sempabwa was clubbed to death in front of the Taba bureau communal.[21]

Here we have the most direct involvement in the killings by someone who is not himself a killer. Should Akayesu be held to be more responsible for the genocide than those who followed his directives and did the actual killing? Should Akayesu, who merely incited, be punished more severely than those who actually murdered?

Each of these cases will get a much more careful analysis in later chapters of this book. But some of the conceptual and normative problems with the crime of genocide and its prosecution are now hopefully clearer. Those who instigate or incite genocide and hence most epitomize the general intent to destroy a social group are, in that respect, not those who kill or assault, etc. So there is a diffusion of responsibility throughout a group, the members of which may be responsible for genocide. And it will be difficult to sort out who is most responsible and who less so, especially given that the crime of genocide is a collective crime, not an individual one. Murder is not an international crime, although it may be part of the crime of genocide. I next turn to a summary of the arguments that will be advanced in the following chapters.

VI. Summary of the Arguments Advanced in the Various Chapters

The parts of the book are organized around various conceptual and normative puzzles that arise when one considers the international

---

[21] *Prosecutor v. Jean-Paul Akayesu*, Trial Chamber Judgment, paras. 14–15.

jurisprudence of genocide. I will now say a bit about each of these parts and summarize some of the conclusions reached. Part A considers the criteria for identifying social groups. After the introductory chapter, Chapter 2 explores various historical approaches to the nature of groups. In particular, I describe the approach taken by nominalists such as William Ockham, Hugo Grotius, and Thomas Hobbes. I end the chapter by sketching my own nominalist account of the nature of social groups. In Chapter 3 I discuss an international commission's attempt to set out a basis of social group identification in cases such as genocide. I critically draw on the commission's view. My view is that social group identification requires both in-group and out-group recognition of a class of people as members of a certain group.

Part B asks what the harm is of intending to destroy a social group. In Chapter 4 I consider the possibility that genocide, like crimes against humanity, harms all of humanity. I partially accept this recommendation, and partially reject it. I agree that there is a type of harm to all of humanity that is the harm of genocide, but I argue that it is to each human individual, not to humanity as a whole. In Chapter 5 I defend a version of the "status harm thesis" as the basis of the harm of genocide. In this view, the harm of destroying a social group is that individuals suffer a significant loss in that their group identity is destroyed. This makes the harm of genocide not morally unique, but still quite significant.

Part C discusses a host of problems having to do with the act and intent elements of the crime of genocide. In Chapter 6 I consider the *actus reus* element in the crime of genocide. I argue that certain acts, of cultural genocide and ethnic cleansing, should be included as acts of genocide. I then set out a general account of the act element of the crime of genocide and defend it against various objections. In Chapter 7 I consider the *mens rea* element in the crime of genocide. Here I argue that there are actually three mental elements: a general intent to do certain acts, a specific intent to accomplish the destruction of the social group by performing these acts, and a collective intent to destroy the group. I then propose various revisions to the way the *mens rea* of genocide is understood and defend it against some objections. In Chapter 8 I distinguish motive from intent and argue that motive should not be an element in the crime of genocide, despite the way some of the delegates to the Genocide Convention understood the "as such" part of the definition of genocide, although I allow that motive can play a role in mitigation of punishment.

Part D considers who should be prosecuted, and who should be most severely punished, in genocide cases. In Chapter 9 I address the special acts of complicity that are characteristic of so many genocides. I sketch the various types of complicity, and I defend a general theory of complicity. In addition, I try to explain what the boundary is between legal and moral complicity, and why it matters so much for genocide cases. In Chapter 10 I discuss the concept of incitement, arguably the most important of the special acts that constitute genocide. Without acts of incitement it is unclear how widespread genocides can occur where lots of killing takes place over a very short period of time. I am especially concerned with the role that the media plays in such cases. In Chapter 11 I ask whether genocide can occur without central planning, ultimately answering in the affirmative. I return to the previous discussion of incitement and compare it to the more standard case of instigation. I then apply my understanding of the various ways that acts can be organized to produce genocide, and I defend the view that some inciters are often those most responsible for genocide.

Part E examines two special problems related to genocide. In Chapter 12 I ask whether humanitarian wars should be waged to stop genocide. I point out that humanitarian interventions are still wars, and thus they have all of the worries about loss of civilian life associated with any waging of war. I argue that in some cases, but fewer than is normally thought, humanitarian intervention can be justified to stop or prevent genocide. In Chapter 13 I consider whether criminal trials in the aftermath of genocide make matters worse for the goal of long-run reconciliation. In this final chapter, I spend time reconceiving political reconciliation so that it does not follow the normal model of the two-person marital reconciliation. I return to the idea of bystander complicity, arguing that criminal trials can advance rather than retard the goals of reconciliation by giving wider latitude to defense attorneys and generally to rule-of-law issues than often occurs in international criminal trials.

When genocide was effectively disconnected from crimes against humanity and placed into its own most highly censured category, a change occurred that is very hard to justify. Throughout this book I argue for a somewhat deflated idea of genocide, aware that such a deflation risks offending people whose group has been the subject of genocide in the past. I do not mean to offend, but merely to proceed where the better arguments lead. Emotional appeals should not decide the issue, either in a court of law or in a theoretical inquiry. Genocide is in my view still one of the worst things that people can do to one another. But it is not morally unique in its horrendousness, and it is not the crime of crimes. Nonetheless, criminal trials should be held for those most responsible for genocides, and quite severe punishments should be meted out against these individuals if convicted.

In the next two chapters, I will set out a general account of social groups and apply it to particular conceptual and normative problems in the way that protected groups are understood in the international jurisprudence of genocide. This discussion will set the stage for my attempt to address a series of complex normative and conceptual questions about the law of genocide. I feel it is important to begin with a discussion of the metaphysics of the group, even as I recognize that many nonphilosophers will find some the discussion tedious. My advice is to skim through this material if such metaphysical discussions are not your cup of tea.

PART A

THE NATURE AND VALUE OF GROUPS

2

Nominalism and the Constituents of Groups

In this and the next chapter, I set out a general approach to group[1] identification and then apply it to the case of genocide. In the current chapter, I will discuss and defend a nominalist approach to groups. In a sense nearly everyone today has nominalist sympathies, for hardly anyone believes that abstract terms such as "Armenians" have reality independent of the individual members. But there are various kinds of nominalism. It is only a "super-nominalist" supposedly like Hobbes who thinks that agreement about the meaning of some abstract terms could really only be established by a civil authority, and it is unclear that even Hobbes held this extreme view.[2] I will spend the first half of this chapter rehearsing some of the most prominent views of nominalists in the late Medieval and early Modern periods. I will then spend the second half of the chapter providing a defense of a nominalist view of the constituents of groups.

In the first section of the chapter I will examine some of the views of the first nominalist philosopher, William of Ockham. In the second section I will discuss some of the views of the most prominent nominalist political philosopher, Thomas Hobbes. In the third section I will build on the views of Ockham and Hobbes to construct my own account of the constituents of groups. In the fourth section of the chapter I will tackle the difficult question of how to determine which groups can be

---

[1] In the ensuing discussion I use the term "group" when the more common term in philosophy is "social group." I do this because the term social group in international law has a narrow technical meaning that is not the meaning I want here.

[2] Leibniz apparently used this term to refer to Hobbes. See Martha Bolton, "Universals, Essences, and Abstract Entities," in *The Cambridge History of Seventeenth Century Philosophy*, edited by Daniel Garber and Michael Ayers, New York: Cambridge University Press, 1998, vol. I, p. 193.

harmed. And in the final section I will address several objections to the nominalist view I have here set out.

I. Ockham's Nominalism

William of Ockham (1285–1349) was a Franciscan monk who taught philosophy and theology at Oxford, as well as in France and Germany. He is best known today for his methodological principle, the so-called Ockham's razor, which urged that we cut away all unnecessary thoughts until we employ the least number of assumptions and concepts that would still explain the experience or sustain the thesis. This methodological principle was most important in discussions of entities. "Entities are not to be multiplied without necessity," Ockham asserted.[3] Ockham seems to have followed his own methodological advice in that he embraced a version of nominalism with respect to entities. Ockham's parsimony about entities led him to be quite critical of assigning independent existence to communities and other groups. Concerning entities, Ockham claimed: "Something is said to be one improperly and loosely, as when a kingdom is said to be one, or a people, or the world is said to be one."[4] Rather, Ockham argued that we should not go beyond the individuals that compose these groups in talk of existing things.

For Ockham, there are many "thought-objects" in the mind that do not correspond to existing objects. As he said: "Furthermore, fictions have being in the mind, but they do not exist independently, because in that case they would be real things and so a chimera and a goat-stag and so on would be real things. So some things exist only as thought-objects."[5] This is the basis of Ockham's nominalism, namely, "his refusal to construe abstract terms as names of entities distinct from the individual things signified by abstract terms. Ontologically, this means that the only things that there are, are individual substances and equally individual qualities."[6]

Ockham said very little about groups, but his general ontological position is one that I find especially illuminating for understanding

[3] Quoted in Ernest A. Moody, "William of Ockham," in *The Encyclopedia of Philosophy*, edited by Paul Edwards, New York: Macmillan, 1967, vol. 8, p. 307.
[4] Quoted in Jeannine Quillet, "Community, Counsel, and Representation," in *The Cambridge History of Medieval Thought*, edited by J. H. Burns, New York: Cambridge University Press, 1988, p. 537.
[5] William of Ockham, *Ockham: Philosophical Writings*, translated and edited by Philotheus Boehner, O.F.M., London: Thomas Nelson and Sons, 1957, p. 42.
[6] Moody, "William of Ockham," p. 311.

the identity conditions for groups. He does spend some time trying to show that Socrates exists but that humanity does not. Indeed, at one point Ockham says that "humanity" seems to connote that there is a name of an existing thing that "signifies a nature composed of body and intellective soul." And yet, Ockham says, this suggestion "is hopeless."[7] Humanity is something that can be predicated of individuals such as Socrates, but this fact of predication does not entail that humanity exists in the same way that Socrates does. Indeed, humanity seems to exist only as a thought-object. In the remainder of this section I will draw on that discussion to try to explain Ockham's articulation of one of the most famous versions of nominalism.

It could be argued that humanity exists as more than a thought-object, namely, as inhering in the collection of individual persons, such as Socrates, who compose it. Ockham denies that humanity exists in this way. For Ockham, humanity is an abstract term, and Socrates is a concrete term. It is true that the abstract term has a "concrete counterpart," and the concrete term has an abstract counterpart.[8] But these terms certainly do not signify the same things, and whatever the abstract term signifies that is different from the concrete term, there is no existence to the abstract term. It is false to say that these abstract and concrete terms signify the same things, and also false to say that what is differently signified by the abstract term must have independent existence. This, I take it, is what Ockham means by saying that abstract and universal terms are merely thought-objects.

Abstract terms are more than concrete terms, but only as thought-objects. It is false to infer that abstract terms, such as humanity, must have independent existence because they signify more than their concrete counterparts, such as Socrates. Ockham's razor does not allow such a supposition as long as there is a more parsimonious one, namely, that the abstract term is different as a thought-object than is the concrete term that is its counterpart. There is no reason to add that the abstract term must also differ in that it has an independent existence different from the concrete term. As Ockham says, "concrete and abstract terms do not supposit for distinct things."[9] Humanity is not a proper subject, if this means that it is an independent existing thing.

---

[7] William of Ockham, *Ockham's Theory of Terms* (Part I of the *Summa Logicae*), translated by Michael J. Loux, South Bend, IN: St. Augustine's Press, 1998, p. 62.

[8] Ibid., p. 63. Counterparts are what a term refers to.

[9] Ibid., p. 64.

Another possibility is that the abstract term signifies what is common to the concrete terms that form its counterpart. In his discussion of genus and species, Ockham discusses this alternative and ultimately rejects it. What is common could merely be the matter of the particulars. So color could be said to be the genera of which individual colors are the species. And yet even though color is what each color has as its material element, color is not itself an existing thing, even though it may stand for what is common to colors, or to colored objects, which themselves exist. In any event, Ockham argues, even if the genus is part of the definition of the species, "it is false to say that the definition is really the same thing as the thing defined" or even that the definition is anything other than a thought-object.[10]

Groups are like colors in that they are abstract terms that have as their counterparts concrete terms, that is, individual persons. Groups are indeed different from these counterparts, but that does not mean that groups must have independent existence. For groups might differ from their counterparts only in that they are different thought-objects than individual persons. Indeed, on my account groups are individual persons related to each other in various ways. The "related to" element of groups makes them different from discrete individual persons. But this does not mean that groups exist in reality. Groups are nonetheless abstract names that can be talked about, and indeed perhaps must be mentioned in various accounts of phenomena. If so, Ockham's razor would allow for them to be so mentioned. But even this would not confirm that groups have independent existence, just as is true of parts of definitions.

Ockham's nominalism is a very good place to start to think about groups, and Ockham's razor is a good methodological principle, especially for those who are minimalists in social theory like myself.[11] For we should not multiply entities needlessly; and the positing of groups as entities is indeed a questionable practice, perhaps especially in international law. The question that Ockham left unanswered, and that Hobbes later attempted to deal with, is how we determine when talk of abstract entities makes sense, and in particular when it makes sense to talk of a group that could be said to be identified as the subject of such crimes as genocide. That will be our main topic in Chapter 3. For the present

---

[10] Ibid., p. 93.
[11] See my discussion of minimalism in May, *Crimes Against Humanity*, ch. 1.

chapter, we need to do a significant amount more work to make sense of how to understand the constituents of groups.

II. Hobbes as a Super-Nominalist?

In *Leviathan*, Hobbes distinguishes four uses of names, two of which are important for our purposes. Names can either "serve as Markes, or Notes of remembrance," or names can act as "Signes" when many people use the same word to signify to one another their common experiences.[12] Universals might be signs of what is common to individuals, and this commonality might be itself an existing thing that allows for the universal to be something different from the aggregation of individuals. But Hobbes is clear that universal names merely call to mind one of a number of individuals that were thought to be similar. As he says, "there being nothing in the world Universal but names, for the things named are every one of them Individuall and Singular."[13] Hobbes's nominalism in this respect is quite similar to that of Ockham. In an earlier work, Hobbes says that "names common to many things... are the images and phantasms of several living creatures" and nothing more.[14]

If Hobbes is a super-nominalist, as Leibniz asserts, it is perhaps because he contended that names have significance only within a linguistic context that the speakers of a language have agreed to.[15] Because language is a matter of convention, then names would be conventional as well, and would have to be dependent on at least a loose agreement.[16] This position would get especially radical if it were Hobbes's view, because in *Leviathan* he also asserts that "*True* and *False* are attributes of Speech, not of Things." If speech, the use of spoken names, is a matter of convention, then so would be truth and falsity. But in the very next sentence Hobbes allows that there can be error that is not merely a matter of convention, "as when wee expect that which shall not be."[17] Yet he also says that "Nature it selfe cannot erre." This admission, it seems to me, makes

---

12 Thomas Hobbes, *Leviathan* (1651), ch. 4, edited by Richard Tuck, New York: Cambridge University Press, 1996, p. 25.

13 Ibid., p. 26.

14 Thomas Hobbes, *De Corpore*, part I, ch. 2, in *Body, Man, and Citizen,* edited by Richard S. Peters, New York: Collier Books, 1962, p. 37.

15 In *De Corpore,* Hobbes talks of the use of names as lawful or not, perhaps indicating that he sees the determination of how to understand metaphysical entities as a matter of someone having legislated. See ibid., p. 35.

16 See Bolton, "Universals, Essences, and Abstract Entities," p. 193.

17 Hobbes, *Leviathan*, p. 27.

Hobbes not quite so radical as he seemed to be, especially in Leibniz's view. For here we see Hobbes admitting that there is something like falsity, namely, error, that is, not merely a matter of the conventional ascription of names. The question then becomes whether enough of what is normally called falsehood can be assimilated to error to make Hobbes's notion of truth and falsity not quite as radical as it first appears.

This raises the question of how we can tell the truth of various claims about the kinds of things that can act and be acted upon, a crucial concern for determining today whether groups can be harmed by genocidal policies. Hobbes claimed that there were two kinds of persons who can be properly said to act. Natural persons are said to own their own words and actions, where here the terms "person" and "actor" are synonymous within the same individual. Artificial persons, by contrast, are represented as acting by having the actions of natural persons attributed to them. When a natural person acts for another natural person, the first is said to bear the person of the second. Or to put the point in slightly different terms, the second person acts vicariously through the first person.

In the case of artificial persons, they all must act vicariously through natural persons. The reason for this is fairly simple. According to Hobbes, artificial persons are either animate or inanimate. Animate artificial persons are multitudes or collections of natural persons. These artificial persons are capable of acting, that is, capable of intentional action where there is a single will, when they have been made one. The only way, in Hobbes's scheme, that such a multitude can be made one is when they each consent to allow one natural person to represent them all.[18] Inanimate artificial persons (for example, churches, hospitals, or bridges) cannot act at all or give others the right to act for them, except when the owners or managers of these inanimate things do so.[19]

There is an ontological claim that follows from Hobbes's analysis of action, namely, that only natural persons can be said properly to act on their own. This comes out clearest when Hobbes says the following: "And because the Multitude naturally is not *One*, but *Many;* they cannot be understood for one; but many Authors, of every thing their Representative saith, or doth in their name; Every man giving their common Represented, Authority from himselfe in particular."[20] As we saw

---

[18] Ibid., pp. 112–13.
[19] Ibid., p. 113.
[20] Ibid., p. 114.

above, Hobbes had argued that all collective entities must be understood as individuals considered severally. Now we see him arguing that collectivities' actions must be conceptualized as the acts of particular natural persons as well. If so, this would be a natural extension of Hobbes's argument, but certain problems remain unresolved in Hobbes's texts. For the analysis just rehearsed turns on the idea that an entity can act intentionally only if it has a will. Collectivities seem to lack a will of their own and hence must have a will, if they do, vicariously.

What remains unclear is whether this same analysis of action can be applied to other possible attributes of collectivities, such as groups. Can collectivities be harmed only in the person of individuals who are members? It is not clear that collectivities need a will to be harmed, and hence not clear that such harm must also be understood as the vicarious harm to individual persons. For this reason, it is not clear how radical a view Hobbes espouses, especially in the passages of *Leviathan* we have been examining.

Quentin Skinner has argued that the key to Hobbes's account of artificial persons is to ascertain which natural person has the authority to act for the artificial person. The answer is that it is the natural person who has dominion over the artificial person, either by literally owning that inanimate object like the bridge, by being a guardian, or by having brought it into being. But what is interesting for our consideration of groups is a fourth means of authorization, namely, where the authority "proceeded from the State."[21] It is such a consideration that plays into the hands of Leibniz and his claim that Hobbes was a super-nominalist because Hobbes thought that significant acts of naming had to be established by civil authority. Of course, Skinner's interpretation of Hobbes does not hold that all significant acts of naming had to be established by the State, but he does recognize the State as one legitimate form.

Once again there is a question of whether we are to understand the attribution to a collectivity of action and of harm in the same way. Part of the answer here will depend on whether we are talking about an animate person or inanimate object, and which of these two is the best way to understand groups. Perhaps groups are like children in that groups are natural not artificial, but not that they are natural in the way that adult human persons are, because they are incapable of independent action in their own right. Yet, if a group is like a child, there is no reason

---

[21] See Quentin Skinner, "Hobbes and the Purely Artificial Person of the State," *Journal of Political Philosophy*, vol. 7, no. 1, 1999, pp. 1–29, especially p. 17.

to think that the group cannot be harmed, as a group, the same way that the child can be harmed, as a child, not merely through the natural person who "personates" the group or the child. To be harmed, it is not necessary that one be capable of independent action, but only that one have interests that can be adversely affected.

In the next section, I will draw on the nominalist considerations of Ockham and Hobbes, as I attempt to lay out a nominalist account of groups that will make sense of claims that groups can be harmed, and this will, I hope, also allow us to begin to ascertain which groups might be properly said to be subject to genocide. My account will be inspired by Ockham and Hobbes, but will have to diverge from them because the questions I pose were never directly addressed by either of these important philosophers. Groups are indeed a kind of artificial person or abstract name that must be understood in terms of the natural persons and concrete names that are the counterpart to them. In the final sections of this chapter I will turn to the difficult question of how to think about whether these groups can be harmed.

III. An Account of the Constituents of Groups

My own account of groups is nominalist in that like Ockham's view it does not recognize the independent existence of groups. My account is also like Hobbes's view in that it sees groups as artificial persons, at least for purposes of understanding them as agents. In my earlier work on groups I constructed an account that still seems to me to be a good place to start, but I will now make some changes to the view in this section. I argued that groups are

1) Composed of individual human persons
2) Who are related to each other by organizational structure, solidarity, or common interests
3) And who are identifiable both to the members, and to those who observe the members, by characteristic features.[22]

Each of these constituents of groups will need to be discussed in detail in this section.

Nominalists are not the only theorists to think that groups are composed of individual human persons; indeed, nearly every type of theorist would agree. But to say that groups are composed of individual human

[22] May, *The Morality of Groups.*

persons does not yet tell us much about how to identify them positively. It really only rules out such things as bridges that on the nominalist view are also artificial entities. What is needed is an account of when a collection of individual human persons composes a group, or on the nominalist account, when a collection of individual human persons can properly be named as a group (where the group name is an Ockhamite counterpart to the individual name).

The key metaphysical constituent of groups is the relationship that obtains among the individual human persons. When there is a sufficiently strong relationship, then it may make sense to talk of a group in addition to the individual human persons, and it also may make sense to talk of these individual human persons as members of the group. For the group to be talked about as an agent, there must be an especially strong relationship among the members that allows for individuals to act together, namely, that allows for joint action. Typically there is some kind of organizational structure with one or more persons clearly assigned to act for the group. I have argued that some groups, such as mobs, can act without organizational structure, but only if the relationship of solidarity among the members is especially tight.

Merely having common interests does not typically allow for a group to "act," or to be called an "actor." The reason for this is that having common interests may motivate the individual members to act on their own, but it may not motivate them to act together in a way that can be described as a group acting. As we will explore in the next section, having common interests may be sufficient for being harmed, as opposed to being an actor. But this is not always true and will depend on how strong the bonds of common interest appear to be. Of course, from a nominalist standpoint these bonds are themselves not really existing things, but rather ways of talking that have as their counterpart what is occurring within individual human persons, typically at the psychological level.

In identifying groups, the last of the three conditions listed earlier is the key. What matters most is whether individual human persons can, and do regularly, recognize certain individuals as members of specific groups. In the rest of this section, I will explain why it is that such identification must be made by both what I will call in-group and out-group individuals. By in-group individuals I mean those individual human persons who are the putative members of the group whose identity is in question. By out-group individuals I mean those individual human persons who are not members of the putative group in question. In my view, both in-group and out-group individuals must identify the group and its members for the group to have group status. I will refer to this as the publicity condition.

The publicity condition is a nominalist principle that requires that groups be identified not merely by those who are its members. Because nominalists follow Ockham's razor, we do not recognize the legitimacy of names unless there is good reason to do so. And for a name to meet this condition, as Hobbes argued, it cannot be merely privately recognized. The publicity condition is a nominalist principle that requires that groups be identified not merely by those who are its members, and not merely by those who observe these individuals from an "objective" distance. Nominalists follow Ockham's razor, and so we don't recognize the legitimacy of names unless there is good reason to do so. And for a name to meet this condition, as Hobbes argued, it cannot be merely privately recognized. Names make sense only when they form a part of discourse, and at least minimally this rules out private naming. As I will indicate, there is also a priority given to naming, or its conceptual equivalent, when the naming is not restricted to just a small portion of a linguistic population.

Another reason for requiring the publicity condition is to make sure that the name or concept of a group is not secretly or clandestinely restricted just to those individuals, especially in an out-group, who would abuse the idea of the group. Stereotypes, and other mischaracterizations of individuals as being grouped a certain way, may arise when such private naming occurs. If the in-group members think of themselves as a group, and no one else in the larger society does so, there is also the risk that these individuals could be in effect stereotyping themselves. For if the characteristic that is used for such identification is not one that out-group members can recognize, then the link between naming and identification is broken.

On my nominalist account of group identification for international crimes, both the members of the putative group and those outside the group must recognize individuals as members of the same group. There must be in-group recognition as well as out-group recognition. Once this occurs, then a group can be named properly and said in a sense to "exist." But such existence of a group remains distinct from the existence of individual persons, who are the real things in the universe and constitute groups only insofar as these individuals have certain things in common.

Nominalism is deeply skeptical of talk of groups, but there is nonetheless sense to be made of such talk. In a way, nominalism is a thoroughgoing reductivism or deflationism in that it calls for us to look behind the group talk for the individual persons and their relationships. Nonetheless, there is a way in which it makes sense to talk as if there are groups, the members of which can be identified. Much recent work has been done on how such identifications can be made for groups that act intentionally. Much less attention has been paid to the subject of this part of my chapter, namely, how to identify which groups can be harmed, and how such identification can be made in a meaningful way so that various questions in law and public policy can be addressed.

IV. Groups That Can Be Harmed

To be properly named a group, collections of individuals must have certain features that can be attributed to them. In most of the literature on this topic in recent years, stress has been laid on the conditions necessary to attribute intentional agency to a collection of individuals. But in genocide cases, it does not matter much whether a putative group can act; what matters is whether the group can be destroyed. It may be that when individuals have common interests this is sufficient in some cases for the individuals to be said to constitute a group that can be intentionally destroyed, even though the group cannot properly engage in intentional action in its own right.

"Being harmed" is a predicate that can be attached to many different kinds of things. But there must be a sense in which the thing in question coheres sufficiently so that one can speak of it before and after the harming act and still be referring to the same thing. If a group has interests, even if those interests are nothing more on the nominalist view than merely the common interests of the members, it may be possible to harm, or destroy, that group. For harm is perhaps best understood on the model of a serious setback to the interests of the thing in question, and so if a thing does indeed have interests, or can have interests attributed to it, there is a sense that that thing can be harmed in virtue of setbacks to those interests.[23] Of course, the next question is: what is the difference between saying that the group has been harmed versus saying that the individuals have been harmed in virtue of harm to common interests?

---

[23] See Joel Feinberg's treatment of this idea in his book *Harm to Others,* Oxford: Oxford University Press, 1984.

Hugo Grotius, commonly recognized as having had a significant influence on Hobbes as well as being the father of international law, states a view similar to the one I want to defend when he says the following:

> It cannot be denied that a people may cease to exist. The extinction of a people may be brought about in two ways: either by the destruction of the body, or by the destruction of that form or spirit which I have mentioned. A body perishes if the parts without which the body cannot exist have at the same time been destroyed or if the corporate bond of union has been destroyed. ... A people's form of organization is lost when its entire or full enjoyment of common rights has been taken away.[24]

In the terms that Grotius employs we can make sense out of the idea of genocide and the corresponding idea of the intention to destroy a group. The body of the group is nothing more than the individual human persons who are its members, and the form of the group is the common interests that exist among these members.

A very important practical question concerns whether a group can be destroyed even though its body, its members, have not all been killed. And here Grotius gives us a good answer. The group may be destroyed if what constitutes its form is destroyed, even though the body, the individual human persons who are its members, remains alive. Think of a very loosely structured group, such as that group of people who form a fan club for a certain sports team, and where all have a common interest in that sports team. If for some reason all of these individuals lose interest in the sports team, or if the sports team becomes disbanded, the fan club could also be destroyed even though the individual human persons who were its members are all still alive.

The next question concerns how we identify which groups can be harmed or destroyed in the way contemplated by such bodies as the Genocide Convention. The answer follows from the above analysis in that the group must be sufficiently coherent that it has what Grotius called a "form." But what sort of "form" is that? At least part of the answer is that the "form" must be one that can be recognized both internally and publicly. But this is not enough. There must also be a certain kind of stability of the form, not something fleeting and insignificant, if we are to say that the harm or destruction of the group warrants a response in terms of political or military action to stop the harm or to prevent it from occurring.

---

[24] Hugo Grotius, *De Jure Belli ac Pacis* (On the Law of War and Peace) (1625), translated by Francis W. Kelsey, Oxford: Clarendon Press, 1925, pp. 312–13.

Groups are generally identified by the features I discussed in the previous section of this chapter, and we can build on that analysis to understand which groups can be harmed significantly enough to warrant a major response. Principally this identification will be based on the relationships that exist among the members, especially the common interests. But not all common interests will do, for some of these interests are relatively insignificant, others are not publicly recognizable, and others, although publicly recognizable, are not recognized by the members as being significant. Here we have three criteria that can be applied to begin to answer the question of whether a putative group is one that can be harmed and then for which some remedy can be sought.

To determine which groups can be identified as having been harmed significantly enough to warrant a major response, we must ascertain when the common interests of the members are significant. Consider an example. Does it make sense to say that people with auburn hair constitute a group that can be harmed or even destroyed, over and above harm or destruction to the group's individual members? Having auburn hair is something that is perceptible by those within and those outside the group. Indeed, it is very hard to miss. But for auburn-haired people to be a significant group, it will matter whether the members see themselves as having common interests with the other members. It will also matter how nonmembers react to members of the group, not in their individuality but as group members. These in-group and out-group reactions are the main source of determining whether a group is one that can be harmed significantly, as one might expect on a nominalist construal. From that perspective, what counts the most are people's perceptions and conceptions, because groups do not have any more robust existence than is found in those two sources. I next take up some objections to my account. In the next chapter I will employ this nominalist framework for specifically addressing the protected groups that can be subject to genocide.

V. Objections

One objection to the nominalist account I have set out is that I have confused nominalism with methodological individualism in making the harm a function of what happens to individuals seen as primitives. Constitutive theorists argue that the lone individual is not the paradigmatic normative actor, but rather "to be an actor is to be constituted as such within a social practice."²⁵ Constitutive theorists could also be nominalists, but they would understand harm in terms of the social practices in which individual agents are embedded.²⁶ Similar to what I set out above, the insider perspective is very important to this theory, but that perspective is not alone definitive of whether a group has acted in a way that causes harm. So a constitutive theorist would not necessarily oppose much of what has been said in this chapter, but would take issue with the idea that nominalism should be linked with understanding harm in terms of individual agency.

I subscribe to a group-based model of harm that is not meant to be thoroughly individualistic. Indeed, significant social action occurs when individuals act in ways that are organized, and where the organization itself cannot be reduced to features of the individuals. Individuals operate as members of groups, and this group membership is significant, whether it is due to common structure, solidarity, or common interests. In particular, my idea of "common interests" could be understood as requiring that the context be taken into account, especially the context of the specific practices individuals participate in. But unlike the constitutive theorists, I do think that talk of social practices is itself fictitious because it does not posit a reality that exists independently of individuals. I do follow constitutive theorists in thinking that we can talk sensibly about groups being harmed, but the harm does ultimately inhere in the individual members of the group. Although it is important that the individual be a "member" of a group if the group is to be harmed, it is also true that the harm ultimately inheres in the individual.

So I accept the point made by constitutive theorists and others that a thorough-going individualist account of groups, especially of the harm to groups that is involved in genocide, is not plausible. What is needed is an account of group harm that is framed in terms of individuals and the relations that obtain among individuals. Constitutive theorists are right to place emphasis on the social practices that individuals are engaged in, especially the memberships those individuals have. But it is not true that we can dispense with a serious regard for these individuals in the social practices. It is in this way that my view cuts a path between the

²⁵ See Mervyn Frost, "Constitutive Theory and Moral Accountability: Individuals, Institutions, and Dispersed Practices," in Toni Erskine, editor, *Can Institutions Have Responsibilities?* London: Palgrave/Macmillan, 2003, pp. 84–99, especially p. 86.
²⁶ Ibid., p. 91.

collectivists and the radical individualists, without committing me to the problems that have plagued both views over the years.[27]

Another objection to the nominalist account I have set out is that nominalism is too robust a theory for what I need, because the main moving force of my view is the publicity condition and some acceptance of an authority condition.[28] This objection maintains that there is a sense that the publicity condition can establish groups in nearly any way one can imagine. As long as some authoritative individual publicly proclaims that a certain collective of individuals is to be treated as being a group, then the group is constituted as having existence. The classic debates about nominalism are somewhat beside the point. The objection concludes that it doesn't require a deep metaphysical understanding to see the point that authority can provide such a public basis for identifying groups.

I considered a similar view when I discussed the claim that Hobbes was a super-nominalist in that he appeared only to accept the legitimacy of groups when a sovereign had recognized these groups. I gave reason to doubt that this was Hobbes's view. In any event, I find the super-nominalist position to be unsatisfying in several respects. First, in most legal situations it is highly controversial who is the authoritative determiner of which collections of individuals should be recognized as a group. Second, in the international arena, where questions of international law relating to genocide are decided, it is even more contentious who the authoritative determiner of group identity is, because of the unsettled nature of international law. Third, even if it is clear who the authoritative determiner is, and even if acts of the authoritative determiner satisfy the publicity condition, it is unclear why such considerations have normative force without some theory such as that provided by nominalism.

Nominalism, at least as I have construed it, is a theory that provides a metaphysical and normative rationale for thinking that publicity is important in group identification. The idea, as I expressed it above, is that collectivities and other abstract names are fictions in that they do not have a referent in the existing universe. Nominalists thus not only endorse a certain way to identify groups but also indicate why there is a problem about group identification in the first place. Unless there is a clear recognition of the group by those individuals who themselves have

---

[27] See my discussion of this issue in *The Morality of Groups*.
[28] I am grateful to John Lango who pressed this objection.

reality, we lack a firm basis in reality for talk of groups, and for evaluating them.

A third objection to consider comes from those who follow Ockham more closely than I did in the previous sections. On one account, that of Calvin Normore, Ockham does not allow that processes or events can exist.[29] On similar grounds, the relations of which I spoke, such as common interests, would seemingly not exist either. Ockham's nominalism would then contradict a Hobbesian view because even the relations that make it the case that the collection of individuals is more than the sum of its parts would not have reality. On this account, Ockham would merely say that any grouping of individuals "does not require making anything new at all but merely requires rearranging things which already exist."[30] For this reason it seems that there is not much sense to my claim that groups are individuals in relations, because the relations are nothing more than the way that individuals are arranged.

In my view, relations exist, but not in the same way that individuals do. Relations, such as having common interests, are just arrangements of individuals. But such arrangements cannot be reduced to individuals in terms of their psychological states. The arrangements, as the word implies, have a kind of reality, a secondary reality that goes beyond the psychological states of the individuals who are so arranged, but not a primary reality of the sort that individuals have. For Ockham, the only individuals that are totally independent are God, angels, and humans. On Normore's reading of Ockham, even nonhuman animals and pieces of wood have reality only in a secondary way because they are not independent of other individuals. But secondary existence can have conceptual and normative significance.

Groups can be identified by whether they satisfy the publicity condition by being constituted of individuals arranged in certain ways. A question remains of whether the publicity condition requires a public understanding of group membership by both in-group and out-group members. Ideally, both would be true, but I have also suggested that the most important is that the out-group members identify members publicly. I here leave open the question of whether this would be sufficient for satisfying the publicity condition. But in most cases, nominalists will want to have signs that both groups engage in such identification.

[29] Calvin G. Normore, "Ockham's Metaphysics of Parts," *Journal of Philosophy*, vol. 103, no. 12, December 2006, pp. 737–54.
[30] Ibid., p. 747.

Satisfying the publicity condition is a way for certain arrangements of individuals to have a secondary reality and to make it possible for us to talk of certain groups as in a sense existing and subject to harm. In this way I tried to set the stage for thinking about which groups are coherent and stable enough to be harmed or destroyed and for which some kind of remedy or response was called for. But I only set the stage for such a discussion. In the following chapter I will apply this model of understanding group identity to recent issues that have arisen in the international law of genocide.

It will turn out that our work on the conceptual foundations of groups in this chapter will be of special relevance to genocide in international criminal law, which is defined in terms of the intention to destroy a protected group. It has been notoriously hard to identify groups in the law of genocide and harder yet to explain why it is that only certain types of groups are subject to genocide. In the next chapter I turn to the task of providing a new understanding of how to formulate the definition of genocide that will be satisfying to nominalists and others who do not recognize the independent existence of the groups that are said to be the object of the attacks definitive of genocide.

3

Identifying Groups in Genocide Cases

The [ICTR] Chamber notes that the Tutsi population does not have its own language or a distinct culture from the rest of the Rwandan population. However, the Chamber notes that there are a number of objective indicators of the group as a group with a distinct identity. Every Rwandan citizen was required before 1994 to carry an identity card which included an entry for ethnic group. ... The Rwandan Constitutions and laws in force in 1994 also identified Rwandans by reference to their ethnic group. ... Moreover, customary rules existed in Rwanda governing the determination of ethnic group, which followed patrilineal lines of heredity. ... The Rwandan witnesses who testified before the Chamber identified themselves by ethnic group. ... Moreover, the Tutsis were conceived of as an ethnic group by those who targeted them for killing.[1]

Currently in the international law of genocide there is a debate about whether groups should be defined objectively, on the basis of criteria that anyone can apply, or subjectively, where only the perpetrators decide who is a member of a group and even what are relevant groups. As we have seen, genocide is defined as "the intent to destroy, in whole or in part, a national, ethnical, racial, or religious group, as such,"[2] so it matters quite a bit how groups are identified. Indeed, in the Rwanda "genocide" there was, and remains, much dispute about whether the victim group, the Tutsis, were indeed a group of the sort that could be the subject of genocide and hence a group that could seek redress in international law for the harms that the Hutus perpetrated against the Tutsis. In the quotation that begins this chapter, the tribunal also seemingly draws a distinction between objective and subjective factors, although what are called objective might be challenged.

---

[1] *Prosecutor v. Jean-Paul Akayesu*, Trial Chamber Judgment, paras. 170–1.
[2] Convention on the Prevention and Punishment of Genocide; Rome Statute of the International Criminal Court, July 17, 1998, Article 6.

William Schabas says that the subjective approach was used in the Rwanda trials when it was determined that "the Tutsis were an ethnic group based on the existence of government-issued official identity cards describing them as such." He goes on to say: "This approach is appealing up to a point, especially because the perpetrator's intent is a decisive element in the crime of genocide. Its flaw is allowing, at least in theory, genocide to be committed against a group that does not have any real objective existence. ... Law cannot permit the crime to be defined by the offender alone."[3] In this chapter I will discuss how a nominalist might respond to Schabas's worries.

Another debate bears on the first. This debate concerns whether there must be physical destruction, not merely cultural destruction, of the group for genocide to take place. The question arises most evidently in the case of putative genocide against a religious group. The religion could be destroyed without the physical destruction of the people who are the members of the religious group, for instance, when the members are forbidden to practice their religion. This so-called cultural genocide is not currently recognized as genocide proper in international law, and at least in part this is because cultural genocide mainly involves a loss to the mental lives of the people in question but seemingly not something objectively tangible. In this chapter I will also set the stage for explaining why such a view seems confused on a nominalist perspective.

From a nominalist perspective, there is not such a significant divide between objective and subjective means for identifying a group in genocide. As we saw in the previous chapter, nominalists generally do not think that groups have reality or existence. Rather, groups are mere "names" that partially stand for our experiences, and about which judgments can be made. Indeed, groups are artificial, just as are States, universities, or corporations, in that they are made-up by humans. Because of the lack of reality of groups, they must be identified by subjective perception and self-perception. This in itself is not a problem, because most identifications are made on the basis of perceptions, and because perceptions are made by subjects they are all to one extent or another subjective. But the problem arises when one attempts to determine what sort of test can be employed by a judge or jury about whether the perceptions are stable enough to be the basis for group identification in law.

In his paper "The Model of Rules I," Ronald Dworkin frames the debate about legal positivism by linking legal positivists such as H. L. A.

---

[3] Schabas, *Genocide in International Law*, p. 110.

Hart with nominalism: "In their view, the concepts of 'legal obligation' and 'the law' are myths invented and sustained by lawyers for a dismal mix of conscious and subconscious motives. ... They are ... unreal. ... We would do better to flush away the puzzles and the concepts altogether, and pursue our important objectives without this excess baggage. This is a tempting suggestion, but it has fatal drawbacks."[4] Dworkin says that many adherents of nominalism "bluff" in that they continue to use the terms and concepts they regard as unreal. This is an important point, but Dworkin also admits that when the details of the practice, of referring to such concepts, are laid bare, they may indeed be "thick with illusion." His point is that the claimed lack of reality has to be argued for, not merely bluffed. I will try to avoid this flaw in what follows.

In this chapter I will first examine a seemingly nominalist approach taken by the International Commission of Inquiry on Darfur established by the United Nations Secretary-General in 2004. Second, I will build on the analysis of the Commission's findings to develop a more satisfactory account of how to identify groups for purposes of genocide law. Third, I will confront arguments advanced by William Schabas against the nominalist approach. Fourth, I will discuss other objections that could be raised to the strategy of identification that I have sketched. Finally, I will indicate how international law should change to accommodate this understanding of group identification. Throughout I argue for a somewhat more expansive way of thinking of groups in the international law of genocide, while recognizing that significant conceptual puzzles with the whole idea of group identification still remain.

I. The Report of the International Commission of Inquiry on Darfur

On January 25, 2005, the International Commission of Inquiry on Darfur issued a report on whether genocide was occurring in the Darfur region of Sudan. In section II.I of the report, the commission attempted to define genocide. Here is how the commission summarized the current state of international law:

> In short, the approach taken to determine whether a group is a (fully) protected one has evolved from an objective to a subjective standard to take into account that collective identities and in particular ethnicity

[4] Ronald Dworkin, *Taking Rights Seriously*, Cambridge, MA: Harvard University Press, 1977, p. 15.

are, by their very nature social constructs, 'imagined' identities entirely dependent on variable and contingent perceptions, and not social facts, which are verifiable in the same manner as natural phenomena or physical facts.[5]

Although the commission does not define its terms, we can infer from the context that "objective" refers to something factual and unchanging whereas "subjective" refers to something constructed and variable. I will shortly refine these concepts, but suffice it here to think of them in the rough way employed by the commission. Ultimately the Commission of Inquiry finds fault with the purely subjective approach to identifying groups.

Here is how the commission expresses the problem with the subjective view, and explains how it is possible to move back toward an objective view:

> Moreover, it would be erroneous to underestimate one crucial factor: the process of formation of a perception and self-perception of another group as distinct (on ethnic, or national, or religious, or racial grounds). While on historical and social grounds this may begin as a subjective view, as a way of regarding the others as making up a different or opposed group, it gradually hardens and crystallizes into a real and factual opposition. It thus leads to an objective contrast. The conflict, thus, from subjective becomes objective. It ultimately brings about the formation of two conflicting groups, one of them intent on destroying the other.[6]

This complex conceptual analysis of group identification is in line with certain nominalist conceptions.

The Commission of Inquiry came up with the above proposal in response to the problem of how to characterize tribes, such as the Fur, Massalit, and Zaghawa tribes that were the object of attacks and killings in the Darfur region of Sudan. The problem is that these tribes "speak the same language (Arabic) and embrace the same religion (Muslim)" as the tribes that were attacking them. Because of intermarriage, the groups have become blurred in social and economic terms.[7] Generally speaking, tribes have not been recognized as the object of genocide in international law. But the tribes in Darfur appear to be different from normal tribes, at least in the Commission of Inquiry's assessment.

[5] The Report of the International Commission of Inquiry for Darfur to the United Nations Secretary-General, Pursuant to Security Council Resolution 1564 of 18 September 2004, Geneva, 25 January 2005, para. 499.
[6] Ibid., para. 500.
[7] Ibid., para. 508.

Over the last decade, polarization has occurred to such an extent that the tribal identities of the tribes in Darfur have become "crystallized" in a way that can make them count as groups for international law purposes. Such crystallization seems to have occurred for the most part because of conflicts over scarce resources that greatly intensified in-group and out-group identification. Both attacking group and victim group see one another as belonging to hostile groups. The Commission of Inquiry concludes: "For these reasons it may be considered that the tribes who were victims of attacks and killings subjectively make up a protected group."[8] The commission implied that this was because "crystallization" had occurred. Nonetheless, the Commission of Inquiry said that genocide was not occurring in Darfur because the perpetrators lacked genocidal intent, that is, the attacking group was not trying to destroy the victim group as such, but rather only attacking for counter-insurgency reasons.[9] For my purposes, what is significant in the Commission of Inquiry's findings is the analysis of the way that groups are identified in hard cases such as tribes.

A similar point is made by the International Court of Justice's case *Bosnia v. Serbia.* The court says that "the Parties essentially agree that international jurisprudence accepts a combined subjective-objective approach." For genocide to have occurred there must have been "a collection of people who have a particular identity." It is not enough that the group be defined negatively, such as the group of "non-Serbs." Instead the group must be identified positively, as was true at the time of the drafting of the 1948 Genocide Convention, "with specific distinguishing well-established, some said immutable, characteristics." In addition, "when part of the *group* is targeted, that part must be significant enough for its destruction to have an impact on the group as a whole."[10]

People generally are members of multiple groups. As a teenager I was a member of the "religious" group of Roman Catholics, the "national" group of Americans, the "racial" group of Caucasians, the "ethnic" group of Germans, as well as many other only somewhat less significant groups, such as the "demographic" group of "Baby Boomers," the "political" group of antiwar activists, and the "informal social" group of high school debaters. In a sense, a person is merely the constellation, or

---

[8] Ibid., para. 512.

[9] Ibid., para. 518.

[10] *Case Concerning the Application of the Convention on the Prevention and Punishment of the Crime of Genocide (Bosnia and Herzegovinia v. Serbia and Montenegro),* International Court of Justice, 26 February, 2007, Judgment, paras. 191–6.

intersection, of a large number of group memberships. To single out just one of these group memberships for purposes of identifying who one is misses the fact that there are many, many other group memberships that that person could also be identified with.

In addition, many groups are like tribes in that they blend, at least partially, into other groups of the same category. Roman Catholics and Anglicans have blended into one another despite Henry VIII's having separated the Church of England off from the Vatican. Intermarriage between Catholics and Anglicans further blurs the border between these two religious groups. And racial groups, arguably the only group recognized by the Genocide Convention that is biologically based, are dramatically affected by intermarriage. In 30 years of university teaching in the United States, I have observed how hard it has become to tell a student's "race" by observing him or her, if the category of "race" makes sense anymore in "melting pot" societies such as the United States in any event.

Tribes are especially problematic because they are typically defined by birth lineage, and such lineages will cross between tribes because of intermarriage and cultural cross-fertilization. This is the reason that is initially given by the Commission of Inquiry for thinking that subjective considerations of construction rather than fact must enter into group identification. But once such subjective considerations play a role in group identification, judgments by third parties are hard to make, and so it seems hard to see how an external authority, such as a judge or jury, could make such identifications in a way that would play an important, if not the key, role in a trial. The tribes in Darfur, as well as the ethnic groups in Rwanda, pose an especially difficult problem for courts that are mandated to determine if genocide, involving the intentional destruction of a group, has occurred. The Commission of Inquiry makes a very good case for thinking that tribes are problematic, especially in light of intermarriage among Sudanese tribes that already share so many features in common, such as religion and ethnicity. Subjective considerations will have to be used to differentiate the members of one tribe from another.

But the commission also makes a very important point when it argues that various other factors can make group membership firmer over time, even when the group is defined initially by largely subjective considerations. In Darfur the in-group and out-group identifications, even though both were initially based on mere subjective perception and self-perception, became solidified as a struggle for scarce resources forced an arbitrary, but nonetheless real, set of identifying markers on these two groups. If both the perpetrator group and the victim group are clear about the borders between these groups, then there is a sense that what was once merely subjective takes on the character of being objective. In the next section of this chapter I will attempt to build on this important point and to make sense of the metaphors of "crystallization" or "solidity" that occur when some groups previously merely subjectively identified seem to become objectively identifiable.

II. A Conception of Group Identification

I wish to defend a version of the view espoused by the Commission of Inquiry in how to identify groups in difficult cases such as that of tribes. It seems to me that the Commission of Inquiry was right to say, although I'm not sure they fully understood the implications of what they said, that otherwise difficult groups can be identified as protected groups in genocide cases if there is *both* stable in-group self-perception *and* out-group perception of the members as all forming a coherent group. Here we do not run into the problem, identified by Schabas, of having the perpetrator group alone determine group membership, although as we will see in the next section, Schabas undoubtedly will object to this scheme nonetheless. If both perpetrator group and victim group members agree on the border of the group, then there is enough "reality" to the group for anyone with nominalist sympathies like me. If groups are merely artificial constructs, then it is not clear how much more we would want than that two very different kinds of people agree in naming a group, and identifying who are the members of a group.

Problems result when the out-group, that is, the perpetrator group in this case, solely defines the in-group, that is, the victim group. It may be sufficient to say that the victim group has in some limited sense been harmed in order to say that the victim group was identified by the perpetrator group and then persecuted on this basis. But that "the group" has been harmed, rather than merely that individuals were harmed because of their perceived group membership, becomes the difficulty. And things get much worse when one tries to show that there is an intentional decision to destroy a group, where the group only "exists" in the minds of the members of the perpetrator group. For there to be intentional destruction of a group that warrants international intervention, it seems that there must be more to the "group" than this, even if one is a nominalist. This is not to deny that some sort of harm, other than genocide, could be occurring, and that would warrant international prosecutions.

For the nominalist, one of the most important conditions of identifying groups is that there be a kind of public recognition, in the manner of naming that has occurred. Private acts of identification do not rise to this level. Typically there must be some authoritative act of naming of the sort that would occur if a government were to recognize the creation of a new corporation because of the filing of articles of incorporation with the relevant branch of the government. The question before us is whether something short of such an official act could still be publicly accessible enough to constitute an identification of a group, similar to an act of "naming." It is my contention that when both the perpetrators (out-group) *and* the victims (in-group) recognize the existence of a group that is being attacked, then this is sufficient for the group to "exist" and be the subject of the sorts of harms that characterize genocide, namely, the intent to destroy the group.

One might wonder why I have placed so much weight on the publicity condition. At least in part, as I will explain, the publicity condition is a test for whether there is a consensus of sorts in the society about the naming of a collection of individual people as a group. It is possible for such a consensus to emerge without the two factors that I have stressed, namely, the in-group and out-group identification of the same collection of people as constituting a group. But having these two factors both present is a very good sign that there is a consensus of sorts within a society to name a certain group as coextensive with a certain collection of people. This consensus is then important because it means that this naming is not likely to be arbitrary or merely private and hence subject to abuse of various sorts. The publicity condition is a kind of "reality" check for group identification. The publicity condition makes it much more likely that there is a group that people are referring to, and that it is the same group whether one is a member of the group or someone outside the group. Here is how we move from subjective to something approaching "objective" identification.

The term "subjective" generally refers to the mental states of a particular person, having its "source in the mind;" the term "objective" generally refers to "that which is external to the mind," as the Oxford English Dictionary puts it most concisely. I will generally follow this way of understanding subjective and objective. But it should be noted that in discussing groups from my nominalist perspective the term "objective" will apply to what is perceptible, not what is external to *all* minds, and it is for this reason that I put such emphasis on the publicity condition. This condition concerns features of a group that are publicly perceptible, not merely perceptible to the members of the group themselves. But even on this construal of what "objective" means, it is still misleading to say that groups have objective existence, because we are still dealing with perceptions of characteristics of individuals, not characteristics of groups per se.

One might also wonder why it is not sufficient for a group to self-identify for that group to count as a group that could be the object of genocide. Again, on my nominalist view, this would depend on the publicity condition being met. If the members merely privately speak of themselves as a group, this would be quite different from having members who publicly do so. Private "naming" does not normally open the group up for public acts such as those involved in genocide. Indeed, there must be enough recognition outside of the group that there is a group for it to be said that an out-group is trying to destroy the in-group. Recognition of a group by an out-group cannot easily occur if the in-group only self-identifies and does not publicly proclaim their putative status as a group so that other nongroup members can also identify this victim group and its members, or if the identifying features of the group are only perceptible to the members of that group.

An objection might be raised at this stage concerning intention. If in criminal law generally it is enough to require that people have intentions to harm others, why is that not sufficient in the case of genocide, and hence why is the subjective view not my view, because one of the elements of genocide should surely be the subjective wrongful intent of the defendant. But another element of the crime of genocide, as an international crime, is that there be a genocidal campaign that the individual is contributing to, in order for the *actus reus* to be satisfied. We certainly might want to say that it is wrong of the individual to do what he or she is doing intentionally, independent of what else is going on around the person, but his or her crime is not an international crime unless it connects to what is going on around the person, as I explained in the first chapter. The international crime of genocide is a mass crime, where the individual's act, which might otherwise just be a hate crime, is part of a larger campaign to destroy the group.

In my view, the publicity condition is one of the most important considerations in group identification. One could ask why such a condition should be given pride of place. In Chapter 2 I rehearsed some of the metaphysical reasons for such a view. Here I will instead focus on the practical reasons. The most serious practical concern is that we not undercut the value of groups by trivializing their identity conditions. If a group decides to oppress all of those people who wear eyeglasses, this looks like a nearly arbitrary designation of victim-group membership. Of course, if it is already well known that members of a given socioeconomic class wear eyeglasses as a way to self-identify as group members, then things seem quite different.

In this context we can think of Pol Pot's purge of intellectuals and professionals in Cambodia. That it was well known that certain features such as the wearing of eyeglasses could identify members of a given class may not be sufficient for the group to be an object of genocide, but we are moving more in that direction than when a perpetrator group makes this determination arbitrarily or in private. The genocide in Cambodia is often called "auto-genocide" because it was perpetrated by members of one group against members of the same group. Yet this is not quite true. For if the wearing of eyeglasses did mark the members of a certain class in Cambodia, both for those who were members of the class and for those who were not members, then the genocide looks less like "auto-genocide" and more like other forms of genocide where one group seeks to destroy another group.

The combination of out-group and in-group recognition of certain features as markers of the "existence" of a group is generally a telling sign of the possibility that such a group could be the object of harms such as genocide. The out-group identification is crucial because without it there is no good reason to see the attacks against individuals as also intentional attacks against a group. For someone to intend to attack a group, that person must believe that there is a group there, in some sense of that term. And this means that the attacker must have criteria for picking out the members that are transparent, or at least that others in the society can recognize, including the victims. Ideally, one would also look for the kind of broad public recognition that goes beyond the perpetrator and victim group, but I do not believe that this is also necessary.

The in-group identification makes it more likely that the group "exists" in more than just the minds of the perpetrators, and that the harms will be group based and not merely individual. By this I mean that the individuals must see themselves as forming a group that is under attack for the attack to be based on group membership. If the individuals do not see themselves as forming a group, then there are no clear-cut membership conditions of the group. Of course, such conditions can be foisted upon the individuals by the out-group. But if despite what the out-group does the in-group members simply don't see themselves as "members," then it is far more likely that the "group" is fully a figment of the minds of the out-group than that there is a "group" that exists in the sense that any member of the society would recognize it.

Metaphysically the identity conditions of a group are: (1) individual human persons, (2) related to each other by organizational structure, solidarity, or common interests, and (3) identifiable, to the members, and to those who observe the members, by characteristic features. In the current section, I have been explaining why I think that the third condition is especially apt for the identification of groups as objects of genocide. I have been suggesting that this last condition be called the publicity condition and have specified its own conditions further. If we were to accept my proposal, then the number of groups that should be officially recognized as the potential objects of genocide would increase from the current four: racial, religious, ethnic, and national groups. At least one advantage of this proposal is that some coherence will be given to the current nearly incoherent set of groups recognized as objects of genocide. In the next sections, I will tackle significant objections that have been raised to my proposal. I will also provide additional reasons to think that my proposal has merit from both a practical and a metaphysical perspective.

III. Objections from William Schabas's Perspective

William Schabas has taken a decidedly nonnominalist position with regard to the identification of groups in genocide cases. Indeed, he argues that there must be some "objective existence" for people to count as groups in genocide law.[11] Unfortunately he provides little by way of details of this metaphysical view. Nonetheless I will try to sharpen his critique and then address his various objections. Schabas's general strategy is to try to show that the four categories of groups that the Genocide Convention recognized, namely, racial, ethnic, national, and religious groups, all overlap and "define each other" as national minorities that are subject to harms based on ethnic hatred.[12] Although these groups are not completely nonvoluntary, at least they are groups that people rarely leave.[13] He then argues that it is a mistake to expand the

---

[11] Schabas, *Genocide in International Law*, p. 110.
[12] Ibid., p. 119.
[13] Ibid., p. 137.

list beyond these four categories, and certainly a mistake to allow for a subjective interpretation of which groups should be protected in genocide law, because then we would have to recognize groups with "no real objective existence."[14]

My response has several parts. First, it is not at all clear that the four categories of groups – national, racial, ethnic, and religious – can be clearly distinguished from gender groups or political groups in terms of anything approximating "objective existence." That the four groups listed in the Genocide Convention might be connected to each other is no reason to think that only these groups should be listed in that convention. Schabas is right to say that there is a historical reason for why just these groups are listed, namely, that the subject of the Holocaust, Jews, arguably overlapped with all four groups. But that reason has no bearing on the metaphysical issue he alludes to as the central issue in deciding whether or not to list a certain group as a possible subject of genocide.

Second, it is not at all clear what Schabas means by "objective existence" when it comes to group identification. A distinction can indeed be made between subjective and objective means of identifying groups – with the latter category reserved for identification that is not merely based on what the members of one group think. Indeed, the better distinction is really between subjective and intersubjective. But Schabas seems to want more than this – something "physical," as he says. Yet he then points out that there really isn't any clear bloodline method of identifying even the four groups listed in the Genocide Convention. In any event, other than saying that the four categories are based in the historical fact of national minorities such as the Jews during the Holocaust that were subject to persecution, Schabas does not give us much else to go on. In the rest of this section I will try to provide an argument that could support Schabas's claims and then suggest how a nominalist could respond.

I suppose the strongest argument in favor of Schabas's position is that one needs something to perceive in identification if any kind of third-party assessment, such as that in law, is going to have a chance of succeeding. We could then add to this that only certain perceptible characteristics have been the basis of persecution over the centuries – not hair color, but rather skin color; not club membership, but religious membership; not geographic home, but rather home within political

[14] Ibid., p. 110.

borders. As was said above, tribes pose an especially hard problem, because it is implausible to say that they have not been subjects of persecution but that only ethnic groups have been. Yet, even in the case of tribes, one could regard them as merely small, close-knit ethnic groups of a certain sort, as indeed seems to be happening in discussions of ethnicity today. In any event they are often identifiable based on perceptible characteristics such as facial features or cultural practices.

In support of Schabas's view, one could argue that if there are no clearly perceptible characteristics, it will be very hard for a judge or jury to ascertain whether there really is a group that was being persecuted instead of there merely being harms directed at discrete individuals. Unless these characteristics are in fact connected to a real existing group that remains stable over time, there will be no good reason to treat persecution based on these characteristics as normatively important. Schabas's view seems to be that grounding claims of group persecution, or genocide for that matter, in perceptible characteristics is the only real alternative to allowing the members of a particular group to have a kind of exclusive or private say over who is a member of a given group.

Nominalists could reply to this argument, which I am attributing to Schabas, that they do not deny that groups need to be identified by perceptible characteristics. What they do deny is that it makes sense to talk of these characteristics as being grounded in some objective existence of the group. In my group-based construal of nominalism, there must be characteristic features of a group that are perceptible for it to make sense to talk of group membership at all. Group-based characteristics are common features that individuals share with other individuals. That individuals share features with one another does not mean that groups exist in which these features inhere. Rather, there is no reason to postulate the existence of a group merely because there are common features that individuals share. And there is no reason that such a group must exist for judges and juries to be able to tell if there is persecution or genocide being conducted against individuals on the basis of common perceptible features. Of course, it will be convenient to talk about the individuals who have the common features as constituting a group, but this need not commit us to the objective existence of this group.

It is my view that genocide as a crime still makes sense without there being objectively existing groups. For the intent to destroy a group would mean the intent to destroy all, or a significant number, of those individuals who have certain common features. And value may be given to the "group," in that those individuals who have these common features are organized, or cohere, in a certain way that itself has value. If there is a kind of consensus such that we can "name" the group and treat the group as if it were an existing thing, that is enough for there to be genocide or persecution waged against the group. Indeed, naming is such a crucial social marker that in some ways it doesn't matter whether anything in objective reality corresponds to the names at all. I will not make the assumption that there is no objective reality, but only that whatever features there are of such reality, groups are not its constituents.

Schabas is certainly right to worry that genocide could end up being meaningless if there is nothing that corresponds to group names. But the main reason for this is that then no special value would attach to the loss of groups and hence no special harm to the destruction of a group over and above the destruction of individual persons. I will explore the idea of the harm of genocide in Chapters 4 and 5. Suffice it here to say that whatever is the value of a group, and the disvalue of the loss of a group due to genocide, that value need not be dependent on the group having objective existence. Indeed, in the next part of the book, I will argue that the best way to characterize such value, and disvalue, is in terms of how individuals are affected when they lose a part of their identity or when others who share significant history with them no longer feel able to protect their rights in various ways.[15]

IV. Other Objections

I wish now to respond to various other related objections against my account. First, let us consider a metaphysical objection. Because I earlier built on the Commission of Inquiry's model, it is appropriate that both of these objections come from the commission concerning the way I have diverged from its initial model. Although recognizing the importance of subjective factors in how collective identity can be shaped,[16] the commission says that a group becomes subject to genocide only if there has been a transformation, a "crystallization," from subjective into objective fact. For otherwise, the commission suggests, there will not be "two conflicting groups, one of them intent on destroying the other," without such crystallization.[17]

[15] See Larry May, "How Is Humanity Harmed by Genocide?" *International Legal Theory*, vol. 11, no. 1, Summer 2005, pp. 1–23.
[16] Report of the International Commission of Inquiry, para. 499.
[17] Ibid., para. 500.

I have agreed with the commission that both self-perceptions and perceptions of others are crucial for group identification. The objection I have gleaned from the commission is that this is ultimately not enough. Crystallization is not mere metaphor for the commission, but something that factually transforms. Yet it remains unclear what the commission means by "factual opposition" or "social facts."[18] Nominalists can still talk of facts, and, indeed, from the late Middle Ages until the present, nominalists have made their case for thinking that social facts do not turn on objective reality.[19] Social facts, like groups themselves, are individuals organized in various ways. Social facts may require more than individuals in that the way these individuals are organized or structured, the organizational or other structure, is not itself reducible to individuals; but there need not be existing groups. And the context will matter quite a bit. In this chapter I have restricted myself to the context of identifying groups that can be the object of genocide. The kind of organization of individuals required for the identification of a group subject to genocide may involve more factors than if the group was being identified for other matters.

My response is to begin by noting that social facts about groups subject to genocide involve more than individual persons; but the "more" does not involve the postulation of more entities. Rather, we need only talk about shared beliefs, or "we" beliefs, as Tuomela and Searle call them.[20] Individuals need to have beliefs about how they will interact with other individuals, and these beliefs need to be the same for a number of individuals for these shared beliefs to constitute a social fact. The agglomeration of social facts can then indeed form "groups" without there being social facts that have as their objects independently existing groups. I have explored this metaphysical issue in greater detail elsewhere.[21] In the case of genocide ascriptions, the "facts" involve the consensus among individuals and groups that I have been discussing by speaking of both in-group and out-group recognition.

Second, the Commission of Inquiry also raises a significant practical objection when it in effect declares that all identification by means of perception is really subjective, not objective.[22] Because of this supposed

18 Ibid., paras. 500–501.
19 See Raimo Tuomela, *A Theory of Social Action,* Dordrecht: D. Reidel, 1984; Margaret Gilbert, *On Social Facts,* London: Routledge, 1989.
20 John Searle, *The Construction of Social Reality,* New York: Free Press, 1995.
21 See May, *The Morality of Groups.*
22 Report of the International Commission of Inquiry, para. 501.

fact, the commission seems to imply that there must be something stable underlying these perceptions from a legal point of view, so rules can be interpreted and applied consistently. The commission then endorses having a list of those groups that can be subject to genocide, which allows for some expansion, but not the loose expansion that is based solely on subjective perceptions. Problems of proof seem to become quite difficult when we move beyond objective considerations.

Making a list is a way to stipulate which groups can be subject to genocide. Such a strategy surely can alleviate practical problems of proof. But solving such problems by a stipulation, especially if the list is exclusive and the exclusivity is not based on strong conceptual and normative grounds, as is seemingly the case in the Genocide Convention, makes of the law a hollow shell. Of course, it is true that criminal law generally is becoming more and more a matter of statute rather than common law, but as Mill argued, the criminal law also needs to have moral support if it is to be respected and not merely adhered to out of fear or indifference. Fidelity to law requires that law be grounded in normative concerns that people can identify with. Merely selecting four types of groups out of many other similar groups, as has been done in the case of genocide, does not breed fidelity to international law, itself already infirm in the domain of fidelity.

Third, the commission members could respond that there is more here than a random list of four types of groups, because these groups cohere in a certain way and are normatively grounded in the worldwide horror that was expressed at the Holocaust. In the attempt to destroy the Jewish "race" Hitler targeted a group for elimination that overlapped with all four groups eventually listed in the Genocide Convention. Jews are certainly a "religious" group, and at least as far as Hitler was concerned, they were also a "racial" group. The Jews in Europe had a distinctive culture and language and so could arguably be said also to be an "ethnical" group. Jews were not necessarily also a "national" group in the sense of being members of a single nation-State. But if we think of nations as extended tribes, then Jews could also be said to be a "national" group. So the four types of groups were not arbitrarily selected, but cohered in that they were chosen to exemplify the group that was the subject of the Holocaust and the persecution of which had given the primary impetus behind the Genocide Convention's ban.

The major problem is that although the Jews do arguably count as a group that overlaps with all four categories of group in the Genocide Convention, there could certainly be a group that did not overlap with all four of these categories that also was targeted for elimination with horrible consequences. Another major group targeted by the Nazis, the gypsies or the Roma, also seem to meet this fourfold designation. But, in addition, the Nazis targeted homosexuals and disabled people, and yet they do not fit into any of the four categories. So, if the Nazi practices are to be the benchmark for what counts as genocide, we still are left in the dark about why these four groups, and only these groups, are listed. At very least the list needs to be expanded.

It would also be a strange strategy to say that because the Jews, and the gypsies, overlapped with four group categories, then any group from that set could be the object of genocide. Why not instead say that genocide can occur only against groups that are such a mixture of religious, racial, ethnic, and national groups? That would make the case of the Jews, and the gypsies, really paradigmatic for the international law of genocide. Unless the Jews, and the gypsies, are to be paradigmatic, then it is also no longer clear that just these four groups are the ones to count as potential objects of genocide. And especially if the idea is to find a collection of groups among which known objects of persecution overlap, it would certainly seem to make sense to add some gender and disabled groups here as well, so that the Nazi campaign against homosexuals and the disabled could count also as genocide. Indeed, ethnicity often overlaps with gender, as in the case of the persecution of the so-called Korean comfort women by the Japanese during World War II. Thus, it is not at all clear how the Nazi Holocaust could be used to defend the restricted list of groups in the Genocide Convention.

V. Some Proposed Changes in International Law

In light of the discussion above, I now offer some proposed changes in international law, recognizing that these changes are unlikely to be accepted in the near future. I begin with a change in the very definition and elements of genocide that is now listed in the ICC statute exactly as it was also listed in the 1948 Genocide Convention. First, we should no longer list just four groups, but instead at very least these four groups should only be examples of groups that could be the object of genocide. Second, a clause will need to be added after the four illustrative cases that will make it clear what the criteria are for deciding what other groups to include. Third, some kind of rule needs to be articulated that would make it possible to determine when a new proposed group clearly could not qualify as a group subject to genocide. I will take up each of these proposals in turn in this final section of the chapter.

The current formulation of the definition of genocide, in both the Genocide Convention of 1948 and the International Criminal Court's Rome Statute of 1998, says:

> 'genocide' means any of the following acts committed with intent to destroy, in whole or in part, a national, ethnical, racial or religious group, as such.[23]

My first proposal is to change the end of the definition so that it now reads:

> 'genocide' means any of the following acts committed with intent to destroy, in whole or in part, *a group, such as* a national, ethnical, racial or religious group, as such.[24]

Such a change will allow for other groups that are very much like the four originally listed types of groups also to be the object of genocidal harms that can be redressed in international law.

The second change is to add a clause to indicate what the four exemplary cases of groups have in common. This is a much harder task than the first, but I provide a possible construction, as follows:

> 'genocide' means any of the following acts committed with intent to destroy, in whole or in part, a group *that is relatively stable and significant for the identity of its members,* such as a national, ethnical, racial or religious group, as such.[25]

Of course, the term "relatively" is meant to give some latitude here, and would actually be needed to make sense of all of the original categories with the possible exception of racial groups, because the others can be changed, just not easily in most cases.

Given the second change, it is possible that the third change, meant to indicate what is ruled out, may not be needed because groups that lack stability or significance are also clearly ruled out. But on the supposition that a bit more guidance is needed, I offer the following third change:

> 'genocide' means any of the following acts committed with intent to destroy, in whole or in part, a *publicly recognized* group that is relatively

---

[23] Rome Statute.
[24] Italics added to indicate proposed wording change.
[25] Again, I add italics to indicate proposed wording change.

stable and significant for the identity of its members, such as a national, ethnical, racial or religious group, as such.

This limitation is meant to indicate that potential groups, such as the Cambodian case of those people who wear eyeglasses, would potentially fit the definition only if the group of those who wore eyeglasses were indeed recognized publicly as a group, and not merely recognized as such by the perpetrators, but otherwise that group would not be a possible subject of genocide. In the Rwanda case, the issuing of identity cards by the government to those who were Tutsis would seemingly also meet this condition because the identity cards met the publicity condition.

So, putting my three proposed changes into italics, I would change the existing definition and elements now to read:

> 'genocide' means any of the following acts committed with intent to destroy, in whole or in part, *a publicly recognized group that is relatively stable and significant for the identity of its members, such as* a national, ethnical, racial or religious group, as such.

Given all of these changes, the facts are such that the Cambodian eyeglass wearers would probably not constitute a group that can be the object of genocide, but the Rwandan Tutsis would. In light of our discussion above, this seems to be the result that was to be hoped for.

In this chapter I have explored difficult conceptual and normative issues in how to identify groups that can be the object of genocidal harm and that can potentially be redressed in international law. I have also made a practical proposal about how to change the identity conditions so that those conditions better reflect careful conceptual and normative thinking about these matters. I have certainly not solved all the problems in this nearly intractable problem set, but I have made a start, and one that I think is fairly plausible and can be built on by others who are also interested in solving the definitional problem that has so vexed tribunals, convention drafters, courts, and international commission members for many years. Along the way I have also suggested that there may have been genocide in Cambodia even though the victim group did not fit under any of the four categories of the protected group currently recognized in international law. I will say more about this issue in future chapters.

PART B

THE HARM OF GENOCIDE

4

Harm to a Group Itself

In the next two chapters, I will address the value of groups and try to explain what the harm is when a group is destroyed. In the previous chapters, groups were shown to have no clear reality of their own. If this is true, then it seems that the value of groups would not be based on anything of their own either. But perhaps there are other ways to think of the harm to a group. I will examine three strategies. In the current chapter I will try to explain the harm of a group's destruction in terms of the loss to the group itself and also consider another strategy that the harm to a protected group entails harm to another group, humanity. Ultimately, both of these strategies will prove problematic. In the next chapter, I will try to explain the harm of a group's destruction in terms of a loss to the group's members. This strategy is less problematic, but still not completely satisfying, calling into question at very least the "supreme" value of loss of a group, and perhaps also rendering problematic the idea that genocide, as the intent to destroy a group, is the worst of all acts.

In the first section of this chapter, I will explain why groups have played such an important role in international law and how this could be true even though the destruction of a group does not necessarily mean that any person is killed. In the second section of this chapter, I then provide an analysis of the various ways that it might be thought that groups matter morally. In the third section, I explore some of Hannah Arendt's views about why genocide, especially in the case of the Holocaust, is harmful to those who do not have, or have lost, the protection of a State. In the fourth section of this chapter, I build on Arendt's account to explore the idea that groups have value insofar as they protect human rights. In the fifth section of this chapter, I explain why the

Arendtian hypothesis will not explain the supreme value awarded to
social groups in international law, but this discussion sets the stage for
seeing the value of groups, and the harm of their destruction, in terms
of what is lost for the individuals who are group members, a task that is
then taken up in the next chapter.

I. The Legal Right to Life of Groups

In the International Court of Justice case *Bosnia v. Serbia*, the Court
comments on the Genocide Convention: "The drafting history of the
Convention confirms...Genocide as 'the denial of the existence of
entire human groups' was contrasted with homicide, 'the denial of the
right to live of individual human beings.'" William Schabas points out
that this is too simple because genocide, unlike the crime of murder, is
"directed against the entire international community rather than the
individual."[1] But the crime of murder is also seen as primarily a crime
against the domestic community, not primarily a crime against an individual. There is a difference between the tort of wrongful death, which
is fully about what happened to an individual person, and the crime of
murder, which is prosecuted by the public organ of the State standing
in for the harmed community.

Historically, the crime of genocide has been linked with that of
"denationalization."[2] This historical treatment of genocide points to an
obvious fact: a group can be destroyed without killing any of its members. One can destroy a group by disconnecting the members of the
group from the group, for instance, by forbidding them to speak their
native language or by dispersing them so that any group coherence is
destroyed. Once that is accomplished, the members are normally forcibly reincorporated into another nation, as Lemkin pointed out.[3] But it is
also possible merely to leave these "denationalized" people alone, as so-
called stateless people, like the Jews in many parts of the world who also
lost any sense of having rights. Indeed, one of the harms of genocide
is that a people is disconnected from its natural protective structure
where the members are left to fend for themselves as individuals without recognized rights, perhaps even without recognized membership in
humanity, as we will later see.

---

[1] Schabas, *Genocide in International Law*, p. 6.
[2] Ibid., p. 28.
[3] Lemkin, *Axis Rule in Occupied Europe*, pp. xi–xii.

In international law the concept of a "group" plays a prominent role, although largely unexamined and undefined. The Universal Declaration of Human Rights says that education "shall promote understanding, tolerance, and friendship among all nations, racial or religious groups."[4] The Genocide Convention of 1948 speaks of "national, racial, ethnical, or religious groups" as the only entities that, when assaulted, could be the object of genocide. But why are these groups the object of international law's chief prohibition? What is the harm if one of these groups is destroyed? I will provide a beginning of an answer to these questions.

It may be that certain groups have significance because their memberships are based on immutable characteristics, on the basis of which no individual should be discriminated against. Or perhaps certain groups have significance because they are permanently in a minority status in a given society, on the basis of which we should not allow the State to exercise its tyrannical majoritarian rule. The Akayesu decision of the ad hoc International Criminal Tribunal for Rwanda gives an argument that seems to rely on both of the above factors by declaring that "stable and permanent groups" are the ones protected by the Genocide Convention. The court says that "a common criterion in the four types of group protected by the Genocide Convention is that membership in such groups would seem to be normally not challengeable by its members, who belong to it automatically by birth, in a continuous and irremediable manner."[5]

Yet "birth" does not seem to be a clearly relevant factor, because one can undo any of the group memberships that one is born into, with the possible exception of race. Perhaps one could claim that there is a prima facie right that one not be discriminated against on the basis of groups that one did not initially join but into which one was thrust at birth. But Lockeians will quickly point out that most people have "exit options," and it is the failure to exercise them that constitutes a kind of tacit consent to remain a member. Once one chooses not to exit a social group that one could exit from, this undermines the claim that henceforth group membership should be an illegitimate basis for discriminatory treatment.

---

4 Universal Declaration of Human Rights, U.N. G.A. Res. 217A, 3 U.N. GAOR, U.N. Doc. A/810, at 71 (1948), Article 26.
5 *Prosecutor v. Jean-Paul Akayesu*, para. 652. The ICTR Appeals Chamber was critical of this position.

The idea that the harm of genocide has to do with the destruction of a group "as such" is the most difficult of the ideas of the Genocide Convention. For the words "as such" seem to take the individual out of the mix – it is the destruction of the group, not the destruction of the individual members, that seems to be the key.[6] It seems that it is not the loss of rights of these individuals, but the loss of the group itself, that is supposed to be characteristic of the crime of genocide. And yet, it is very unclear what precisely the harm is when a group is lost, especially when it merely happens that the members of the group are assimilated into another group, or simply reformed into a new group with a different identity. With the loss of one group it does not follow that there is even one less group in the world, and hence hard to see why that loss is the crime of crimes.

Some groups, such as racial or ethnic groups, cannot be destroyed without destroying the individual members, indeed, all of the individual members. In the debates at the Genocide Convention "Iran saw a distinction between groups whose membership was inevitable... and those of which membership was voluntary... it must be admitted that destruction of the first type appeared more heinous in light of the conscience of humanity, since it was directed against human beings whom chance alone had grouped together."[7] Here it is clear that genocide was thought to be most heinous when violence was occurring due to racial hatred. But racially motivated violence can be group based and not directed at the destruction of the group "as such." And as Brazil's representative to the Genocide Convention pointed out, even forced assimilation is not necessarily a wrong because it can be part of a "perfectly normal assimilation in new countries."[8]

There are also groups, such as those based on religion or nationality, that can be changed, although in many societies these changes are rare. To destroy these groups is not quite as much of an outrage as it is to destroy a group the members of which cannot voluntarily leave. But these are the groups I will focus on because it is thought that genocide is the worst of all crimes, even though genocide committed against religious or national groups does not necessarily mean that even one person is killed or tortured. For racial groups, genocide is truly terrible

[6] It is therefore interesting that many of the drafters of the Genocide Convention saw these words as mainly adding a motive element to the other elements of this crime. I explore this idea in Chapter 8.

[7] UN Doc. A/C.6/SR.74 (Abdoh, Iran).

[8] UN Doc. A/C.6/SR.133 (Amado, Brazil).

because destroying the group, even in part, means killing many individual persons. Yet this is only one of the four types of group that the Genocide Convention is aimed at. I will focus on voluntary groups so as to try to see why the destruction of the group "as such" is the worst of crimes that should be punished more severely than crimes of violence by one person against another. The main task of the rest of this chapter is to try to determine precisely what is the wrong of destroying voluntary, as opposed to involuntary, groups.

II. The Wrong of Genocide

Genocide, as understood in international law, does not necessarily involve any killing. But the actions that genocide does cover are extremely repugnant, and the kind of actions that would surely divide a community or nation. The definition of genocide in international law seems to imply that it involves doing what would make the group to be destroyed, where this may entail only that the group is permanently dispersed, as in ethnic cleansing campaigns. I will later endorse this interpretation of the Genocide Convention. Today judges have ruled that ethnic cleaning does not count as genocide, but they have not urged that the definition that allows for this possibility be changed. Genocide can also involve the infliction of serious suffering even if no one is killed, an interpretation I have also endorsed. Once again, the ICC prosecutors have said that they will not prosecute genocide cases that do not involve large-scale killing, but the definition certainly allows for it. Only the first, and arguably the fourth, of the five acts would involve killing. In these cases there is no requirement that the killing be conducted on a massive scale, for it may involve only the killing of a few of the members of a group.

At least if we look only at the legal definition of genocide, the moral uniqueness of genocide is not based on it clearly being worse than or even different from other atrocities. Yet some cases of genocide, such as the Holocaust, elicit such a visceral reaction as to give us pause in thinking of genocide as anything other than the worst, or one of the very worst, of crimes. Some but not all cases of genocide appear to be the worst of crimes and are also seemingly the hardest for a community to get over. Perhaps this is because of what the individual perpetrators do during genocides. Yet, as we will see, the perpetrators of genocide, or at least those who were most deserving of punishment, turned out not to be moral monsters. The individual acts of genocide were generally no more horrible than would be true of other international crimes. So it seems it must be the victims that make genocide special, and this would mean a focus on the group that is to be destroyed.

Having indicated that genocide does not necessarily involve massive killing, or even any killing at all, I will explore what else about genocide might make it an especially serious, and possibly supreme, international crime. The most obvious candidate for the uniqueness of genocide is that it involves the destruction of a group. All other international crimes are defined in terms of the harm to individuals, and only genocide is primarily defined in terms of a harm to a group instead of to an individual. But this fact of genocide does not yet get us to see what is morally significant about genocide. For we still need to investigate what it is about groups the destruction of which might be of, perhaps supreme, moral importance.

Perhaps groups could be understood like species. With the destruction of only just one species the rest of nature is adversely affected because there is less diversity for evolutionary selection to proceed upon. The problem with this possibility is that it is very unclear why groups should be thought to be similar to species in this way. It may be true that one less group in the world means less diversity, but it is not clear what is equivalent to natural selection in species that would be equivalently hurt in the domain of groups. Groups do not propagate, although it is true that their members do reproduce, as is also true of the members of species. Perhaps groups provide a wealth of genetic diversity for the evolutionary development of their individual members. Unfortunately, a group, even one that is biologically based, does not have the same kind of genetic diversity as does a species. Indeed, a group that is the object of genocide, such as an ethnic group, is often difficult to distinguish from other indigenous ethnic groups in a given region, as was true of the ethnic genocide in Rwanda. Similar considerations apply to religious or national groups.

Racial groups are the most likely to be repositories of genetic diversity that could be important to the rest of the human race. It is important to note that race is not primarily a biological rather than a social category. Nonetheless, it may be true that certain racial groups have a preponderance of members who share a certain genetic characteristic that is not shared by the rest of the human race. And if this racial group were to be eliminated, genetic diversity could be adversely affected. It is now important to point out again that the destruction of a social group does not necessarily mean that all or even very many of its members are eliminated. For this reason, the destruction of a group, unlike the destruction of a species, does not necessarily affect the diversity of the gene pool.

Leaving aside genetic diversity, perhaps group diversity is important for other reasons. Yet whatever those reasons might be, there is one fact that also needs to be mentioned, namely, that when one group is destroyed there may not be one less group in the world. For it may turn out that some of the members of the previous group simply reform as a new group. Perhaps the group is less diverse than it was before, but it is also possible that it is even more so, especially if other people who join the new group bring a new dimension of diversity to the new group that the older group did not possess. Despite what many might believe, groups come into existence and go out of existence with a fair amount of regularity, at least if we consider such things in evolutionary time, rather than in an individual's lifetime.

III. Arendt on Statelessness and Groups

In *Origins of Totalitarianism,* Hannah Arendt worries that the problem with genocide campaigns, especially those that create concentration camps, was not mass killings resulting in the "manufacture of corpses," but that "living corpses" were created. "A period of political disintegration suddenly and unexpectedly made hundreds of thousands of human beings homeless, stateless, outlawed and unwanted." This creation of "living corpses" occurred, Arendt argued, because the "Rights of Man, which had never been philosophically established but only formulated, which had never been politically secured but merely proclaimed, lost all validity."[9] The loss of validity of the Rights of Man came as a result of the failure of States to secure such rights through their own laws, and through the failure of the international community to demand that each person have his or her human rights secured by being granted civil rights in a particular State. Arendt focuses on political disintegration, literally the pulling apart of States where certain minority groups were expelled from the domain of full civil rights protection and left "Stateless" in the sense that no other State came forward to protect their human rights by granting them domestic civil rights.

Arendt argues that in the 19th century it was recognized that the "Rights of Man, supposedly inalienable, proved to be unenforceable – even in

[9] Hannah Arendt, *Origins of Totalitarianism,* New York: Harcourt, Brace and World, 1951, 2nd edition, 1966, p. 447.

countries whose constitutions were based on them – whenever people appeared who were no longer citizens of any sovereign state."[10] In the 19th century theorists realized what seemed "obvious: civil rights – that is, the varying rights of citizens in different countries – were supposed to embody and spell out in the form of tangible laws the eternal Rights of Man, which by themselves were supposed to be independent of citizenship and nationality."[11] When people were forced to be refugees they clearly saw that having inalienable human rights did not afford much protection. "The stateless people were as convinced as the minorities that the loss of national rights was identical with the loss of human rights."[12]

Arendt equates the idea of human rights with "the right of every individual to belong to humanity."[13] States can deny the humanity of whole subgroups – minority groups – within its borders by depriving these groups of their full civil rights and thus undermining the major protection of their human rights. It is for this reason, Arendt says, that "it is by no means certain whether" the protection of human rights by *international* means "is possible."[14] Indeed, "the abstract nakedness of being nothing but human was their greatest danger."[15] As a last ditch attempt to secure their rights, minority group members insisted "on their nationality, the last sign of their former citizenship, as their only remaining and recognized tie with humanity."[16]

The problem is that if an individual human has lost "his place in a community...and the legal personality which makes his actions and part of his destiny a consistent whole, he is left with these qualities which usually can become articulate only in the sphere of private life."[17] In such a position, one's status as a rights bearer can be secured "only by the unpredictable hazards of friendship and sympathy, or by the great incalculable grace of love."[18] But this is to become, at least at law, largely unprotected, where one has no claims to make if one is treated badly. Legal personality is what best secures our rights; without legal personality we lack even the "right to have rights." Racism denies that one

[10]   Ibid., p. 293.
[11]   Ibid.
[12]   Ibid., p. 292.
[13]   Ibid., p. 298.
[14]   Ibid.
[15]   Ibid., p. 300.
[16]   Ibid.
[17]   Ibid., p. 301.
[18]   Ibid.

subgroup in a State merits legal personality, and racism thus denies the common humanity of all humans. When racism is made a policy of the State, then the State denies "in principle... the idea of humanity which constitutes the sole regulating idea of international law."[19]

Arendt gives us a very good beginning at figuring out what is wrong with genocide. Genocide often, but not always, forces a people to become refugees, an outlawed people who have lost the protection of their rights because they have been expelled from a sovereign State and have not yet been accepted into another sovereign State. As refugees, the members of a group that has been excluded from the benefits of the State lack the protection of civil rights, the mainstay of human rights. Arendt focuses on the case of Jews in Europe in the 1940s, who went from State to State not finding a home, and hence were effectively rendered nonhuman. Another example is a group that has been forcibly evicted from one State and now exists in a refugee camp across the border in another State, but where the other State is not accepting the refugees and instead is trying to push them back across the border from which they have come. It is not sufficient to grant Stateless people abstract human rights. What they need is to be accepted into another State with civil rights protections.

There is a rather large role that international law could play in preventing States from creating Stateless people of their disfavored minority groups. Yet international law, at least in Arendt's view, is unlikely to be able to protect the rights of refugees on its own. This was the problem of the League of Nations, which saw itself as primarily the defender of the displaced minority groups in Europe, but the League failed to protect minority group rights. Arendt thinks that similar actions by international organizations are also likely to fail. But what an international organization may be able to do is to prevent, in the first place, the creation of Stateless people by preventing genocides and other horrible crimes that destroy groups or force individuals to be disconnected from their primary social groups that provide the last ditch protection against the lack of rights or the withdrawal of rights by a State.

When a people is excluded from a State, there is an attempt to destroy the people by forcing them to be assimilated into many other States, thereby destroying the character of the group. But it is not initially clear why anyone in the international community should care that

[19] Ibid., p. 157.

there is one less people or social group. It is most obviously a problem
when the members of the group must wander the face of the earth as
refugees, and hence as people who do not have civil rights protection
and hence do not really have human rights either. But what about the
situation where refugees are accepted as members of another State?
Why should it matter that these individuals are not formally accepted
as members of a group but only as individuals who are then pressured
to assimilate into another State? What does their forcible exodus from
a national or ethnic group, ultimately aimed at the destruction of the
group as such, add to the expulsion that renders expulsion such a significant harm even when the individuals have been assimilated into
another State?

Arendt does not provide us with an answer explaining how it is that
harm occurs when groups are destroyed. But she has begun to show us
a way to possibly understand such a harm or wrong by her talk of the
important connection between being a member of a State and having
human rights protections. Most importantly, she has shown that being
a member of a social group is also a way to be protected, or at least
to allow for individuals to be able to put up a last ditch effort against
becoming Stateless and rightless. So, when a person is forcibly removed
from a group, especially a national group, this often may be the destruction of the last opportunity for the individual to have human rights
protection.

IV. Rights in Groups and Rights of Groups

Members of minority groups within a State have rights in two senses: as
members of the State they have civil rights; and as members of a group
they have group-based rights, that is, rights by virtue of their membership
in a group. Arendt focuses on the former but not the latter, and so she
was not able to give a full account of the wrong of genocide, although she
gave significant hints by talking about the importance of political status
as well as friendship. For a State can give an individual a sense of having
human rights formally protected by bestowing civil rights protections
on him or her, but the State cannot give an individual a sense of belonging and purpose, which is often only had through group membership.
Groups can give to their members this sense of belonging and thereby
overcome what Arendt describes, at the end of *Origins of Totalitarianism*,
as the loss involved in loneliness. Indeed, in seemingly an aside, Arendt
coins the phrase "organized loneliness" and calls it "more dangerous"

than tyrannical rule generally.[20] Genocide seems especially harmful for creating large numbers of lone individuals, who have lost the protection of their rights and even the sense of self.[21]

Voluntary, as well as involuntary, groups perform at least two important tasks. First, some groups act as a last refuge for a minimal protection of human rights. Insofar as groups cohere, they have some power that can be exerted against States in behalf of their members. Second, groups provide an important ingredient in an individual's sense of self. When a person is stripped of group membership, he or she is at a loss, lonely even when clearly not fully alone. For in an important sense, the group-less individual does not even know who he or she is, and in that sense has lost his or her self. I discuss this second point in much greater detail in the next chapter.

Genocide is a catastrophic assault on the person, both in terms of the destruction of the last bulwark protecting the rights of the individual, and also in terms of potential destruction of the self. Genocide leaves the individual group member without resources to claim his or her rights as a human, and sometimes without resources even to understand who he or she is. Understood in this way, genocide is not primarily a harm to the group but to the individual person. If so, then it remains unclear why the international community should care so much, and indeed punish above all other acts, the crime of genocide. If genocide is a violation of the rights of individuals in groups, and not a violation of the rights of groups, then we are still a long ways from understanding genocide as a unique harm.

As Arendt says, "We are not born equal; we become equal as members of a group on the strength of our decision to guarantee ourselves mutually equal rights. Our political life rests on the assumption that we can produce equality through organization."[22] Groups are necessary to bridge the gap between the promise of equality for all humans and the actuality of diversity. Humans in their diversity must overcome the animosity that diversity inspires to attain the promised equality. In a provocative comment, Arendt says that "It seems that a man who is nothing but a man has lost the very qualities which make it possible for other people to treat him as a fellow-man."[23] One of the main things

---

[20] Ibid., p. 478.
[21] For more on the sense of self see Larry May, *The Socially Responsive Self*, Chicago: University of Chicago Press, 1996.
[22] Arendt, *Origins*, p. 301.
[23] Ibid., p. 300.

that membership in a group does is to provide the member with common rights and responsibilities. Stripped of rights and responsibilities, humans are seen as no more than brutes, not individuals to be
respected. And, it appears, that this is the condition that genocide seeks
to perpetuate, namely, to reduce humans with dignity to humans as
mere brutes, as those who are not worthy of respect let alone of rights.
For Arendt, what makes people worthy of equal respect is that they are
recognized as having common responsibilities based on being capable
of taking joint action in the world.[24]

Genocide devalues individuals by depriving them of membership in
groups in such a way that it also renders impossible the keeping of the
promise of equality to all humans. With this loss of equality, the seeds
are sown for the destruction of the rule of law that had replaced "the
old laws and orders of the feudal society."[25] Naked individuals, stripped
of group affiliation, and long ago stripped of feudal class status, are
unprotected and subject to arbitrary rule. And arbitrary rule, especially
of the totalitarian kind, so obliterates even the hope of equality that it
ultimately harms humanity itself. There is thus truth to the claim that
concentration camps were as much an affront to Jews or gypsies as to
humanity as a whole.

Various authors and court opinions have also stressed the harm
to humanity of genocide. Raphael Lemkin says that "the destruction
of a nation, therefore, results in the loss of its future contribution to
the world."[26] In the very influential Krstic case, the International
Criminal Tribunal for the Former Yugoslavia (ICTY) Appeals Chamber
said: "Those who devise and implement genocide seek to deprive
humanity of the manifold richness its nationalities, races, ethnicities,
and religions provide. This is a crime against all of humankind, its harm
being felt not only by the group targeted for destruction, but by all of
humanity."[27]

It turns out that what is important about genocide is that individuals
are forcibly removed from their groups, either by killing or other means.
It does not matter whether the group is actually destroyed or not. But
what if the individuals who have been forcibly evicted from one group

[24] On this point see Larry May, *Sharing Responsibility*, Chicago: University of Chicago
      Press, 1992.
[25] Ibid., p. 290.
[26] Lemkin, *Axis Rule in Occupied Europe*, p. 91.
[27] *Prosecutor v. Radislav Krstic*, International Tribunal for the Former Yugoslavia, case no.
      IT-98–33-A, 19 April 2004, Appeals Chamber Judgment, para. 36.

are then assimilated into another group. Assimilation, especially forced assimilation, still has the consequence that the individual's sense of self is likely to be undermined. For unless the assimilation happens at a very young age, and the assimilating group accepts the new member and bestows friendship-like sentiments upon him or her, the individual will still feel alone. The individual stands to the new group as an outsider and feels that a significant part of his or her self has been removed by being forced from the group that this individual has grown up in. In any event, the key is that an individual feels support from one's primary group affiliation, and there is only a small likelihood that a group that one has been forced to join, after forcibly being removed from a group one was born into, will provide that support. I will discuss this point in greater detail in the next chapter.

If the key to understanding the harm of genocide is not the destruction of the group, why does the Genocide Convention set out this as the main part of the definition of genocide? On the account I have been elaborating, the group's existence is tied to the individual group member's ability to claim as a matter of rights, not merely as a matter of charity, that his or her rights should be protected. And to have the right to make claims one has to have a certain status. What Arendt showed was that it wasn't sufficient merely to have the status of human, for this directed no one to do anything, and more importantly, no one was responsible when rights were not protected, and hence there was no place to turn to make one's rights claims. Groups are important for providing a basis of identity and protection.

At least one meaning of the words "as such" is that these words are added for emphasis so that the *mens rea* of the perpetrators of genocide is defined in terms of not merely diminishing the relative status of the group but ultimately destroying the group by some kind of discriminatory animus.[28] How does this square with my account? At least part of the answer is that even with diminished status a group can still protect its members to a certain extent. Indeed, there may be incidental diminution of the status of the group that is based merely on the relative rise of the status of other groups. Perhaps this up and down status of groups is inevitable over time. But what genocide is supposed to be about is the intentional destruction of the group, depriving the group of its status of being able to protect the rights of its members. Such a crime, although not appearing significant when stated so blandly, may be quite

---

[28] For much more on this topic see Chapter 8.

significant but probably is not the greatest of crimes, as we will see in the final section of this chapter.

V. Objections

In the extensive literature on rights, one dominant view sees rights as claims to specific goods. But it is not enough that one can make claims for various things, and even that some moral sanctioning power can be appealed to when those claims go unanswered. In addition the rights-claimant must have a certain legal status within a particular political society. On this construal of Arendt's position, one must be an equal, at least before the law, to everyone else in the society. If one is not in the majority in the society, then one must have some clear status as a minority member that entitles one to make claims against the majority of the State. In this context, being a member of a recognized and respected minority group will provide a foot in the door to having equality before the law even if one is a member of only a tiny minority.

As an example, think of black slaves in the United States South before the Civil War. They had certain limited rights, effectively what their owners were willing to grant them as a matter of charity, or perhaps even pity. But after the Civil War, and especially after the passage of the 14th Amendment to the United States Constitution, Blacks in the United States had rights as a matter of equal legal right. One might think that because the key seems to be a function of equality of rights, it is unclear what role groups play in the guarantee of rights. The response is, as I indicated above, that being a member of a group provides one with an aid in pressing one's rights as a bulwark against the denial of the equal protection of the laws.

We now can begin to see why genocide might be one of the most important crimes in international criminal law. Genocide is wrong because it is a denial of one of the chief protections against human rights abuse. But somehow I suspect that this explanation of the wrong of genocide will not satisfy. Arendt provides us with an important beginning consideration, but only a beginning. The so-called rights of man do not secure human rights, because in the abstract they offer few if any protections. Indeed, although genocide violates the "rights of man," not much, in her view, follows from that. There should be institutions that will provide remedies when rights are violated. For Arendt, international institutions are not able to do much, and have not done much historically. This is why she links civil rights with human rights. When a whole group of people is deprived of their civil rights, as occurs most dramatically in genocidal campaigns, the human rights of those people is also harmed, and so humanity is harmed. But we would still need a more sophisticated basis for linking civil rights protection with certain groups, such as those racial groups that do not themselves generally have much political power.

One might wonder what Arendt would say today about the new set of international institutions that have arisen to deal with human rights complaints and their proposed remedies. I am thinking of the regional human rights commissions, such as the European Commission on Human Rights, as well as the ad hoc and permanent international criminal courts. Perhaps these commissions and tribunals will be seen as the new last bulwark for the protection of human rights. So in addition we might also wonder whether the role of groups will be diminished in protecting human rights, and hence whether the attempt to destroy a group should continue to be seen as the greatest of crimes in international law. Genocide will still be an important, although not the worst, crime in the constellation of international crimes, because it deprives people of something significant for their status as rights bearers.

We have come to this point of seeing the harm, but not the overriding harm, of genocide by treating genocide as a crime primarily that harms individuals, not primarily as a harm to the groups that are targeted themselves. If one wants to continue to defend genocide as the worst of all international crimes, after the rise of new effective international institutions for redressing human rights violations, one might look to some other theory of the harm of genocide, perhaps to other ways that the loss of group membership affects the lives of individuals, such as when individuals are stripped of significant meaning in their lives, and even in their deaths.[29] But in doing so one must pay heed to Arendt's arguments, and those of many of the people who represented States at the 1948 Genocide Convention. Groups do not have value in themselves; the value of groups is in terms of how they affect individuals.[30]

The destruction of a group, where most of the members are also killed, is a truly terrible crime. But this seems to be primarily because of the widespread killing of individuals involved. The destruction of a group, where individuals are not killed, is harder to see as a great crime. I have tried to make sense of the harm of genocide largely in

[29] See Chapter 5 for more on this topic.
[30] See May, *The Morality of Groups*.

Arendtian terms. I believe that the arguments have been successful in showing how the destruction of social groups might harm humanity. But I worry that these arguments are undercut by the rise of effective international institutions that take the place of social groups in providing a last bulwark against human rights abuse. If nothing else, the rise of these institutions, perhaps paradoxically, makes it harder to see what the harm of genocide is. And there are certainly other possibilities if the world moves increasingly toward a cosmopolitan State. In such circumstances, will genocides be more acceptable? This would also be a very odd result.

Another objection to the Arendtian approach to the harm of genocide is that not all groups listed in the Genocide Convention have historically been protectors of the human rights of their members. As I said, racial groups rarely provide protection for their members because they do not generally have much political power. In addition, racial and ethnic groups have "group boundaries" that are porous and often unclear, so the status of a member of the group is often contentious. National groups may be better in this respect, because they are often declared by fiat, and some have provided significant protection of rights historically, although certainly not uniformly so. It is only certain national groups that Arendt is primarily thinking of in her arguments in *Origins of Totalitarianism*. Religious groups are somewhere in the middle. Some religious groups have historically protected their members, but the membership conditions are often not well articulated.

A further objection to the Arendtian view brings us back to the idea of humanity. If a person is stripped of his or her civil rights, this does not necessarily mean that the person's human rights have been adversely affected, and hence it is unclear precisely why loss of civil rights would mean that humanity is harmed. It is true that human rights without some protections are not truly human rights. But civil rights are both underinclusive and overinclusive as human rights protectors. Some civil rights, such as the right to be paid a minimum wage, are narrower than, and not normally included in the list of human rights. Other civil rights, such as the right to be a citizen, are broader than what is normally included in lists of human rights. There is not a tight fit between civil and human rights. So even when civil rights are protected there will be important human rights that are not protected.

In the next chapter I will continue to pursue the question of what is the harm of genocide. I will build on the idea that the harm cannot be understood in terms of killing individuals, even massive killing of individuals. And I will try again to explain the supreme moral importance of the harm of genocide in terms of what is happening to the individuals who are members of a group that is the subject of genocide. Here loss of status will be a key consideration, although precisely what is lost due to genocide will remain somewhat elusive.

5

Harms to Identity and Status
of a Group's Members

In the previous chapter I explored the idea that the harm of genocide is that the group is harmed or that in some sense humanity is harmed. Although there is a sense in which all of humanity is harmed when genocide occurs, this is also true of other international crimes as well. The crime against humanity, as its name would suggest, is also a crime for which the harm can be characterized, at least in part, as adversely affecting humanity. To find what makes genocide uniquely harmful, and perhaps supremely harmful, in international law, something else needs to be identified as the basis of the harm of genocide.

In this chapter it will be important to note that the crime against humanity, called persecution, involves attacks made against a population based on group membership. In this respect the crime of persecution differs from the crime of genocide only in the reference to group destruction. It is thus the reference to group destruction that is the unique characteristic of genocide. And it is this characteristic that needs to be shown to make matters worse than if it were not present. I will argue that the destruction of a group does not make genocide the worst of crimes, although I also argue that the destruction of a group is one of the worst of harms.

In my view, the harm of genocide is best understood in terms of the effects on the status or identity of the members of a group. But the harm to status or identity is not like what Claudia Card has called "social death," and because of this, because the harm of genocide is less than the harm normally associated with death of individuals, it is my view that we should not continue to talk of the harm of genocide as morally unique and worse than all other international crimes, and hence we should not think of the crime of genocide as the crime of crimes. Nonetheless, the harm of genocide is quite a serious harm and indeed one of the worst harms among international crimes, and crime in general.

In the first section of this chapter, I will begin by rehearsing how the debate about the harm of genocide has been affected by a consideration of the paradigm historical case, that of the Holocaust. I argue that the Holocaust had certain unique features, not shared by other genocides, that make it not a good example to study to ascertain what the harm of genocide is in general. In the second section of this chapter, I will compare the harm of persecution to that of genocide as I look for the moral uniqueness of genocide having to do with individual harms. In the third section of the chapter, I will critically discuss Claudia Card's important attempt to understand the harm of genocide, ultimately giving reasons to dismiss her suggestion. In the fourth section, I consider a new strategy, partially inspired by Card's account, called the loss of group status model. In the fifth section of the chapter, I respond to some objections to my view.

I. The Holocaust as a Model of Understanding Genocide's Harm

Let us begin with a brief discussion of the important and highly controversial use of the Holocaust in debates about genocide. In the extensive literature on genocide, it is common to find a premium placed on a deep respect for the experiences of those who have suffered from genocide. One finds important testimony from the victims, and their family members, as well as soul-searching attempts to explain what would have motivated humans to do such horrible things to fellow humans. In earlier chapters I asked what theoretical account can best be given of the harm of genocide, especially when not too many are killed. Thinking of the Holocaust is useful as a vivid reminder of the way that genocide produces strikingly horrendous suffering of humans, most of whom are innocent and many of whom are children.

It is difficult to think of genocide without thinking of the paradigm cases of genocide, and especially the Holocaust. There is ample evidence that those responsible for drafting the Genocide Convention, which occurred only a few short years after the end of the Second World War, were similarly and strongly influenced by the Holocaust. If one were Jewish and living in Central Europe in the early 1940s, there would surely be very few if any losses that one could experience that are worse than what would have been lost had the anticipated annihilation of the entire Jewish people by the Nazi government been successful. And even without the completion of the "Final Solution," the sheer number of deaths and untold misery caused by the Nazis in their attempt to destroy the Jewish people is nearly unparalleled in human history and stands as a stark example of all that is horrible about genocide.

Many subsequent instances of genocide have involved large-scale complicity within the larger population, where even the relatives of the victims are often complicit. Many will object that the Holocaust is different, and I will be the first to agree. As Hannah Arendt and others have argued, there was complicity among some Jewish leaders in the Holocaust,[1] but this was undoubtedly not on the scale that has occurred in other genocides. And the "evil" that was manifest in the Holocaust did not have the kind of ambiguity that many other genocides have had. Indeed, when people visit Auschwitz or the other death camps, many are literally sickened by what they see. The conclusion seems obvious: international law must deal directly with the perpetrators of genocides such as the Holocaust, if there are any others, in the clearest terms, for this type of wrong is certainly among the worst. Yet, as we will see in subsequent chapters, it is not always clear who is responsible for what has occurred in many recent genocides.

Berel Lang has argued that it is important to conceptualize genocide with the Holocaust always as the paradigm example. He argues that

> historical paradigms – exemplary causes – are components of that history, as similar structures have otherwise, in other areas, also figured in the history of human ideas and acts. There is nothing surprising or problematic in the claim that we come to know what moral principle is – or, [what]...evil principle [is] – by encountering [it] first in history, by seeing there, close up, its transformations and its consequences. It is indeed difficult to know what the alternative to this, as a basis for the history of ethics, could be.[2]

If we follow Lang's suggestion, and think of genocide and the Holocaust as inextricably intertwined then it will be easier to understand why many have seen genocide as the worst of all possible international crimes. In general I do not disagree with Lang about keeping paradigm cases in mind when we examine a moral concept.

---

[1] See Hannah Arendt, *Eichmann in Jerusalem*, New York: Viking Press, 1963.
[2] Lang, *Act and Idea in the Nazi Genocide*, p. 29.

Yet it is also true that the concept of genocide has been, and is currently being, used for many cases other than the Holocaust.[3] I do not dispute that we should see the Holocaust as one of the most horrible moral atrocities of all time. But insofar as genocide covers more than one case, indeed more than even its main exemplar, we cannot rest with the easy task of explaining the moral wrong of the Holocaust alone to understand the much larger concept of genocide. The alternative to what Lang suggests is to look first at the exemplar but then also at the whole range of phenomena that fall under the concept of genocide.

Paying too much attention to the exemplar of the Holocaust may make it difficult to understand the rest of the phenomena, especially insofar as the rest of the phenomena may not elicit the visceral condemnation that is elicited in considering the Holocaust. As I said, I am not opposed to the idea that exemplars and paradigm cases can often elucidate a concept. But if these cases are too closely associated with the concept, it becomes very difficult to know how to deal with other cases that also seemingly fall under the concept. Concepts are larger than individual instances that fall under them. And, it should go without saying, the category of genocide is larger than the Holocaust.

There is also a problem with the way the definition of genocide was so closely tied to the example of the Holocaust. In Chapter 3 I argued that the definition of genocide, with a list of only four groups that can be the object of genocide, is conceptually insupportable. One needs to remember that, at least according to one authority, the four groups – racial, ethnic, national, and religious – were chosen because they best represented the constellation of groups that all intersected with the Jewish people who were the subject of the Holocaust.[4] As various scholars and practitioners have tried to defend the definition of genocide first announced in the Genocide Convention, they have generally failed to account for why just these four groups can be the subject of genocide. Disconnecting the exemplary case from the concept of genocide again seems called for. For this reason and the reasons advanced earlier in this section, the harm of genocide should not be drawn with reference to the Holocaust. But there may be other reasons why genocide is morally unique, reasons that I will explore in the next section of this chapter,

---

[3] See the cases discussed in the book *Is the Holocaust Unique?* edited by Alan S. Rosenbaum, Boulder: Westview Press, 2001.

[4] See Schabas, *Genocide in International Law.*

before discussing my own solution to the question of what is the harm of genocide that would make it quite bad but not uniquely immoral or harmful.

II. Comparing the Harms of Persecution and Genocide

In international law, genocide differs from persecution, which is a crime against humanity, in that persecution is an assault against a person based on that person's group membership, but that is not necessarily based on an intent to destroy the group. So one conceptual question is: what is the moral difference between genocide and persecution that would make genocide significantly worse than persecution? To make for a fair comparison, we need to think about persecution on the scale that genocide normally occurs, namely, to think of both of these as mass crimes.

So we can think of 1,000 people killed as mass persecution, where each is killed because of his or her ethnicity, and compare that crime to a genocide where 1,000 people are killed with the intent to destroy the ethnic group in question. There certainly is a difference between the first case and the second, but is there a significant moral difference so that we are entitled to say that the second case, of genocide, is worse than the first case, of persecution? I will explore various possible ways to answer this question in the affirmative, finding all of these responses unsatisfactory, but one less unsatisfactory than the others. Given that many people seem to have the intuition that the question should be answered in the affirmative, then despite its problems the basis for this intuition is probably that other harms are more likely to occur as ancillary to the mass crime in the case of genocide than in the case of persecution.

Because I am a nominalist, as discussed in Chapter 2, I will not spend much time worrying about whether groups themselves have value completely independently of individuals. Groups are not like species in that they have value for the diversity of the gene pool. And groups are not like communities because groups don't necessarily cohere and provide support for their members. Even if they did provide such support, the value of the group is surely mainly in what can be provided for the individual members. Some groups may be repositories for cultural heritage, although this is much more likely to be true of communities rather than groups, and certainly is not true of such groups as racial ones.

Although it is true that persecution normally affects fewer people than genocide, it seems to be a mistake merely to let this contingent fact color our analysis of the comparative harm of these crimes. And although both of these crimes are like hate crimes, it is also true that genocide seems to be a more severe reaction based on group hatred than does persecution, because genocide involves the intent to destroy the entire group. But the definition of genocide in international law involves the clause "in whole or in part," so it is countenanced that the harm of genocide may not be a more severe reaction in terms of consequences than is true of persecution because the harm may affect only a part of the group, as is normally also true of persecution, even though the aim is ultimately to destroy the whole group.

The most plausible, and yet by no means unproblematic, basis for the moral difference between persecution and genocide is that the latter risks more ancillary harm than does the former. If one engages in a campaign of persecution, one is not as likely to continue to perpetrate additional persecutions or other crimes against the target social group, as in genocide where the whole point is to aim at the ultimate destruction of the group itself. Hence, in genocide it is more likely than in persecution that there will be continuing harms after the initial ones, because genocide involves the additional intent not only to harm current group members but also to destroy the group itself. As we will see in subsequent sections, although these harms are to individuals, especially to their group identities, the harms all cluster around loss of status and identity in a way that makes genocide especially harmful even if not uniquely or preeminently so.

The moral uniqueness of groups could be understood not in terms of the moral uniqueness of the group per se but in terms of what the group means to the individual member. This is surely the idea that animates the strong visceral reaction that many people have when they hear news of a genocide. Individuals form a strong attachment and derive significant elements of their identity from the groups of which they are members. And if the individuals are forced not to be members of a particular group, even if there is no significant loss of life of the members of the group, these individuals will often feel a very significant psychic loss and social disorientation. When individuals are forced out of groups, there are indeed morally significant consequences to those individuals. The kind of harm involved is likely to spread across large segments of a population, even including those segments not under direct attack.

When we shift to see the value of a group not in terms of the loss of the group per se but in terms of what the group means to the individuals who are members, we also make it harder to explain the possibly unique moral character of genocide. For many things affect the mental lives of individuals, and the negative effects are likely to lie along a continuum rather than fall into a hierarchy that has clearly defined borders. This is not to deny that the destruction, or attempt to destroy, a group will often entail enormous psychic costs to these members, but only to indicate that other things will also entail harsh psychic costs, such as loss of a member of one's family, that would render the moral uniqueness of genocide suspect. Indeed, it seems that the loss of a family member would normally produce more psychic distress than would the forced disconnection from one's group. And such a loss can occur in a wide variety of cases for a wide variety of causes and motivations.

In the previous chapter, I cited some of the work of Hannah Arendt as giving us a beginning understanding of the harm of genocide that turns on the loss of the protection that a group offers to its members. Such protection is often the last bulwark that prevents the individual from being lost and alone in the world. In what follows I will explore this idea in more detail as I compare the strategies of seeing genocide's harm in terms of social death and loss of status or identity. Both of these strategies are consistent with the thrust of Arendt's moving discussion of what Jews suffered during and after the Holocaust, and also with the accounts of other genocides in the late twentieth and early twenty-first centuries.

III. Genocide and Social Death

Claudia Card has provided an initial solution to the puzzle of why the harm of genocide is considered special, even if not unique. She argues that "What distinguishes genocide is not that it has a different kind of victim, namely groups (although it is a convenient shorthand to speak of targeting groups). Rather the kind of harm suffered by individual victims of genocide, in virtue of their group membership, is not captured by other crimes."[5] Card presents genocide as involving what I have elsewhere called group-based harm, harm that befalls individuals, but does so by virtue of some reference to the group membership of those individuals.[6] As she says, "It is not just that one's group membership is the occasion for harms that are definable independently of one's identity. When a group with its own cultural identity is destroyed, its survivors

---

[5] Card, "Genocide and Social Death," p. 68.
[6] See May, *The Morality of Groups*.

lose their cultural heritage, and may even lose their intergenerational connections."[7]

Card draws on a literature from sociology to describe genocide. Here is how she characterizes the harm of genocide:

> To use Orlando Patterson's terminology, in that event they may become 'socially dead' and their descendants '*natally alienated*,' no longer able to pass along and build upon the traditions, cultural developments (including language), and projects of earlier generations. The harm of social death is not necessarily less extreme than that of physical death. Social death can even aggravate physical death by making it indecent, removing all respectful and caring ritual, social connections, and social contexts that are capable of making dying bearable and even of making one's death meaningful. In my view, the special evil of genocide lies in its infliction of not just physical death (when it does that) but social death, producing a consequent meaninglessness of one's life and even of its termination.[8]

For Card, social death means that something equal to, or perhaps worse than, physical death has occurred. Card characterizes the harm here as a loss of what makes one's own life meaningful, and what would make one's death bearable.

I am inclined to think that Card is on the right track in characterizing the harm of genocide in terms of social death. Such a characterization allows us to account for the feeling of hopelessness and despair of those who lived through a genocidal campaign. It also allows us to see why, even when there isn't much killing, the harm of genocide still seems to be extreme. What Card has not fully explained is the way that groups play a role in genocide and why it is that the destruction of a group that one identifies with is as important, and perhaps more so, than the destruction of other parts of a person's identity, such as gender, age, place of birth, place of residence, profession, and kin.

I suppose that some of the identity characteristics just mentioned could be understood also by reference to groups, such as profession and kin, but this is not necessarily true. In identifying with a profession, a lawyer or doctor could be thinking of the tasks that he or she performed and the good that was achieved, rather than having any explicit connection to the others who performed the same tasks and had the opportunity to do so much good. It is certainly true that one's group often plays a major role in determining identity, but other factors seem

---

[7] Card, "Genocide and Social Death," p. 73.

[8] Ibid. At the beginning of this passage, Card is quoting from Orlando Patterson's book *Slavery and Social Death*, Cambridge, MA: Harvard University Press, 1982, pp. 5–9.

to be important as well. So, if one loses one's group identity, one might not be sent into despair or meaninglessness, for there are other aspects of one's identity that are seemingly unaffected by the loss of a group characteristic.

Yet group affiliation, especially concerning groups that one is born into, is often the main ingredient in one's identity. In my view, this is because of the way in which we are such social creatures. In this, Card is right to talk of something such as social death as the key to understanding the harm of genocide. As social beings, a large component of our identities concerns our groupings, the way that we are connected with other individual human persons into distinct clusters of people who are able to support each other in various ways and to provide significant sources of interaction: friendship, companionship, intimacy, comfort, conversation, and a wide range of opportunities to share experiences. Group affiliation provides these significant components of one's identity. And although one could find new groups to provide some of these factors after loss of one's primary group, something more seems lost that cannot be made up if one is forced out of a group that one was originally born into, or if one's group was significantly demeaned.

Card also makes the important point that even one's death, not just one's life, loses meaning because of genocidal campaigns. I wish to explore this important point in more detail. Even if one is not killed in an untimely manner by genocide, Card claims that one's eventual death may be adversely affected by that genocide. I suspect that what she has in mind is that a person's death has meaning insofar as one can see that the life led had a purpose and accomplishments, and that one of the most significant ways that lives have these features is when the people are part of a group where roles and purposes are reasonably well defined. More importantly, one's identity is often intimately linked to one's group memberships. While alive one is recognized by these memberships, and when one dies one is, at least in part, remembered in terms of the social memberships one had and the social roles one played.

One can wonder, as Aristotle did, about whether the dead really have interests that are harmed in a straightforward way by what happens after their death. But at the moment, I am discussing the less controversial topic of whether what happens just before death affects the quality of one's death. Surely there is something to this general point, because a person who is tortured before death has a much worse death than one who is not.[9] On this model, it also seems sensible to say that a person who has lost significant group affiliations before death has a worse death than a person who does not. But it is less clear to me that the death would be completely meaningless because of such a loss caused by genocide. A person can have accomplishments even after being stripped of significant social attachments, as was true for many German Jewish refugees after the Nazi Holocaust. Indeed, although these lives might have had less significant meaning because of the genocide, surely most still had meaning both in life and death. Nonetheless, I agree that even death is less meaningful for those people who did experience genocide than those who did not.

Both a person's life and death are adversely affected by genocide, even if a person is not killed directly by the genocidal campaign. Groups that one is born into, such as ethnic, racial, national, and religious groups, normally have a role to play in one's identity that is hard to replace. Loss of such group affiliations does indeed leave many people feeling rootless or ungrounded. As I said, it is possible for some people, over time, to find other groups to attach themselves to and to begin to identify with those groups. Card is right to think that when genocidal campaigns strip away group membership from individuals, those people are left with something like a feeling of death, even if it is only social and not physical death. And even one's death can be rendered less meaningful by genocide. The idea of social death captures, at least in part, the very significant loss that comes from the destruction or attempted destruction of a group of which one has been a member since birth.

As we will next see, the idea of social death does have some conceptual problems that warrant a change to a somewhat different characterization of the harm of genocide, but one that is certainly in the same ballpark as Card's social death thesis. The social death thesis does indeed help us explain why genocide is seen as one, if not the worst, of the harms that can befall a human person. And it is for this reason that genocide is seen as the worst of crimes. I do not think that this inference is well supported, but I understand why people draw the inference. As Arendt pointed out, not only is group membership important for identity, but also for a kind of security that comes from associating with others for the protection of one's rights. In the next section I will criticize but also build on Card's views and then employ my own account of the harm of

---

[9] See Henry Shue, "Torture," *Philosophy & Public Affairs*, vol. 7 no. 2, Winter 1978, pp. 124–43.

genocide, the "loss of group identity and status" view, to examine why genocide is not morally unique but nonetheless immoral and extremely harmful.

IV. Loss of Status and Identity

The idea of social death carries with it ideas that are somewhat misleading and do not fully capture the harm of genocide. That the social death thesis is both too broad and also too narrow should not be seen as diminishing this significant effort to identify the harm of genocide. I will build on the social death account, but will ultimately support a different view that hopefully does not have the same problems as exist in the social death account. Thinking of the harm of genocide in terms of social death is misleading in several important ways, yet these are ways that lead us to a very fruitful reconceiving of the harm of genocide.

I begin with some criticisms of Card's view that I began to explore in the previous section. First of all, the term "social death" is too strong in that it implies that the entire social part of a person has died as a result of the genocide. As I indicated above, many, if not most, people will be able to go on with their social lives after surviving genocide. The lives may very well be enormously impoverished, but people will normally be able to form new social relationships and social roles partially to replace those lost by the genocidal campaign. Second, although the lives and deaths of the victims of genocide will be impoverished because of the loss of some group-based identifications, other group-based identifications will remain, perhaps even unaffected by what has occurred in the genocide. And, third, although genocide does affect the meaningfulness of both one's life and death, it is likely that there is still some meaning to life and death even after genocide. The idea of social death is too strong a term to capture the harm of genocide. But this idea is certainly on the right track. As we will see, loss of identity is one of the most important things that constitute the harm of genocide.

A loss of group identity is associated with a loss of status. In general, I will follow Arendt and Card and argue that the harm of genocide is a status harm. I have already said quite a bit about this kind of harm in the previous chapter. Status harms affect many aspects of a person's life, although not as profoundly as death. When one lacks status as a group member one also loses significant rights protection, including even human rights protections. But there are significant differences between the metaphor of death, a biological concept, and status, a social concept.

The status harm caused by genocide affects some of the most significant of a person's rights, chiefly by affecting a person's social identity. The harm of genocide is that individuals are stripped of one of their group identities, with a corresponding loss, normally not permanent, of who they are and what roles they have in the larger society, as well as a loss of the sense of self that sustains them as a source of meaningfulness for both their lives and their deaths. As one can see, this view is similar to the social death thesis. Genocide involves a loss to the individual of many aspects of one's life that are dependent on group identity and identification. The loss of group identity thesis holds that genocide does involve a very serious harm, and that harm is not captured by other kinds of harm that are recognized as international crimes, such as war crimes, crimes of aggression, or crimes against humanity.

The loss of group identity, even if it comes about only for those in a particular region and not across the entire group, is significant. There are three factors here. First, group identity forms a part of the mechanism by which people are recognized and identified in society. Social recognition is important for one's status and standing in society, where one is visible, not invisible, to one's compatriots. Second, group identity forms a significant component in how a person acknowledges and remembers who he or she is, a way of locating the self in a sea of factors and influences. Here collective identity forms a part of collective memory, which strongly influences individual memory. Third, group identity often plays the role that Arendt discussed, where a person derives support from fellow members who aid in the protection of interests and rights of the members. In this way there is sometimes a bulwark against loneliness and aloneness that would make one vulnerable to loss of rights protections, as is true of those who are Stateless.

The three factors of external recognition, self-acknowledgment, and rights protection are linked with each other in various ways. For the Arendtian account we discussed in the previous chapter, the first two factors are the ways that the members of a group are recognized and recognize each other as having a certain status that carries with it a certain level of rights-protection. Of course, when a group is under attack as occurs in genocide, the identification of a group's members is what triggers the perpetuation of harms across the group, or at least that part of a group that coheres in a given geographic region. What was once a form of recognition and acknowledgment that protects the individuals as members of a coherent group becomes a source of harm that is more likely to spread from one person to another when the group itself is targeted for elimination as occurs in genocide.

The solidarity of some groups is made possible by the forms of identification, and there is then a link to the status of the group that each, or many, members feel. Persecution can be the catalyst that intensifies harm, but it is my contention that genocide is worse than persecution, in most cases, because the spread of the harm is rendered so much more likely if the members of the group are not merely targeted because of their group membership, but also because the perpetrators seek the group's ultimate destruction. The harm to individuals is more likely to continue if there is this aim of destruction of the group "as such" and not merely that the individual members are made to suffer. This will not always be true but is made more likely because of the larger plan of group destruction that typically exists in genocide cases, as we will see in Part D, because once there is coordinated behavior, there is the greater likelihood of harms spreading beyond an initial subgroup of members of a group that is under attack.

Another strategy may be to argue that genocide should be seen as involving some physical deaths, contrary to the way the Genocide Convention understood it, but closer to how it is being treated in international criminal law today. The task would then be to indicate that what makes genocide worse than other forms of killing is the added dimension of the loss of group identity for the survivors.[10] The problem here is only to explain why some killing in genocide, plus the loss of group identity for the survivors, is worse than massive killing in other atrocities that do not involve such loss of group identity and status, and also worse than extreme persecution based on group membership. We are thrown back on the question of what precisely is the harm of loss of group identity, and whether it is indeed equivalent to or worse than random massive physical death. As I have said, I remain skeptical that such an argument can be successful, even in the case where we amend the definition of genocide so that at least some killing must be involved.

One of the key differences between the social death thesis and the loss of identity and status thesis is that the kind of harm of genocide is not characterized as involving anything equivalent to physical death. Loss is a very different metaphor than death. Yet there are strong similarities nonetheless, especially if the loss involves something very important

---

[10] Berel Lang suggested this strategy to me in correspondence on March 25, 2006.

to the person in question. At the time the loss of one's reputation, for instance, is for many people almost as bad as death itself, even if the loss of reputation may over time be overcome. Indeed, many philosophers, Aristotle included, have said that some harm can occur even after someone is dead, because of loss of reputation. Loss can be a very serious harm, just not quite as serious normally as death in any of its forms.

The social death thesis is problematic in just this way, namely, that it tries to show that genocide involves something that is worse than massive physical death. Perhaps having an account of genocide in terms of social death would indeed correspond to the sentiments of many of the victims of genocide, especially Holocaust survivors. But it is very hard to work out theoretically, as I have been arguing throughout this chapter. Instead, we may have to settle for a thesis, something such as the loss of group identity and status thesis that does capture the phenomenon but is not as satisfying to some of the victims as one might have hoped. Conceptually, though, we will have a more defensible account of genocide on the basis of which international law will be firmly grounded. In the remainder of this chapter I will add more detail to my loss of group identity and status thesis by responding to various objections that a critic could make against my proposal.

V. Objections

One could object at this point that I am simply giving too little weight to the true horrors of genocide that are illustrated in the many deeply wrenching accounts given by genocide survivors. One can think especially of the accounts of Holocaust survivors and the very deep anguish that they felt and that has been documented many times in films and print sources. The Holocaust should not color all of our insights into genocide, but it also should not be underestimated either. One might ask how one can worry about such fine distinctions such as whether the harm of genocide is best seen as a type of death or a type of loss. Isn't this the kind of insensitive rationalizing of genocide that victims groups have objected to over the years, and that have so divided members of genocide studies programs?

As I suggested earlier, I aim to discuss genocide in a way that is somewhat sensitive to those who have focused on the victims, but my aim is indeed primarily theoretical. From a theoretical perspective, it matters what is the best account of the harm of genocide given the variety of things that the term "genocide" covers in international law. In addition, it is important to articulate the harm of genocide so that when there are those who try to diminish its significance, we have something to say that is not merely an emotional telling of the facts. The field of law generally is in this sense rational rather than emotional, although the kind of consequences to those who are made to stand trial for international crimes such as genocide are often much more severe than those that are meted out merely in the court of public opinion. In later chapters I will turn to how the conceptualization of the harm of genocide affects such things as the justification of humanitarian intervention undertaken to stop or prevent genocide. Most importantly I will also link this discussion of the harm of genocide to the responsibility of individuals for its perpetration.

A second objection to consider concerns my earlier defense of nominalism. If there really aren't social groups independently existing in the world, why think that there is a real harm from loss of group identity or status? The loss of group identity and status thesis seems to require that there is a "group" for there to be loss of "group identity." Yet my discussion in earlier chapters seems to preclude me from holding that there is such a group that could be the source of this "group identity," the loss of which is the basis for the harm of genocide. If one is a nominalist, the harm of genocide seemingly cannot be so closely linked to a group, and this is especially true if the ontological status of groups is as infirm as I suggested in previous chapters. Nominalism about harm should be as difficult to overcome as is nominalism about the ontological status of groups.

My response to this objection is to point out that I did not earlier deny that it can make sense to talk of groups, although I did argue that the ontological status of groups was infirm. Talk of groups has to be grounded in what is happening to individuals, and my loss of group identity and status thesis seemingly does that. In addition, things are different if one is speaking of the characteristics of group membership, rather than groups themselves. This is because group membership is a relation among individuals, not necessarily a feature of an independently existing thing, a group. Indeed, the kind of group identity that I have been speaking of is best understood in terms of the psychological states of individuals, most especially how these individuals identify themselves, and are identified by others. In acknowledging this fact, I must acknowledge that the harm of genocide then is also primarily psychological, excluding the killings and other physical assaults associated with genocide but by no means unique to genocide. Such an admission opens me up to the charge that genocide is not as catastrophic as it is normally thought. As will become clear, I will make that admission.

A third objection to my loss of group identity and status thesis is that, like Claudia Card, I too have exaggerated the importance of the harm of genocide by making it seem as if loss of group identity cannot be compensated by the gaining of new identities of at least some of those people who have suffered through genocide. I had argued that the social death thesis exaggerated the harm of genocide by making it seem as if all the people affected by genocide had suffered something comparable to death. Similarly, it could be argued that my loss of group identity and status thesis also exaggerates the harm of genocide in making it seem as if all the people affected by genocide had suffered an irredeemable loss. Yet, because people have more than one group identity, and may acquire new ones, the loss is not as significant as I have suggested.

I must admit the thrust of this objection, namely, that if what makes genocide unique is the loss of group identity and status, the unique harm of genocide is indeed not nearly as bad as it is often portrayed. I have tried to make it clear that I do not follow in the footsteps of those who have attempted to characterize genocide as uniquely or supremely morally important. The main harm of many genocides is that which is shared in common with some of the worst of the crimes against humanity, and also with some other international crimes, namely, physical destruction primarily of human beings and communities. There is a significant harm to genocide, but it is not so significant as to make it much worse than these other crimes. So I concede the thrust of this objection, and yet I do not think that such an admission damages what I have said about genocide's harm in previous chapters.

A fourth objection is that I have not adequately captured the kind of loss experienced by people who have lived through a genocidal campaign with my idea of loss of group identity and status. This loss of group identity may indeed be part of the loss here, but it is only a part and not by any means the whole story. Loss of community and loss of significant elements of one's family are also often involved in the harm that individuals feel as a result of suffering through genocide. My thesis risks trivializing the loss by seemingly focusing only on certain psychological factors that in and of themselves are not as significant as other factors that are importantly connected to the experience of genocide. If the major harm that extends across all cases of genocide is purely psychological, then genocide should not even be equated with crimes against humanity and other international crimes. Indeed, genocide might not even count as an international crime at all because the harm involved in genocide is not of the sort that would have an impact on the world community or on humanity, what I have elsewhere argued is the hallmark of international crime.[11]

In response, let me point out that in my view genocide does, and must, involve some physical destruction as well as psychological harm if it is to be prosecuted as an international crime. In looking for what makes the harm of genocide unique, I have not meant to give the impression that the special harm of genocide is the only harm connected to that crime. Indeed, it is my view that the special harm of genocide is not by any means the main harm of genocide. It is for this reason that I suggest that genocide should be treated as one of the crimes against humanity. The large loss of life, or the risk of such a loss, is the main harm that is associated with both genocide and other crimes against humanity. There are some interesting differences between genocide and the crime of humanity called persecution, some of which I have already explored and some of which will be the subject of discussion in later chapters. But I do not mean to deny the difficulty of prosecuting genocide cases when there is no physical harm but only psychological harm. Such a difficulty, though, is similar to the difficulty of prosecuting other serious international crimes, especially other crimes against humanity such as persecution.

In the Nuremberg Statute, the crimes that now constitute genocide were not separated out of the relatively new general category of crimes against humanity. This was true even though the Holocaust was surely the model for crimes of this sort. In recent years when genocide was elevated, and removed from the category of crimes against humanity, this was done because it was thought to be important so as to pay homage to the victims of the Holocaust. But I have argued that there is no good conceptual or normative reason to make all of the crime of genocide fit into a special and supremely important category of international crime. Having said this, I will not let this conclusion affect my analysis in the remainder of the book. I will generally proceed in a way that is indifferent to whether genocide is morally unique and superior to other crimes or not. But we will encounter several other related serious conceptual and normative puzzles about genocide nonetheless.

---

[11] See especially the discussion of the idea of "the international harm principle" in ch. 5 of May, *Crimes Against Humanity*.

PART C

ELEMENTS OF GENOCIDE

6

Genocidal Acts: Destroying Groups in Whole or in Part

How does one decide whether or not genocide is occurring? The most obvious strategy is to see if there was an explicit plan, such as in the case of the Holocaust, to eliminate an entire group from the face of the earth. Short of that strategy, one looks to see whether or not there is intent to destroy a group by having a large number of the members of a group attacked or killed. Genocide can be occurring, and yet it may not be the case that the whole group is being destroyed all at once. But the problem then becomes to figure out how much of the group has to be destroyed for it to count as a genocide. In the next three chapters I will look at the elements of the crime of genocide, the factors that mark the fact of genocide occurring, namely, the element of collective intent as well as the elements of individual act and intent associated with the collective intent to destroy a group.

In the current chapter I will discuss the *actus reus* of genocide in light of the ontological debate about joint action. This debate will shed light on the seemingly arbitrary determination of how many members of a group have to be assaulted or killed for it to constitute "destroying a group in part." This question is not merely one of arbitrarily picking a number, or some other stand-in such as "significant number," as the United States has successfully proposed as a "reservation" to the original genocide statute, although this was a good place to begin. In the current chapter I wish to focus conceptually on acts, even as I realize that it is nearly impossible to keep act and intention separate in practice.

The crime of genocide is defined as "any of the following acts committed with intent to destroy, in whole or in part, a national, ethnical, racial, or religious group, as such." Article II then gives what is supposed to be an exhaustive list of these acts:

a) Killing members of the group
b) Causing serious bodily or mental harm to members of the group
c) Deliberately inflicting on the group conditions of life calculated to bring about its physical destruction in whole or in part
d) Imposing measures intended to prevent births within the group
e) Forcibly transferring children of the group to another group.[1]

Genocide is said to involve the commissions and omissions of many people, although how many is unclear.

And so the problem becomes one of determining what the "in whole or in part" section of the intent requirement tells us about the act element of the crime of genocide. How many killings, bodily injuries, or transferring of children must be inflicted on the members of a group for it to count as an act of genocide? How are we to understand the U.S. reservation to the genocide convention, now pretty much accepted as part of international law, that the "part" must be "significant"? And what do we do with the fact that many of the acts in the list above involve not only acts but also intent dimensions? How do we make sense of acts, such as "d) Imposing measures *intended* to prevent births within the group," which clearly contains an explicit intent dimension?[2] I will attempt to answer some of these questions in what follows, although some of the most important questions will remain puzzling.

In the first section of this chapter, I will examine what is meant by the act element of the crime of genocide, paying particular attention to the question of how many such acts must be involved for the acts to count as meeting the act element of the crime of genocide. In the second and third sections, I will address two very controversial omissions in the list of genocidal acts, the destruction of cultural life in Section II, and ethnic cleansing in Section III. In the fourth section I will provide a revised characterization of the act element of the crime of genocide that allows for a more expansive list than that which is currently provided in international law. In the final section, I address some objections to my revised understanding of the act element in genocide cases.

---

[1] Convention on the Prevention and Punishment of Genocide; Rome Statute.
[2] In the *Case Concerning the Application of the Convention on the Prevention and Punishment of the Crime of Genocide (Bosnia and Herzegovinia v. Serbia and Montenegro)*, para. 186, the court also recognizes that the acts in the genocide convention "themselves include mental elements."

I. The Act of Genocide

The idea of the act of genocide, initially, is problematic simply because of the ambiguity of the term genocidal act. Does the term refer to the act of an individual person or to an act of a group? Genocide cannot normally be carried out by a single person, so it would seem that a person's act couldn't be an act of genocide. So perhaps the term "genocidal act" can apply only to group action. But because groups cannot be easily put into the dock, then no one could be prosecuted for genocide because no individual could meet this *actus reus* element of the crime of genocide. There is a third possibility, namely, that the genocidal act is the act of an individual that fits into a pattern of similar behavior that aims at the destruction of a protected group.[3]

If genocide involves "a pattern of similar behavior" across a population, then one of the key conceptual questions becomes how to establish that an individual's act of killing or assaulting a member of a protected group was indeed part of a pattern of behavior rather than merely an isolated act. It then seems hard not to make the characterization of the act depend on the intent of the individual in the dock. The question would be whether or not the individual intended his or her act to be part of this pattern. If so, then it is a genocidal act, and if not, then it is merely an isolated act of violence. But perhaps there is some other way to make this determination about the act element without appealing to the intent element.

One strategy is to look to the context of the surrounding acts. It would be odd indeed if the context fit the pattern of an organized effort and yet it turned out that the acts were related to each other only by coincidence. Of course, it is not impossible that this could occur, just very unlikely. Another factor to examine is whether there was anyone who had set the stage for an organized effort occurring by having incited or planned the organization. If this had occurred, then again it is quite likely that the individual acts that are occurring and seem to fit the organized model do so because they are part of a pattern. Once again, this is not a certainty but only another factor that makes it more likely than not that the individual acts fit into a single pattern of behavior, and are not merely related by coincidence. Once there is a pattern discovered, it is more likely than not that there are concerted actions, not mere isolated individual acts.

---

[3] See the discussion of circumstances in Clark, "The Crime of Aggression."

Another strategy that employs a mental element, but not one of intention, asks whether the person who engages in the act is aware that others are behaving similarly. If it is also known that these other people see themselves as acting in a concerted manner, and the person nonetheless acts in ways that conform to the pattern of the others' behavior, then it is again more likely than not that the individual act is related, not merely coincidental, to the pattern of behavior. And if the individual person intends to contribute to the concerted effort, even though he or she does not intend what the others intend, it is even more likely that the individual's act forms part of a pattern of similar behavior with these other acts.

Patterns of similar behavior help to link the act of an individual to a group act that could be described as genocide. In this case the individual's act as well as the group's act could be called a genocidal act. But this is primarily because the individual's act is actually part of the larger concerted genocidal act. There is a distinction between the genocidal act of an individual person who may be prosecutable in an international court and the genocidal act of a group of people who are engaged in concerted action. I propose that only when the individual's act can be linked to a pattern of similar behavior by others is the act element of the crime of genocide satisfied.

The term "genocidal act" has been highly contentious in recent years. At the time of the Rwandan atrocity, many States drew a distinction between genocidal acts occurring versus genocide occurring. The underlying assumption seemed to be that one could have genocidal acts without full-scale genocide. I wish to explore how this might be possible, ultimately criticizing this idea. We can begin this inquiry by noting that there could be genocidal acts but no genocidal intent, and hence no genocide occurring. There could be acts of mass killing, for instance, that could lead to the destruction of a group, and yet there is no clear aim to have the destruction of the group occur. This might be a case of genocidal act with no genocide occurring.

Although on one level this strategy might seem plausible, on another level it is unclear whether the act that is not attached to genocidal intent can plausibly be described as a genocidal act. Here, once again, the question becomes how to distinguish genocide from persecution. If one engages in violence toward a person because of that person's group identity, this would be a classic case of persecution. For it to be a case of genocide there must be, in addition, the *intent* to destroy the group. At least on this construal, there could not be genocidal acts that did not have attached to them genocidal intents. So the acts that are occurring could be acts of persecution, but would be misnamed as genocidal acts.

Another possibility is that there could be a single genocidal act, or perhaps even a set of such acts occurring, and yet there would not be enough of them to count as a full-scale genocide. This returns us to the point made by the United States that the "in whole or in part" proviso of the genocide definition must be understood to mean something like "in substantial part." In my view, this reservation, lodged by the United States, might be a good start. Genocide involves a circumstance surrounding individual acts that makes it plausible to say that the individual acts form a larger action such as genocide. Without such a proviso, there could be genocidal acts occurring, but there are not enough of them to constitute a full-fledged genocide.

Again, this appears to be plausible, until one recognizes that the acts in question would not be properly genocidal acts if they did not contribute to a genocide. If the circumstances of genocide are not present, because the level of violence does not cross the threshold of significant violence, the individual acts would not be part of a genocide either, and in this sense these acts would not be "genocidal." The violent acts that are not deemed to be significant enough to count as genocide would not themselves be genocidal because there were not enough of them for one of these acts to count as part of a pattern of similar behavior.

Finally, one might ask why the adjective "genocidal" couldn't be applied to acts independently of whether the noun "genocide" was appropriately applicable. This question is especially important when we are discussing incitement to genocide or attempted genocide, crimes that use the term genocide but that are also inchoate crimes in the sense that the crime can occur without there being completed genocide occurring. If it makes sense to say that there was incitement to genocide without there being a genocide, why couldn't there be genocidal acts occurring without there being genocide? The adjectival application without the noun being applicable could be merely a kind of inchoate use.

My response to this point will have to be brief and somewhat incomplete, because a full-scale examination of this issue will be needed when we get to consider incitement and other inchoate crimes associated with genocide in later chapters. Initially, I would contend that this strategy might make a certain kind of sense so that one could say that a genocidal act is only a kind of inchoate act. Inchoate acts are ones that do not require completion. Here think of attempts. We might talk mean-ingfully about "attempted murder" where a plan of murder is begun but not completed. Genocidal acts could be acts where genocide is begun but not completed. If we take this tack, then it may indeed be possible to separate the *actus reus* of genocide from the *mens rea*, even though the *mens rea* is the most important element. I will later give reasons to worry about this strategy.

II. Acts of Cultural Genocide

In the next two sections, I will look at two cases of controversial geno-cidal acts. I engage in this exercise to test the conceptual limits of the idea of genocidal acts, not necessarily because I think that changes are likely. I begin with acts of cultural genocide. The debates surround-ing the Genocide Convention considered, but ultimately rejected, the inclusion of acts of cultural genocide under the genocide statute. To get a sense of what cultural genocide means, consider the following proposal made jointly by China, Lebanon, Poland, the Soviet Union, and Venezuela.

> In this convention genocide also means any of the following deliberate acts committed with the intention of destroying the language or culture of a national, racial, or religious group on grounds of national or racial origin or religious belief:
> (1) prohibiting the use of the language of the group in daily inter-course or in schools, or prohibiting the printing and circulation of publications in the language of the group;
> (2) destroying, or preventing the use of, the libraries, museums, schools, historical monuments, places of worship, or other cultural institu-tions and objects of the group.[4]

Another proposal also included the forcible transfer of children to another group. That act was included in the genocide statute, but the rest of the proposal was rejected.

In this section I will ask whether there are good reasons to exclude cultural genocide from the list of acts that satisfy the *actus reus* of geno-cide. This question is similar to the question we investigated in an ear-lier chapter about whether there are good reasons to leave out other groups, such as gender or political groups, in the protected groups of the definition of genocide as well. The conclusion will be very similar as

[4] UN Doc. E/AC.25/SR. 14.

well, namely, that there are reasons to limit the reach of the genocide statute, but the way in which it is limited is not clearly justifiable. Indeed, I will argue that acts of cultural genocide should be included as punishable acts in international law.

One of the arguments advanced against including cultural acts in the genocide statute was advanced by Brazil at the time of the drafting of that statute. The delegation from Brazil warned that "some minorities might have used it as an excuse for opposing perfectly normal assimilation in new countries."[5] In my view, Brazil's objection is a significant one, but not one that should jettison the whole idea of including some kind of cultural genocide in the definition of genocide. There is a distinction between normal assimilation and cultural genocide that could be maintained, if one is careful in drafting. Indeed, initially one could simply distinguish between forced assimilation and unforced assimilation. More controversially, one could then try to distinguish between forced assimilation that has a devastating impact on the group and forced assimilation that does not have this effect.

Another curious objection raised by many of the delegates was that cultural genocide was a human rights issue and for that reason not something that should be included in the genocide statute. Today it is rare to draw a sharp line between international criminal matters and human rights matters. Indeed, many theorists defend the International Criminal Court as well as the earlier ad hoc international tribunals in human rights terms.[6] Mass atrocities almost always include massive violations of human rights, especially the human right of bodily integrity. But it was common for many years to distinguish between humanitarian crises and human rights crises. The former but not the latter could be understood in terms of the failure of mercy rather than duty, strictly understood.[7] But it is not evident why this distinction would help in the case of genocide because genocide seems clearly to involve massive failures at the level of both mercy and duty.

It is true that the destruction of a group is different from an assault on the human rights of the members of the group. As I argued above, though, groups do not have status and value independent of the status and value of the individuals who make up these groups. So the destruction of a group is a wrong mainly as it affects individuals who are

---

[5] UN Doc. A/C.6/SR. 133 (Amado, Brazil).
[6] See Ratner and Abrams, *Accountability for Human Rights Atrocities in International Law.*
[7] See my discussion of this issue in *War Crimes and Just War.*

members, or as it affects those humans who are not members but who are nonetheless adversely affected when genocides are allowed to occur. Thus, it remains odd to think that cultural genocide would be thought of in terms of human rights and not think of traditional genocide also in those terms, something that I will propose in later chapters of this book. Unless some clear demarcation is made, the human rights argument is simply not persuasive as a reason to exclude cultural genocide from the genocide definition.

One last point to consider is the argument that if cultural genocide were to be included in the genocide statute, it would dilute the importance of that statute. The dominant sentiment expressed at the Genocide Convention was that genocide should concern the most serious of crimes, and that this meant that it should be restricted largely to physical and biological acts.[8] This restricted way of understanding genocide would amount to minimal interference with the way States conducted their own affairs and also would restrict genocide to the most clearly egregious cases and hence further the idea that genocide was indeed the crime of crimes.

In previous chapters I have already argued that genocide is problematically seen as the crime of crimes when the contours of genocide are drawn in such a way that genocide could involve not much, or any, killing. But I also argued that even if genocide involves lots of killing, it still does not have a strong claim to be the crime of crimes. So including cultural genocide under the jurisdiction of the genocide statute would not dilute it so that it was no longer thought of as the crime of crimes. Indeed, if the point of genocide is that it involves the destruction of a group, then it seems odd not to criminalize all of the most significant acts that could lead to that result.

The acts of cultural genocide seem just as likely to lead to the destruction of a group as those acts currently listed in the genocide statute that involve killing people, and hence just as significant. Denying that a group can speak its native language or practice its traditional religion will destroy the group just as readily as killing some of the members. For this reason, acts of cultural genocide should be included under the definition of the crime of genocide, as can be seen in the "transferring children" act that is already listed under that jurisdiction. I return to this issue at the end of this chapter.

---

[8] See *Prosecutor v. Radislav Krstic*, Appeals Chamber Judgment, para. 25.

III. The Acts of Ethnic Cleansing

Ethnic cleansing, as Elihu Lauterpacht put it, is "the forced migration of civilians."[9] In the case of Bosnia, Lauterpacht argued that ethnic cleansing was a form of genocide because the intent was to destroy at least a part of a group, namely, that part that resided in a certain locale.[10] Lauterpacht here raises a very interesting conceptual issue, namely, whether groups, or parts of groups, can be defined by geographic location rather than membership. Is part of a group destroyed when it is evicted from the land the people want to live on, and have lived on for generations, even though the people can be resettled in another land? I will here support Lauterpacht's somewhat expansive understanding of how to treat "part of a group." Indeed, I will argue that sometimes the acts of ethnic cleansing should count as satisfying the *actus reus* element of the crime of genocide.

The idea of committing acts that are aimed at destroying part of a group is fraught with conceptual problems. The most obvious problem, already discussed earlier, is whether the part could be just one member of the group. Another obvious problem is whether destroying part of a group means that that part must be literally destroyed, never to emerge again, or only temporarily destroyed, in the sense of being rendered invisible for a time. And here is where the problem of ethnic cleansing comes to the fore. If destroying part of a group can mean that some members of the group are temporarily rendered invisible, then dislocating the group, so that it can no longer be easily identified, looks like it could be an instance of intending to destroy the group in part. As long as the destruction of the group in part need not connect to destroying the whole group, then ethnic cleansing might fit the act element of genocide.

William Schabas has argued that there is a significant difference between genocide and ethnic cleansing. He argues that

> it is incorrect to assert that ethnic cleansing is a form of genocide, or even that in some cases, ethnic cleansing amounts to genocide. Both, of course, may share the same goal, which is to eliminate the persecuted group from a given area. While the material acts performed to commit the crimes may

---

[9] *Application of the Convention on the Prevention and Punishment of the Crime of Genocide (Bosnia and Herzegovina v. Yugoslavia (Serbia and Montenegro)),* International Court of Justice, 13 September 1993, Separate Reasons of Judge *ad hoc* Lauterpacht, p. 431, para. 69.

[10] See ibid., pp. 431, paras. 68–70.

often resemble each other, they have two quite different specific intents. One is intended to displace a population, the other to destroy it.[11]

As Shabas notes, the "issue is one of intent."[12] But that is just the problem. If we are focusing on the act element of the crime of genocide, the issue is arguably different from intent. Indeed, Schabas admits that the acts "may often resemble each other."

I would argue that the acts of ethnic cleansing and genocide are often the same acts, for instance, the acts of forcibly evicting a group from its native territory. But even as the acts may be the same, it may be true that these acts have different intents, such as either merely to displace or to begin a process of extermination of the group. What is at issue, however, is whether certain acts should be added to the list of acts in the genocide statute. Before proceeding further, we need to identify some of these candidate acts. But it should be clear that merely thinking that these acts may not be closely related to the genocidal intent element does not necessarily rule them out as possible candidates for being genocidal acts.

Let's consider the act of forcibly displacing a population. This is often thought to be a defining act of ethnic cleansing. Such an act can be performed for many possible intentions. Here I would agree with Schabas that it would matter which intention is displayed in deciding whether the accused committed genocide by performing this act. But the status of the intention need not affect the status of the act, or at least there is nothing in principle that would dictate this result. For this reason, I think that the defining acts of ethnic cleansing could and should be included in the list of acts in the elements of the crime of genocide. But I would agree with Schabas that the act-plus-intent of ethnic cleansing is not necessarily a form of genocide.

In a 2007 judgment of the International Court of Justice, the court recognized that acts described as "ethnic cleansing" may "constitute genocide," but that ethnic cleansing is "not necessarily equivalent to destruction of" a protected group. The court argues that ethnic cleansing may constitute genocide if the acts are those that are proscribed in the crime of genocide and if the intent is to destroy the group as such. But ethnic cleansing cannot "as such be designated as genocide."[13]

---

[11] Schabas, *Genocide in International Law*, p. 200.
[12] Ibid.
[13] *Case Concerning the Application of the Convention on the Prevention and Punishment of the Crime of Genocide (Bosnia and Herzegovinia v. Serbia and Montenegro)*, para. 190.

I would agree that the intent is the key consideration here, but I would disagree with the court about the status of the acts. As I will argue, other acts of ethnic cleansing can, with the appropriate intent, also constitute genocide.

On one level, ethnic cleansing is best treated as simply a set of acts that constitute such things as the displacement of a population. The displacement can be aimed at several distinctly different outcomes. I see some reason to think that displacing a population could aim at destroying the group, at least in part. One way to think of ethnic cleansing concerns the use of a certain tactic to intimidate or harm a population group, and if the harm or intimidation is severe enough, the effect can be that people leave the group, at least as the group has been understood. Or the tactic of ethnic cleansing could be aimed at breaking up a group by moving large portions of the contiguous population into geographic areas that will isolate them from one another and thereby so disrupt the group as to destroy, at least in part, the group itself. And so, if we focus on the acts that count as ethnic cleansing, independent of the aims for which they may be acted, I see no reason not to include these acts in the list of acts that satisfy the *actus reus* element of the crime of genocide.

Ethnic cleansing also raises the interesting conceptual question of how to think about the concept of "a part of a group." Typically, groups and parts of groups are identified in terms of membership. As we saw in the first few chapters, groups should generally be identified in terms of perceptions of those who are outside and those who are inside the putative group. But the identification of part of a group need not follow this model. Parts of groups could be identified solely in terms of factors such as geographic location, as in the case of "the members of my family from Pittsburgh." If all of the members of my family who had been identified by the geographic designation "from Pittsburgh" were to be dispersed, there is a sense in which part of my family has been destroyed.

The difficulty is that if there were no actual loss of members of my family, but only their dispersal, then the loss of part of my family when the Pittsburgh group disperses would not be as important a loss to the family as if a group of members had been cut from the family, or eliminated altogether. But although this is true, it is nonetheless true that there could have been a loss of a part of my family when the Pittsburgh faction was dispersed. The extent of the loss, and whether one could say that it was a significant "part of the group," depends on whether the geographic subgroup was indeed more than just notionally a part of the whole. On my nominalist construal of such metaphysical questions, one can still distinguish between purely notional and well-grounded talk of groups and their parts.

Another question that arises is whether dispersing can constitute destroying. It may be agreed that a part of a group is lost when it is dispersed, but still not acknowledged that this should count as a destruction of a part of the group. Yet there are many cases where dispersion counts as a form of destruction. Think of a collection of particles that have formed into an atom. If the particles are dispersed, as happens in nuclear fission, the atom has been destroyed. If the particles form a part of the atom, and the part is dispersed, the part is similarly destroyed, although the atom is also destroyed in the process. But surely there also can be cases where the part is destroyed by dispersion and yet enough of the rest of the whole is left to say that the whole has not been destroyed, at least not completely.

If a part of a whole can be destroyed merely by dispersing the subparts of the part, then conceptually ethnic cleansing, which involves forced migration and dispersion, could, in some instances, be said to be the destruction of part of a social group. For these reasons, the acts of ethnic cleansing can count as the destruction of a part of a group, and the acts of ethnic cleansing should not necessarily be excluded from the list of genocidal acts. Instead, it is the intent that will matter most in terms of whether the acts of ethnic cleansing are indeed acts that are part of a genocide.

IV. An Account of Genocidal Acts

In this very brief section I will set out an account of the *actus reus* element in the crime of genocide. I will then defend my proposal against objections that might arise from those who would defend the current characterization of genocidal acts in international law, as set out in the first few pages of this chapter, or from other more ambitious ways to characterize the *actus reus* element in genocide. I see my view as a compromise that is conceptually defensible. As I have been explaining, it seems somewhat arbitrary to separate acts from mental states in this way, and indeed the list of acts currently in the genocide statute already mixes intent elements with act elements, as in act (d) "Imposing measures intended to prevent births within the group." But I will continue to try to keep these elements separate, waiting until the next chapter to discuss the *mens rea* elements.

First, I propose that there be an addition to the chapeau of the definition of genocide before providing a list of these acts. I believe that the chapeau should say something such as: "acts such as the following." This addition will make the list that follows not exhaustive, although there could still be guidance about the possibility of including other acts. The addition of the words "such as" will allow for expansion and also give guidance about how much expansion is allowed. Just as the addition of a similar phrase meant that the list of groups that could be subject to genocide was not exhaustive, so the list of acts will no longer be seen as exhaustive either, giving much greater flexibility for considering new types of cases in the future. This will deal with one of the major drafting problems caused by attempting to have a coherent and exhaustive list.

Second, I propose that the list itself be lengthened by at least three acts in order clearly to allow for cultural genocide and ethnic cleansing to fall under the *actus reus* element of the crime of genocide. Here are three acts that I believe should be added to the list of the five acts already listed in the genocide statute:

> Prohibiting the use of the language of the group in daily intercourse or in schools
>
> Prohibiting the printing and circulation of publications in the language of the group
>
> Forcing migration of civilian members of a significant subsection of the group.

The combination of these additions with the change in the chapeau will better capture the idea that in some cases such things as cultural genocide and ethnic cleansing can be the basis of genocide charges.

Putting all of these changes together with the existing proposed changes to the definition from previous chapters gets us the following:

> Genocide involves any acts *such as the following acts* committed with intent to destroy, in whole or in *substantial* part, *a publicly recognized group that is relatively stable and significant for the identity of its members, such as* a national, ethnical, racial or religious group, as such.
> a) Killing members of the group;
> b) Causing serious bodily or mental harm to members of the group;
> c) Deliberately inflicting on the group conditions of life calculated to bring about its physical destruction in whole or in part;
> d) Imposing measures intended to prevent births within the group;
> e) Forcibly transferring children of the group to another group;
> f) *Prohibiting the use of the language of the group in daily intercourse or in schools;*

> g) *Prohibiting the printing and circulation of publications in the language of the group;*
> h) *Forcing migration of civilian members of a significant subsection of the group.*

These changes will improve the definition and give it a more plausible interpretation in terms of conceptual coherence than currently exists. And it will be easier for both the prosecution and the defense to know how to satisfy the *actus reus* element of the crime of genocide.

The idea of requiring *actus reus* as well as *mens rea* elements in a crime such as genocide is to signal that mere thoughts and wishes are not enough to trigger prosecution for such a serious charge. But this does not mean that intent is not important, indeed, that it is not ultimately more important than the act requirement. Rather, something especially harmful needs to have taken place in addition to having the aim of destroying a protected group. Without such harms occurring, it would remain questionable that there should be international prosecutions on the basis of even admittedly horrible intentions. What is true in criminal prosecutions generally, namely, that prosecutions occur only when bad acts have occurred, is even more true in cases that concern the most serious offenses, along with the most severe penalties, for those who are found guilty. Having to satisfy the *actus reus* element of especially serious crimes is among other things a guard against frivolous prosecution of certain individuals for those crimes.

Countering a prima facie showing of the *actus reus* of genocide will be clearer although not necessarily easier to prove with my proposed account of genocidal acts. One of the things that will undoubtedly be exploited by defense counsel is the portion of the definition that concerns "substantial part." The court declared that "when part of the group is targeted, that part must be significant enough for its destruction to have an impact on the group as a whole."[14] The acts listed in the definition, such as killing or transferring children, cannot be isolated acts or too few to be a component of a larger attack on a substantial part of the protected group, and in some sense they must constitute an attack on the protected group, not merely on its members. Here two issues are important for the overall defense of a person charged with genocide.

First, was the act, either taken in itself, or taken as part of a plan, an attack on members of a protected group, not merely an attack on random people in a given population? This is sometimes easy to prove,

[14] Ibid., para. 193.

but not always. It is easy if the people attacked were not all from, or mainly from, the same protected group. But it also may turn out that the people were all from a protected group, but they were not attacked for this reason. In such a case, the act is not one of attacking a substantial part of a protected group. In other cases, it may be that the attack can be so characterized, perhaps because it was known, and yet still fail to meet the *mens rea* elements because the protected group was not being directly targeted.

Second, was the act, by itself or as part of a plan, directed at a significant subsection of the protected group? This second consideration blends together *actus reus* and *mens rea* factors. It is possible to assault members of a protected group, even a substantial number of them, and yet not act so as to assault a substantial part of a protected group. We haven't gotten to the most explicit *mens rea* elements here, namely, that there must be an intent to destroy not only to assault a protected group. Rather we are still mainly at the level of the act. Was the act one that could be characterized as an attack on a substantial part, as opposed to just some less significant part, of a protected group? Defense attorneys will attempt to show that one or another of these factors was not proven by the prosecutor.

There is another somewhat unrelated issue that will come up in defense. Was the act or plan aimed at the destruction of the group, or perhaps aimed only at harming or scaring the group by means of the attack? This consideration is mainly one of intent and will thus have to wait until the next chapter for a full consideration. But we should note at this point how hard it is to keep act and intent consideration separate from one another and hence how hard it is to say that there were genocidal acts occurring but not yet intentional genocide occurring. And when the charge is genocide by means of ethnic cleansing, as we saw above, it will be even harder to show that the dispersion of a group was aimed at destroying the group, not merely creating havoc or as some elaborate mechanism of reprisal, unless reference is made to intent.

V. Objections

I will now take up a series of objections to the proposed revisions of the *actus reus* element of the crime of genocide. First, it could be objected that any attempt to modify the genocide statute, which has remained exactly the same for 60 years, will fail to capture a consensus and could even disrupt the consensus that has been sustained over such a long

period of time. It is well recognized that previous attempted changes to
the genocide statute have met with ignominious defeat. Indeed, even the
attempt to correct the typo in the original genocide statute, to change
"ethnical" to "ethnic," has failed. And there is no reason to think that
a similar fate does not await my proposal. Indeed, the debates about the
changes I have proposed at the time of the drafting of the Genocide
Convention show how hard it is to achieve a consensus to include these
changes.

My response to this objection is that my proposal is a normative one,
not necessarily one that is designed to be adopted in the near future.
As a normative proposal, in a nonideal rather than an ideal world, one
needs to take into account some practical matters, but it is a mistake to
be overly influenced by what has happened in the past, or what is predicted in the future. It may turn out that the future does not resemble
the past, and at least in part this may be because of a gradual movement
toward a greater acceptance of the international rule of law. Indeed, we
are experiencing many indications that the incremental expansion of
the international rule of law has gone far beyond what people predicted
just 25 years ago, especially in the way the International Criminal Court
has developed out of the ashes of what seemed to be the highly unlikely
destruction of the Iron Curtain. Of course, I hope that these recom-
mendations have an effect on international law, but I will not scale back
these proposals merely to make it more likely that they are adopted
soon.

Second, another objection is that my proposal will allow frivolous suits
for genocide.[15] Think of the attempt to prosecute NATO for its bombing campaign against Serbia. The case was weak, but it was taken up on
its merits because of the very high regard given for claims of genocide.
Schabas says that this is a problem that needs to be guarded against by
narrowly restricting the definition of genocide. Having a narrow definition of genocide is the best hedge against frivolous suits succeeding. If
one has to choose between broadening the definition and allowing for
less vigorous enforcement, the choice seems obviously to favor enforcement and hence to plump for the narrower definition, contrary to what
I have claimed in this chapter.[16]

In response, I would deny that we have to make just this choice
between strong enforcement and narrow definition, on the one hand,

[15] I thank Mark Drumbl for raising this objection.
[16] See Schabas, *Genocide in International Law*, pp. 551–2.

versus weak enforcement and broad definition, on the other hand. Indeed, in my view, the idea of frivolous suits is unrelated to how narrow or broad the definition of a crime is. Frivolous suits are made more likely when the law is unclear. But broad definitions are not necessarily unclear, especially if they are only a bit broader than a more narrow definition. A broader rather than a narrower definition can still have quite a precise meaning, and it can thus be clear enough to be adjudicable. And if this is right, then having a somewhat broader, but fairly precise, definition does not contribute to the proliferation of frivolous lawsuits. So, although I worry about the rise of frivolous suits, I do not think this is a reason to reject my proposals about including acts of ethnic cleansing and cultural genocide in the definition of genocide. Indeed, I would contend that whatever little risk there is here is more than outweighed by the good to be done by including these acts as acts of genocide.

In the Yugoslav claim that NATO engaged in genocide there are several additional things to point out that somewhat mitigate the worries that some might have to my proposal. Serbia would have made this claim pretty much regardless of how narrowly genocide is defined. So the issue is whether the claim can be easily shown to be without merit. Again, what is actually in the definition and how clear it is will be crucial. In any event I am not persuaded of the value of being able easily to dismiss such suits. International law, and especially international criminal law, is still relatively infirm. The more trials there are, the better known this type of law will be. But at the moment there is a countervailing risk that too quick a dismissal of charges will be seen as a reason to think that this type of law is more about show than about fairness to all parties. So letting some potentially frivolous suits proceed, at least initially, is not necessarily a bad thing.

Third, it could be objected that the changes I have suggested do not go far enough in that they leave untouched various forms of atrocity directed at groups that should count as genocide, especially cases of very serious persecution that are clearly just as bad as the kinds of atrocity I have now included under the genocide rubric, or other forms of very serious human rights abuse directed at groups. If we do not include certain egregious atrocities, while including only selected others, there will be a strong case for selective prosecution. And when there are serious charges of selective prosecution, a risk is run of creating a highly negative impact on the international rule of law.

I am quite sympathetic to the underlying motivation behind this objection, namely, a concern for consistency within the domain of genocidal acts, otherwise I would not have argued for an expansion of the domain of genocidal acts in the first place. But I believe that just because there is a strong public outcry against a certain practice it does not mean that that practice must be prosecuted as the most serious of crimes, and in any event I have not supported the idea that genocide must be conceived as the most serious of crimes in the first place. Crimes should be prosecuted only when their elements have been met. Of course, one can then ask why the way we understand certain elements should not be changed. And I am sympathetic, as I said, to the idea that elements of crimes can, and sometimes, should be changed, to include some acts that are very similar to acts that are already being prosecuted under the crime of genocide.

To make my position clear, I need to underline that I am opposed to the idea that acts of persecution, even extreme persecution, should be automatically counted as genocidal acts. Contrary to what might appear from the preceding discussions, I think there is some merit to the idea that when persecution is directed at the destruction of a group it is normatively different from other forms of persecution, such as that directed at retaliating against the group. There should be different levels of punishment based on the type of intent that can be proven. The intent to destroy a group does add an important dimension to the character of the harm and crime. I will explore this idea in much greater detail in the following two chapters. Suffice it here to say that there is nothing incompatible between saying that genocide is worse than normal, even severe, persecution, and saying that genocide is not the worst of all crimes. Indeed, nothing I have suggested tells against seeing genocide as not all that much worse than other crimes against humanity, especially extreme persecution.

In this chapter I have surveyed a host of issues about the *actus reus* element of the crime of genocide. I have been especially interested in the question of what it means to destroy a group in part, not merely in whole, as is countenanced by the current genocide definition in international law. I have argued that the act element of the crime of genocide is in need of revision, especially concerning the cases of cultural genocide and ethnic cleansing. Cultural genocide can be just as devastating for a social group's continued existence as the killing of the group's members. I have thus proposed some important changes to the way that the act element of the crime of genocide should be conceived. And in responding to the most obvious objections to my proposal, I have endeavored to render that proposal more plausible than it might otherwise appear.

7

Collective and Individual Intent

The crime of genocide involves both individual intent elements and a collective intent element, the latter involving an intent to destroy a group. The Convention on Genocide, article 2, says: genocide is "any of the following acts committed with the intent to destroy, in whole or in part, a national, ethnical, religious, racial or religious group, as such."[1] In this respect, genocide is different from crimes, even other international crimes. There is a significant difference between persecution, a crime against humanity, and genocide, although there are also significant similarities. In the *Kupreskic* case, the International Criminal Tribunal for the Former Yugoslavia said that "In both categories, what matters is the intent to discriminate...from the perspective of *mens rea*, genocide is an extreme and most inhuman form of persecution."[2] Persecution involves an assault on a population of persons because of their group membership. Like persecution, genocide also involves an assault on a population because of their group membership, but in addition it involves the intent to destroy the group, not merely to harm or kill various members of the group. In this chapter I examine what it means to have such a collective intent, and how it can be proved.

The term "collective intent" in international law is not well understood. Sometimes the term is used to mean that a number of people are working loosely toward the same end, perhaps unbeknownst to one another. To say that there is a collective intent in this sense is just to say that a number of individuals all have roughly the same intent to accomplish the same end. Sometimes the term is used to mean that there is concerted action in that the individual acts of many people are

[1] Convention on the Prevention and Punishment of Genocide; and Rome Statute.
[2] *Prosecutor v. Mirjan Kupreskic et al.*, International Criminal Tribunal for the Former Yugoslavia, IT-95–16-T, Trial Chamber Judgment, 14 January 2000, para. 636.

coordinated so as to achieve a single end. In my view, it is the second, not the first, kind of collective intent that the crime of genocide depends on. It is not mere aggregation of intents, but some type of nonaggregated collective intent that is contemplated in the international crime of genocide, and yet some have found this claim deeply mysterious.

If genocide is seen on the model of the Holocaust, the collective intent element seems to be easily met by showing that Hitler and his top henchmen planned the extermination of the Jews in great detail and then initiated their plan. The plan plus the initiation is a form of collective intent in that the plan organizes the acts of many people and directs those acts toward the destruction of a group. But in Rwanda, there does not appear to have been a central plan to exterminate Tutsis. It is thus harder to see that there was a collective intent to destroy Tutsis, and hence that there was a genocide, in Rwanda. In later chapters I argue that it does make sense to talk of a collective genocidal intent in Rwanda if we examine the role played by the media in inciting the individual acts of many Hutus toward the destruction of the Tutsis. In the current chapter I will discuss the background conceptual issues.

William Schabas talks about what I am calling collective intent as "collective motive":

> For the purposes of analysis, it may be helpful here to distinguish between what might be called the collective motive and the individual or personal motive. Genocide is, by nature, a collective crime, committed with the cooperation of many participants. It is, moreover, an offense generally directed by the State. The organizers and planners must necessarily have a racist or discriminatory motive, that is, a genocidal motive, taken as a whole. Where this is lacking, the crime cannot be genocide.[3]

I will criticize Schabas's view in several respects in what follows, even as I agree with him that genocide is by its nature a collective crime. I will argue that genocide should involve a true collective intent requirement, not merely a collective motive requirement, and that the special intent dimension of *mens rea* also does not satisfy the collective intent requirement.[4]

In cases such as the Rwandan genocide, the collective intent requirement could be met by one or a group of intentional acts of incitement

---

[3] Schabas, *Genocide in International Law,* p. 255; 2nd edition, 2009, p. 305.
[4] In the next chapter, I explain in some detail the difference between intention, or aim, and motive, or reasons for having aims.

if the idea behind the incitement was to excite a group to aim at the destruction of another group, where that destruction would otherwise require a coordinated plan. In some cases the incitement both engages in stage setting and also initiates the campaign of violence. In some cases but not all, incitement could function like direct instigation (which involves explicit planning) in that it supplied the collective intent element that is necessary to prove genocide. But the question I will focus on in this chapter is how to characterize collective intent in such a way so that it can be connected to standard criminal law ways to think about individual intent, that is, *mens rea*.

In the first part of the chapter, I will describe the several senses of what collective intent could mean in the jurisprudence of genocide. In the second part of the chapter I will say something about how collective intent connects to individual intent in genocide cases, especially in cases such as that of the Rwandan genocide. In the third part of the chapter, I will provide a revised understanding of the mental elements in the crime of genocide. And in the fourth section, I will address several objections, including that by William Schabas, to the proposal I have set out in the previous sections. Among the most serious of objections is that collective intent is too abstract an idea to have place in criminal prosecutions, especially in light of the principle of legality. Genocide may be a collective crime, but we still need to articulate its elements in such a way that individual defendants will have the chance to disprove that they were indeed involved in this crime. I will argue that the collective intent requirement of the crime of genocide can be given sufficient clarity and precision so that it will be clear how to establish proof, or offer a defense, concerning this element.

I. Varieties of Collective Intent

Raimo Tuomela begins his recent book *The Philosophy of Sociality: The Shared Point of View* by distinguishing two senses of a group's point of view, what he calls the group members' "shared *we-perspective*": "A we-perspective may be involved both in the case of one's functioning *as a group member* for the group and in the case of one's functioning *as a private person* in a group context."[5] Collective intentionality can occur in either case, although in the latter case it concerns what Tuomela calls a

---

[5] Raimo Tuomela, *The Philosophy of Sociality: The Shared Point of View*, New York: Oxford University Press, 2007, p. 3.

progroup, not a full-blown group that can easily be ascribed collective or group intentions.

Using this initial divide, we can distinguish four types of collective intention. The first, not properly collective at all, is merely the aggregated intentions of individual persons. In some ordinary uses of the term "collective," it is mere shorthand for aggregation of this sort. The second is what Tuomela calls private intention in a group context. The third is Tuomela's individual sharing of intent. The final is a full-blooded collective intent, the intent of a group that is not reducible to the intentions of the individual members of the group. We can dismiss the fourth as an empty set, or if there are any members, then it would be something like an organic State that acts and has intentions all of its own. Yet in the cases we are concerned with, there is no significant "organic" State involvement, even if this is the correct way to understand State acts and intents, which I doubt. In my previous writings I have argued that there are no such mysterious groups with intentions.[6] Even the State should be conceptualized as having intentions only vicariously through the various individuals who serve in various roles within the State structure. This leaves us with three candidates for the kind of collective intent that seems to be contemplated in the genocide statute.

Some commentators think of genocide's intent requirement as involving nothing more than the aggregated intention of my first type. It may be that a number of disparate people have the same aim and set out to implement that aim by acting in certain ways, and then, by a kind of coincidence, the aim is achieved by all of these individual unrelated acts coming together. Although this is a distinct possibility, it is not likely to occur very often. And even if it does occur it is still not clear why we should think that the aim was achieved by a collective aim rather than by coincidence. Instead, genocide is far more likely to require the coordinated efforts of many people, each of whom has some connection to the collective enterprise's aim or intent. In the Rwanda case, it will not be such a simple matter to figure out how the coordination occurs without central planning.

If a group is small enough, a single person could intend to destroy a group by planning to kill all of the group's members. Proof of genocidal intent would be relatively easy because it will merely have to be proved by the statements made, or inferred from actions taken, of what was the intent of this single person. This simple case is not likely to occur very

[6] See May, *The Morality of Groups.*

often, if at all. In international law the groups that are of interest are those that are large and fairly stable. It is possible that a single person could intend to destroy these groups on his or her own, but it is far more likely that carrying out such an intention will require enlisting the help of lots of other people.

A single person could intend to destroy a large group by organizing others to aid in this aim and then motivating them to do so. Again, the proof of this genocidal intent is sometimes easy, requiring only that we examine the person's statements or draw normal inferences from his or her behavior. If there is evidence of planning or explicit organizing, the proof of genocidal intent is indeed easy. But there are other forms of proof as well. Perhaps one of the most controversial is something I discuss in greater detail later in the book, namely, incitement. Here a person, or persons, communicates to others in such a way that these others are excited and act soon thereafter to accomplish what the inciter intends. I will later argue that proof of genocidal intent can be had by showing direct instigation, through planning and initiating, or by showing incitement.

The hard case concerns how genocidal intent can be proved concerning those who are not inciters or instigators, but those who carry out the genocide. In this case it is not normally enough that each person individually acts against another person while aiming at destroying the group because a single individual normally cannot accomplish this aim merely by such an act. This is what Tuomela calls private intention in a group context. There is a sense in which this case is a type of collective intent, but only if we use this term in an extended way. There isn't really a coherent group that has an intention here; it is again more like a coincidence of isolated individual intentions, or so I shall argue.

For the intentions of a group of people to constitute a single intent, there must be some sense in which we can refer to a shared intent in the multitude of individual intentions. If there is no relation among the individual intentions except that those having the intentions are in spatial or temporal contiguity, the intentions do not cohere in a way that would normally allow us to refer to these intentions as all part of a larger intention. Coincidence of time or space is not sufficient for such an attribution. Of course, if there has been communication or interaction among these individuals, and the communication or interaction has influenced these individuals to come to hold similar intentions, then things are different. But then we are dealing with a significantly different kind of collective intention. Similarity of intention that is not brought about by some act remains merely a coincidence of common intention and only very loosely called collective intention. The idea of shared intent is the one that best represents the kind of intent that can constitute the collective intent of genocide.

Let me say a bit more about what Tuomela calls individual sharing of intent. Tuomela talks of this category as involving people acting as members of a group and also as acting for the group. Similar to Tuomela, I have argued that sharing of intention involves individuals seeing themselves as engaged in group-based behavior. I make this claim because I do not believe that groups exist in and of themselves, as I explained in earlier chapters. In my view, the individuals need to see themselves as participating in a joint venture, and they have to aim at so participating although they do not have to share the very same intents that every other member has. In this way the individuals need to see themselves as part of a larger enterprise but not as being parts of a group that has some kind of existence on its own.

In law, questions of proof are crucial. Think of the Rwandan genocide example. The question is how it can be proved that an individual perpetrator of violence does indeed share genocidal intent with those who have instigated or incited the genocide itself. The key will be to prove that the sharing of intention is not mere coincidence but has resulted from some particular act or event that has shaped the intentions of the individuals. Tuomela draws the distinction in terms of whether a person acts as others in the group do out of private reasons or out of some kind of collective acceptance or commitment.[7] In this view collective intent makes sense when the individuals act out of a kind of public reason, that is, one that is based on deliberation and collective acceptance or commitment.

I don't believe that collective acceptance or commitment needs to be understood as involving formal acts of acceptance. What is required instead is some loose sense that the individuals see themselves as participating in a group effort. Indeed, they do not need to have the same intent as the one displayed by those who instigate or incite. Rather, the informal acceptance of what the collective does can occur as a matter of knowledge that by acting he or she is jointly participating, and the venture participated in has as its aim a genocidal act. The proof of shared acceptance or commitment can come from showing that an individual had knowledge that by acting his or her actions would be contributing

---

[7] Tuomela, *The Philosophy of Sociality*, pp. 98–100.

to a group effort. In the next section, I will explicitly link the individual mental states of the participants to the collective intent of the group.

We have now surveyed the landscape of the varieties of collective intent. The truly collectivist idea was found wanting, at least in cases where there was no significant State involvement. The merely aggregated case did not help us out much either, because mere aggregation of intention is only controversially called collective intention. That left two ways to think of collective intent that seem to be apt for genocide cases. As I have just argued, the sharing of intent model seems to be the most promising, although this will depend on how we understand the link between individual and collective intent in this respect.

II. Connecting Collective and Individual Intent

The *mens rea* of genocide involves two distinct types of individual intent requirements, one of which will allow for a linking of individual and collective intent. There is first the intent to kill or assault another person, which is necessary to bring the defendant initially under the genocide statute in a general way. There is in addition a special intent requirement in which the defendant must intend to destroy a group by his or her actions. We have already seen that serious worries are found about how to understand an individual participant's intention to destroy a group. In this section I will argue that the special intent requirement is best seen as either an intent to plan and initiate a collective enterprise, or as an intent to participate in what one knows will be a collective enterprise. If individuals all had to have the same intents, few if any participants in genocide could be convicted.

It may help to consider examples where Anglo-American criminal law requires two kinds of intent. Here are two examples from LaFave and Scott:

> Common law larceny, for example, requires the taking and carrying away of the property of another, and the defendant's mental state as to this act must be established, but in addition it must be established that there was an 'intent to steal' the property. Similarly, common law burglary requires a breaking and entry into the dwelling of another, but in addition to the mental state connected to these acts it must be established that the defendant acted "with intent to commit a felony therein."[8]

---

[8] Wayne R. LaFave and Austin W. Scott, Jr., *Handbook of Criminal Law*, St. Paul, MN: West Publishing, 1972, p. 202.

These examples are often referred to when explaining why it is thought that genocide also has both a general and a special intent requirement.

But in the Anglo-American tradition, serious reservations have been raised against the standard distinction between general and special intent. The U.S. Model Penal Code, for instance, no longer conceptualizes larceny and burglary in the traditional way that LaFave and Scott set out above. The Model Penal Code authors urge that we drop the idea of general intent and characterize the *mens rea* element in terms of specific intents.[9] It could also be argued that one could speak of just one *mens rea* requirement with a complex structure. I will follow in this spirit by arguing that if there is a special intent requirement it is at the shared not at the individual level. At the individual level, it is intending to participate and knowledge of what is so involved rather than each person having the same intent that normally links the individual to the collective, that is, to the genocidal intent. The question is not whether the individual has a genocidal intent, but whether there is a collective plan that the individual intends to participate in and knows the aims of, including the destruction of a group.

Another difficult question is how to link the person who most instantiates the collective intent with the individual acts that are proscribed at law, such as killing. This is perhaps an easier question than the previous one. The inciter, for instance, does not normally kill, or do any of the proscribed acts of the definition in the Genocide Convention. But insofar as the incitement "organizes" these acts, the inciter may be linked to these acts insofar as the inciter instantiates the collective intent requirement. Indeed, the act of "organizing" the killings is also a basis of proof of the intent to do the killings, just as if the inciter were to be the one doing the killings on his or her own. It is in this way that collective intent comes to have pride of place in the crime of genocide.

The person who plans and initiates, or who incites, a genocide more clearly instantiates the collective intent than does the person who merely participates. The reason for this is that planning can organize the acts of others into a joint endeavor. Similarly, as we will see in Chapter 10, incitement can excite and "organize" individuals to act together to reach a common objective. The actions of the one who plans or incites are more reasonably said to instantiate the collective intent than is true of the actions of the individuals who merely participate in the plan or

---

[9] Model Penal Code, sec. 2.02, Comment (Tentative Draft no. 4, 1955), cited in ibid., p. 202, note 4.

who are incited to participate. For this reason the planners and inciters should be more clearly responsible for the collective crime than are those who participate, although those who participate can also instantiate the collective intent as well.

It may be useful to explore in more detail the idea of how an individual intent can instantiate collective intent. As I said above, collective intent is best understood as sharing of intent. In this sense anyone who does in fact share in the intent instantiates the collective intent, but some may do so more than others. If the collective intent is to accomplish a certain objective, such as to destroy a protected group as in the case of genocide, then anyone who sets in motion the means to accomplish that objective instantiates the collective intent and does so more than someone who merely follows along after the initiation. Instantiation is a way to bring to fruition, at least partially, something that is otherwise inchoate.

Although the actions of the planner and those of the participant are both necessary for the fruition, the actions of the planner that so clearly involve the first steps taken toward the end are in many ways more of an instantiation than the actions of the participant. Indeed, the intent of the planner is often nearly indistinguishable from the collective intent itself. The planner plays a more significant role in the sharing of this intent than does the one who merely knows that he or she intends to contribute and knows of what is planned. The participant shares in the intention too, but to a lesser extent than is true of the planner or inciter.

The case against the inciter has two *mens rea* elements to be proved, namely, the instantiation of the collective intent, on the one hand, and the vicarious *mens rea* to do the killing, or other proscribed acts, on the other hand. These two forms of *mens rea* are not the same as special and general intent, as we saw above. It is my view that the vicarious *mens rea* is more like, but not the same as, knowledge than like intent proper, as was also true of the case of the person who does the killing as part of a genocidal campaign. For the person who is incited to do the killing, or other proscribed act, the two mental elements are an intent to kill, or do some other proscribed act, and the aim of at least contributing to a plan or campaign that has or is known to have as its aim the destruction of a protected group.

The link between individual intent and collective intent is the key to the *mens rea* elements of the crime of genocide. And the link is not easy to see in many cases. This is at least in part because the very idea of a collective intent is itself so unclear, especially as it relates to individual intent. Can an individual's intent be the same as a collective intent? Think of the putative and likely intentions of Hitler. As he set out the plan of the Holocaust, there seems to have been both a collective intent through establishing a master plan to destroy the Jewish people and also a personal intent to aim at the same end. The two came together in the mind of Hitler. But in many other cases, those who incited, although they also had the intent to get others to act toward the destruction of a protected group, were not as personally committed to that aim as was Hitler. In this respect we will later examine the Media Case in Rwanda where it is clear that radio and newspaper editors and executives incited a genocide, and yet it is unclear what were the personal aims of these editors and executives.

The most difficult case concerns an individual who does not have the intention to destroy a group but who knows that his or her acts will advance just that goal, and that others are intentionally pursuing that aim. Here the personal intention and the collective come apart at least partially, but they may come together in certain cases. If we require that there is a complete coinciding of these intentions, then there will be very few people who will turn out to be convictable for the crime of genocide. It is rare that there is a person such as Hitler whose personal aims so completely coincide with the collective aim he or she sets in motion. This may not seem to be an especially troubling result unless one believes, as do I, that it is important to hold people responsible for genocide. To hold some individuals responsible for genocide, the mental connection between the collective intent and the individual intent should only be an aim to contribute or participate in the collective enterprise. The individual need not aim at what the plan or campaign aims at, but must aim at participating in that plan or campaign and at least understand what the aims of the plan or campaign are.

Collective intent is, in my construal, shorthand for the intent of a group of people to act a certain way. Some people, such as those who instigate or incite, better instantiate the collective intent, because their intentions and actions set the stage for the concerted behavior. But others can also link to, or instantiate, the collective intent as well by their intention to contribute to a plan that they know has an intent to destroy a protected group. The collective intent of the crime of genocide is the intent to destroy a protected group. But it turns out that this intention element in the crime of genocide is much more complex than is normally realized. There are, as we shall next see, three different *mens rea* elements of the crime of genocide. Yet I will argue that prosecuting the crime of genocide need not prove that a non-leader manifest all three of these *mens rea* elements, but only two mental elements, as in the case of incitement I discussed earlier in this section.

III. Knowledge in the *Mens Rea* of Genocide

In this section I will discuss the relationship between knowledge and intent in *mens rea*, with special emphasis on the *mens rea* conditions of genocide. In his book *Punishment and Responsibility*, H. L. A. Hart argues that foresight of the consequences can be an important basis of criminal responsibility, and so can the failure to exercise foresight.[10] He argues that it makes sense to punish someone not for inadvertence but for omitting to think, not for having a blank mind but for a specific omission. What we hold people responsible for is failing to exercise control in various ways, and failing to attend to certain facts that other reasonable people would attend to can trigger responsibility ascriptions, just as is true for failures to restrain one's passions. Here what is key is that precautions were not taken that should have been taken, and we punish to deter people from such behavior.[11]

I wish to follow Hart in explicating my idea about how to reconceptualize the *mens rea* element of the crime of genocide. In my view, it is not necessary to show that the defendant intended to cause genocidal harm, but only that he or she intended to participate in a plan that had as its intent to cause genocidal harm. It also must be shown that the defendant knew or should have known that the plan would have this effect. In what follows I will defend this idea against a similar view espoused by Alexander Greenawalt that also allows for knowledge to play an important part in the *mens rea* conditions of genocide. Greenawalt fails to see, though, that intent should still play a role, even if the intent need not be to cause genocidal harm. I will argue that intending to participate in a plan is the key to allowing knowledge, or failure to know, to become a basis of guilt.

Greenawalt contends that "the requirement of genocidal intent should be satisfied if the perpetrator acted in furtherance of a campaign targeting members of a protected group and knew that the goal or manifest

---

[10] H. L. A. Hart, "Negligence, Mens Rea, and Criminal Responsibility," in *Punishment and Responsibility*, Oxford: Oxford University Press, 1968, 2nd edition, 1973, p. 140.
[11] See ibid., p. 154.

effect of the campaign was the destruction of the group in whole or in part."[12] Greenawalt argues that knowledge is considered enough to satisfy the *mens rea* requirement in normal criminal proceedings in the Anglo-American and Continental systems of law. In genocide, he argues that what is added is merely that there is "selection of group members on the basis of their group identity" along with the knowledge of the "destructive effects" of this selection on the "survival of the group."[13] In effect, the genocidal intent is transferred from the group level to the individual defendant because of the defendant's knowledge of the consequences of his of her harmful acts.

My view is that Greenawalt supplies too meager an intent requirement for such an important crime as genocide. He misidentifies the problem when he suggests that having a "specific purposive attitude" requires too much. The problem, however, is not one of attitude but of how one comes to find oneself participating in the genocidal plan. The relevant question is did the defendant fail to exercise control in finding himself participating in genocide? Greenawalt also misses the crucial importance of there being a larger plan that encompasses many other acts than merely those of the defendant. And, most important, Greenawalt misses the importance of joining in the plan.

In the debates that led up to the Genocide Convention, quite a lot of discussion concerned how to understand the intent requirement. Nehemiah Robinson comments:

> The majority of the Commission was, however, of the opinion that there was no Genocide without intent and that, if intent was absent, act would become simple homicide. Therefore, according to the wording of Article II, acts of destruction would not be classified as Genocide unless the intent to destroy the group existed or could be proven regardless of the results achieved.[14]

Although I do not completely follow the Commission members, I am more faithful to their concerns about intent that is Greenawalt.

It is indeed crucial that there be a plan that has as its purpose the destruction of protected group in whole or in substantial part. This is the collective intent that is the most important element of genocide.

---

[12] Alexander Greenawalt, "Rethinking Genocidal Intent: The Case for a Knowledge-Based Interpretation," *Columbia Law Review,* vol. 99, 1999, p. 2288.

[13] Ibid., p. 2289.

[14] Nehemiah Robinson, "The Genocide Convention: Its Origins and Interpretation," 1949, reprinted in *Case Western Reserve Journal of International Law,* vol. 40, nos. 1 and 2, 2007–8, appendix, p. 15.

And the way that the individual defendant is linked to the collective intent cannot merely be by knowledge, although that can indeed be part of the story. What is crucial is that the individual intend to participate in the plan, thereby linking his or her own intent to the collective intent of genocide. Where knowledge comes into the picture is as a substitute for intending to destroy the protected group. The defendant need not have that intention, as long as there is some intention that does connect to the genocidal or collective intent. If one buys this part of the story, then it is an easy matter also to see that the knowledge requirement could be satisfied by a failure to know what any reasonable person would have known. In this way we are able to block the claims of those who did participate but claimed that they simply were not aware of what the plan entailed. If any reasonable person would have known the aims of the plan, and the defendant was not blocked from being such a reasonable person, then he or she cannot use lack of knowledge as a defense.

The main problem with strategies like that of Greenawalt is that they do not provide a clear way to connect the defendant's guilty mind to the collective or genocidal intent. Greenawalt makes an attempt by requiring that the defendant knew that he or she was participating in a venture that aimed at the destruction of a protected group. But in my view, unless this was an intentional participating, the defendant's own guilty act does not link to the guilt-making intentional state of the crime of genocide. Greenawalt never provides a clear link to the collective intent because his knowledge requirement is knowledge of the consequences of the defendant's acts, not knowledge of the aims of what the group are. And he puts all of his emphasis on knowledge, thereby allowing the defendant to escape liability by showing that he or she was unreasonably lacking in such knowledge. If he does not allow for this defense, then the whole game is up because he has only knowledge as the link to the genocidal intent.

My view puts emphasis on the intent to participate and thus allows that the knowledge requirement is of only secondary importance, although still of importance. This gives me the opportunity to follow Hart in allowing a "should have known" standard to be a reasonable substitute for what the defendant knew about the plan he or she was participating in. Although my proposal also, like Greenawalt's, diverges from the main jurisprudence on this issue, at least it still captures what is the most important dimension of crimes that require specific or special intent. In general, this requirement picks out crimes that are especially serious and for which punishments will be especially severe.

In recent international case law, it seems clear that some form of intent remains a very important consideration in establishing guilt in genocide cases. In one of the leading cases, the International Criminal Tribunal for the Former Yugoslavia Appeals Chamber judgment in the Krstic case, the conviction for genocide was thrown out because of the lack of intent. Here is how the court argued:

> As has been demonstrated, all that the evidence can establish is that Krstic was aware of the intent to commit genocide on the part of some members of the VRS Main Staff, and with that knowledge, he did nothing to prevent the use of Drina Corps personnel and resources to facilitate those killings. This knowledge on his part alone cannot support an inference of genocidal intent. Genocide is one of the worst crimes known to humankind, and its gravity is reflected in the stringent requirement of specific intent. Convictions for genocide can be entered only where that intent has been unequivocally established. There was a demonstrable failure by the Trial Chamber to supply adequate proof that Radislov Krstic possessed the genocidal intent. Krstic is therefore not guilty of genocide as a principal perpetrator.[15]

Here we see the court rejecting an approach similar to what Greenawalt proposed. Although I do not myself think that this is overriding, I do think that the court's reasoning bears consideration, and weighs in favor of a proposal such as mine.

IV. Revisions to the Mental Element of the Crime of Genocide

In this section I will provide a revised understanding of the mental elements of the crime of genocide. Genocidal intent must involve some kind of collective intent in the sense that the person who is prosecuted must have his or her mental states linked to a kind of we-perspective. In this sense collective intention is better understood as shared intention rather than a full-blown intention of a collectivity. But there are various ways that one can share intentions with others, and hence there are at least two paths that I will indicate below by which a person can be shown to instantiate or manifest genocidal intent. It will be important, then, to revise the way that intent is characterized in genocide prosecutions to reflect this more complicated way to understand genocidal intent than is normally recognized.

What we have seen from the previous section will be important here. It has turned out that the collective intent that is definitive of genocide

[15] *Prosecutor v. Radislav Krstic,* Appeals Chamber Judgment, para. 134.

is normally split among several individuals, making it hard to see whether there is any one person who can be shown to have the collective intent that is involved in the intent to destroy a protected group. There is both the intent to coordinate the acts of others but also the intent to do specific acts of harm, and it is rare indeed that one person manifests both of these aspects of genocidal intent. Yet, although no person normally completely manifests the genocidal intent, some people may come closer than others. And it can be specified what the ingredients are of the overarching genocidal intent, as I will now attempt to do with some precision, or at least with more than is normally shown toward this difficult subject.

In my view, the intention to destroy a group involves two separate paths to satisfy the *mens rea* element of the crime of genocide. This is because three separate intentions are involved in genocide cases, namely:

a) The intent to initiate a concerted effort to destroy a given group
b) The intent to perform a particular act of killing or assaulting, etc. a member of a given group and
c) The intent that by killing, or assaulting, etc,. one contributes to a concerted effort that is known to intend to destroy a given group.

My proposal is that a person must to be shown to manifest either the first intent (a), or both the second and third intents (b and c), but one does not need to be shown to manifest all three of these intents to satisfy the *mens rea* element of the crime of genocide. I shall defend this revised version of the *mens rea* element of the crime of genocide in this and the next section.

Before offering my defense of this view, I wish to indicate what specific changes to the genocide statute would be needed to reflect the analysis of genocidal intent I have set out above. First, the "committed with the intent to destroy" phrase should be changed to give more guidance about how one can manifest this intent. So, I urge that the statute be changed to read:

"committed with intent, *either by directing others to act in a coordinated endeavor or through intending to participate in a coordinated endeavor,* to destroy..."

This change will clarify what it means to intend to destroy a group and also provide some clarity for both prosecutors who must prove the case and defense attorneys who try to show that the accused did not so intend. As I said above, it is crucial that some clarity and precision be added to the statute so that defendants' rights are not jeopardized in terms of the principle of legality in that they cannot know in advance what is required of them and when their liberty will be placed in jeopardy by their actions.

Second, I propose that it be made clear that the "as such" component of the definition of the crime of genocide refers to intent and not to motives. In the next chapter I will present the developed argument for his position. Suffice it here to say that this issue was not at all clear at the time of the Genocide Convention. Some of the delegates to the Genocide Convention saw the "as such" stipulation as signaling that it must be proved that the defendant had wrongful motives as well as wrongful intentions to be guilty of genocide. And some commentators have failed to separate motive from intent. So, because of its ambiguity, and in light of all of this discussion, I propose that the "as such" proviso simply be dropped from the genocide statute.

Putting the pieces together, I propose that the chapeau that sets the *mens rea* elements of the crime of genocide, which currently says:

> "any of the following acts committed with the intent to destroy, in whole or in part, a national, ethnical, religious, racial or religious group, as such"[16]

be changed to the following:

> "any of the following acts committed with the intent, *either by directing others to act in a coordinated endeavor or through intending to participate in a coordinated endeavour that is known to intend,* to destroy, in whole or in part, a national, ethnical, religious, racial or religious group."

These changes, I believe, will make the definition of genocide considerably clearer and more precise and will be a better conceptual and normative statement of what needs to be proved for an individual to be convicted of this very serious crime of genocide.

The *mens rea* element of the crime of genocide is the key to this crime. No other international crime involves such a complex intent element. Although other international crimes require some kind of connection between the collective crime and the individual actor's state of mind, no other international crime requires a showing of a collective intent that must be linked to the individual intent of the accused. In other international crimes there must be a larger crime occurring that the accused participates in, but that larger crime is not so dependent on aiming at a particular result. Crimes against humanity require that there be a mass

[16] Convention on the Prevention and Punishment of Genocide; Rome Statute of the ICC (1998).

assault on a population, and war crimes and the crime of aggression require that there be an armed conflict that the acts of the accused fit into. But only genocide requires not merely a larger setting of violence but that the violence have a specific aim that is linked to the aim of the defendant. Because of this, intention is the key to the crime of genocide and also the basis of most of the conceptual difficulties of this crime. It is for this reason that the *mens rea* of this crime needs to be formulated much more clearly than is true for other international crimes.

There are two distinct ways to satisfy the *mens rea* of the crime of genocide, one involving those who lead or plan and the other involving those who participate. Because of this, confusions have arisen. I will later argue that the people who plan are the ones who should be punished most severely, even though they are not the ones who actually do the killing or other explicitly harmful acts. The problem of how to assign responsibility and punishment is a difficult one. In this section I have only discussed how to think about the elements that need to be satisfied to make out the prima facie case against a given defendant in a genocide case. There are conceptual problems already at this initial sage. I have tried to clarify this problem, although probably not as much as many would have liked. In the next section I address specific challenges to my proposal.

V. Objections

The first objection to consider is that I, along with Schabas and others, am wrong to think that genocide must be a collective crime in the sense that it involves the activity of many people. David Luban has argued that a lone individual who gets access to a nuclear bomb could commit genocide, especially if we focus on the idea that genocide can involve the intent to destroy a protected group "in part."[17] On this analysis, a lone person could manifest the "collective intent" element simply by intending to destroy a collectivity on his or her own. It is for this reason that some have said that it is a mistake to think of genocide as involving collective intent, and hence of thinking of the subject of genocide the way I have done in this chapter.

It cannot be denied that such a hypothetical case is possible and that such a case could indeed be one of genocide. In this sense genocide is

---

[17] David Luban, "A Theory of Crimes against Humanity," *Yale Journal of International Law*, vol. 29, no. 1 (2004), pp. 85–140.

a collective crime only in the sense that it involves an assault on many people who form some kind of collectivity. Genocide need not involve a collectivity acting. But in all of the actual cases of genocide that have occurred, and are likely to occur, genocide also does involve a collectivity acting, because the scale of the assault needs the coordinated actions of many people. Having said this, I should say that I'm not at all sure that much turns on the theoretical possibility that a lone person could commit genocide. The International Criminal Court, along with the ad hoc international tribunals, are prosecuting and are quite likely to prosecute genocide only that involves the coordinated activity of many people.

Second, an objection to the current version of the genocide statute's *mens rea* element is that it is too abstract a basis for proving individual guilt. A similar objection could still be run against my revised version of the *mens rea* element in the crime of genocide. An objection could be that the idea of directing others to act in a coordinated endeavor leaves it too vague what directing means and how much coordination must be shown. Indeed, I set the stage for such an objection by suggesting that incitement could be sufficient for such directing. Incitement is really directing only in the loosest of senses and contributes to the vagueness of the idea of genocidal intent. So, according to this objection, my proposal falls short of solving one of the most serious objections to the current definition of genocide.

My response to this objection is that I have specified what is meant by the intention to destroy by indicating the two principal ways that the prosecutor could prove such an intention. I agree, though, that the idea of directing as well as being coordinated, and even the idea of an endeavor could still use considerable specification. But criminal statues always try to cut a middle path between being specific enough to make clear what is proscribed and being general enough to allow for a myriad of possible cases falling under the statute, especially to cover cases where situations have changed radically over time and are likely to continue to do so. Good future work needs to be done on how to specify the key terms in this element of genocide. I would also add that law scholars and practitioners may well want to consult the growing literature on the ontology of groups, especially the idea of collective intentionality here.[18]

---

[18] See several recent collections of essays on collective intention and responsibility, including the special issue of the *Journal of Social Philosophy*, vol. 38, no. 3, Fall 2007, and *Midwest Studies in Philosophy*, vol. 30, 2006.

In a later chapter I will address the specific issue of how to specify the idea of incitement and especially how it is that incitement can be said to direct or coordinate the actions of others.

A third objection is that the mere participation plus knowledge requirement is not sufficient for establishing genocidal intent. Something like recklessness must also be shown to be fair to the defendants who are facing such a serious jeopardy of liberty. Recklessness is the knowing taking of an unjustified risk that one's action will cause substantial harm. Merely intending to participate and knowing that one contributes to a harmful collective endeavor does not seem to be strong enough, especially in those cases where one's contribution is likely to be very slight. Rather than knowing what the group aims at, one should also have to prove that one's act of participating was reckless in that one took a substantial risk of harming others by what one did. To add a recklessness proviso will make things quite a bit harder to prove on the part of the prosecution, but at a savings for the defendants who have so much to lose if they are convicted of such serious crimes as that of genocide.

My response is quite sympathetic, because I too have worried quite a bit about how to make international criminal statutes fairer to the defendants who must prove their case to avoid significant loss of liberty. And yet, if a person intends to act in a certain clearly harmful way, and knows that by doing so that person may also be contributing to an endeavor aimed at the destruction of a group, it is plausible to think that that person shares in that endeavor sufficiently to share in the genocidal intent, and that punishment could be fairly based on that showing. Requiring a showing of recklessness actually comes very close to what my participation plus knowledge requirement amounts to, because one must intend to act in a certain way knowing that such action will contribute to a certain collective harm, and that a knowing act could certainly be construed as a reckless one in that the risk is indeed normally substantial. I have not phrased this in terms of recklessness, but I believe that my proposal could be so formulated.

Sharing of intent is a very difficult conceptual category, but it can be made sufficiently precise to be the basis of *mens rea* of a crime such as genocide. The main way to make the underlying idea of shared intention more precise is to specify the kind of things that need to be proved. At the beginning of the previous section, I set those conditions out in some detail, and certainly in much greater detail than is normally done in a commentary on a criminal statute's *mens rea* element. In any event, proving that a person had knowledge is considerably easier than proving that the person had an intention. So, although I am sympathetic to this objection, I would point out that I have at least made things better than they are in the current formulation of the *mens rea* element of genocide.

A fourth objection is that for the worst of crimes, such as genocide, more is needed than merely showing that the defendant had wrongful aims; one needs also to show that there was something evil about the defendant, and that means that it must be proved that the defendant had wrongful motives. The history of criminal law, at least its folk history, shows that acts are considered criminal because of the evilness of the actor – terms such as wanton and depraved were often employed to describe the type of person who should be punished for the commission of a crime, as opposed to those who are said merely to have committed a tort. And to mark this evilness, according to this objection, international criminal law should focus on the motives, not only the intentions, of those accused of genocide because motives are what make a person evil or not. In any event, it is not enough that one participates and knows what the goals are of the enterprise one intends to contribute to. Criminal law should mark the very worst of offenses. And if the crime of genocide is supposed to be the absolute worst of all crimes, then it should definitely mark only the very worst of offenses.

My response is that whether or not these claims about the history of criminal law are true, from a normative point of view criminal law cannot easily be defended on this basis. Today criminal law prosecutes intentional actions, not the character of persons, and this is as it should be. The idea that people are evil is itself such a highly contested idea that it surely cannot bear the weight of a criminal prosecution. In the next chapter I will have quite a lot to say about the role that motive should play in criminal trials. I will argue that motive's role should be at the stage where aggravation or mitigation of punishment is being considered, not at the stage where the guilt of the defendant is being determined. Motives should count in decisions about how severe punishment should be, but the idea behind guilt determinations is of a different sort than is captured by inquiries into motives. I develop the argument that motive should not be seen as a basis of guilt but only of mitigation of punishment.

Fifth, it could be objected that my proposal about refining the intent element of genocide does not do justice to the extraordinary seriousness of the harm of genocide. If we are going to try to revise the intent requirement, we should do so, or at least this objection would claim, in a way that better highlights the way that the crime of genocide is worse than persecution in its aim of exterminating an entire social group. The proposal that I have made actually makes the crime of genocide seem more mundane and less serious than it already was, because it allows for prosecutions to go forward where the individual did not necessarily intend to destroy a group. Requiring malice aforethought would be a better way to think of the necessary mental element of a crime that is best seen as the international equivalent of murder (i.e., the killing of a group), rather than something that seems to require nothing more than a weak version of recklessness.

My response is to point out that very serious offenses do not always have the most stringent intent requirement. It is true that rape and murder involve specific as well as general intent requirements. But torture and terrorism do not have such complex intent requirements, and in any event, the structure of the *mens rea* requirement that I have proposed also has quite a complex structure. In this structure there is still a very strong requirement that the accused must be shown to have intended to do significant harm or to have directed others to do significant harm, and in most cases there is a second level of *mens rea* required as well. All in all, I have urged that it be made explicit how complex the *mens rea* requirement is in genocide, and I have also tried to specify it in such a way that the seriousness of the crime is made manifest in ways it was not in the original version of the genocide statute.

The question of what role individual intent should play in crimes that are by and large collective ones is a very difficult one. On one level it seems unfair to try to make an individual responsible for a crime perpetrated by a group upon another group. Indeed, the most appropriate thing to do is to hold the group responsible. But criminal law is not well set up for such proceedings. Criminal law is designed to deal with individual people in the dock. Normally, of course, this is not problematic if the individual is charged with a crime that he or she has fully committed on his or her own. But when an individual is charged with a collective crime such as genocide and that individual did only a part of the crime, something seems to have gone wrong. This is why the individual who is most deserving of conviction and punishment, if anyone is, will be the one who planned the crime, and only secondarily the one who merely participated in it. My proposal for revising the way that intent is understood in international criminal law is meant to reflect this intuition.

In this chapter I have spent considerable time trying to make clear what sort of special intent is involved in the crime of genocide, and how that intent element should be reconceptualized to make it more plausible both conceptually and normatively. I began by investigating the ontological status of collective intent and then applied this idea to the conceptualization of genocidal intent. Then I tackled the difficult question of how collective intention links to individual intention, because it is individuals who are in the dock. And I confronted directly the problem that no individual person typically manifests both the collective intent and the intent to commit a particular harmful act that satisfied the *mens rea* element of the crime of genocide. Indeed, there is a sense that the guilty mind is often split among several people, and the task of deciding which person is most guilty is one of ascertaining who most exemplifies the guilty mind of genocide where that is largely a collective intent. In this and earlier sections, I argued that despite its name, the best way to understand this collective intent element of genocide is as a kind of shared intent, not as a full-blooded intent of a collectivity.

Despite the problem of shared intentionality, I then advanced a proposal about how to change the current formulation of the *mens rea* element of genocide in ways that make it conceptually and normatively more plausible. I argued that we should much more clearly specify the kinds of intent that are involved in genocide and how they can be proven. In this respect, I also argued that it was important to drop the wording "as such" from the genocide definition because it gave the misleading impression that there was a motive requirement as well as a complex intent element in the *mens rea* of the crime of genocide. I ended this chapter by defending my proposal against several important objections, including an objection that was especially troubling, namely, that I was being unfair to defendants in international criminal proceedings, and that motive needed to be part of the elements of the crime to mark the morally serious character of that crime. In the next chapter I continue this inquiry by going into more depth about the distinction between motive and intent.

8

Motive and Destruction of a Group "As Such"

In this chapter I wish to consider the relationship between intent and motive in criminal law, and I will use the international crime of genocide as my main case study. Criminal lawyers, even those law professors who teach criminal law, often confuse motive and intent, and the same can be said of many philosophers. Popular speech certainly is rarely any help because many dictionaries list intention as a synonym for motive. In its most straightforward usage, intent or intention is what is aimed at, and motive is the reason or desire for acting. The standard confusion is easy to see here because it seems obvious that one way to characterize what our actions are aimed at is by reference to the reasons we have for so acting (for instance, the aim of my giving money to my daughter was because I wanted to help her out).

One way to link the actions of an individual to a crime perpetrated by a group concerns the participation of the individual in the larger enterprise. But a better way to indicate the guiltiness of that individual is by reference to his or her state of mind. Did the individual see himself or herself as aiming at the same things that the group did, or at least had the intent to participate in a group plan? Or was the individual's participation merely incidentally related to what the group had as its objective? As we saw in the previous chapter, the individual's intent is the key, and this is true of the way that genocide has come to be defined since the crime was first defined some 60 years ago, in the Genocide Convention after World War II.

In international law the crime of genocide is defined as "the intent to destroy, in whole or in part, a national, ethnical, racial or religious group, as such." One of the oddities of this definition is the phrase "as such." On first inspection, the "as such" phrase seems unnecessary, especially given the rest of the definition. It is even odder, as we will see, that many of the drafters of the Genocide Convention thought that adding the phrase "as such" meant that certain motives would become part of the elements of the crime of genocide.[1] Yet it remains unclear whether the drafters fully appreciated the distinction between motive and intention and hence truly meant to include or exclude motive from a crime that had already been understood to have a special intent requirement at its core.

In the first part of this chapter I will try to disconnect intent from motive, as best I can, and with a little help from Jeremy Bentham. In the second part of the chapter, I will consider the phrase "as such" in the legal definition of genocide and try to explain why this phrase was thought to bring motive into the elements of that crime. In the third section of this chapter, I will explain why I think that motive should not be part of the elements of any crime, and most especially the crime of genocide. And in the final section of the chapter, I will nonetheless explain what role considerations of motive should play as mitigation of punishment for the crime of genocide.

I. Motive and Intent Distinguished

It is common for lawyers to refer to the main idea behind the *mens rea* element of criminal liability as expressing the requirement that the defendant had to have evil motives. But this is to confuse guilty intentions with guilty motives: where guilty intentions are merely having the aim of doing that which it is illegal to do. Evilness doesn't necessarily have anything to do with *mens rea*, in my view, and the criminal law no longer looks to the type of character of the accused to determine whether the accused has *mens rea*. There was a time when criminal law was more closely linked to community moral standards, and when criminals were thought to have a hardened or depraved heart. Today the modern theories of criminal law eschew such categories, except in very restricted use such as "depraved heart murder," which is really only another name for gross negligence, not for an evil character.[2]

Those of us who are concerned about the rights of defendants bristle at the idea that *mens rea* has anything to do with people having evil

---

[1] I was first made aware of the unusual interpretation of this term by references to it in Schabas's *Genocide in International Law*.

[2] See the excellent discussion of these issues in Wayne R. LaFave and Austin W. Scott, Jr., *Criminal Law*, 2nd edition, St. Paul, MN: West Publishing, 1986.

characters. Many defendants may very well be guilty, but in my experience, rarely if ever have they been recognizably evil. In any event it is not
precisely clear what the term "evil" is supposed to stand for. The strong
religious connotations of the term make defense lawyers nervous, and
if "evil" is merely supposed to mean "very bad," why not use that term?
But even so, I'm also not sure what it is to have a bad character, or even
whether it makes sense to talk of character as a set of stable traits.[3] In
any event, I don't think that a person's character should enter into the
determination of his or her guilt, whereas it might be reasonable for it
to enter into their sentencing. To understand this point, we need to be
able clearly to separate motive from intent. This is the task of the current chapter, and I will begin with Jeremy Bentham's helpful account
of motive and intent in two central chapters of his seminal work, *An
Introduction to the Principles of Morals and Legislation.*[4]

Bentham gives a general account of motive, and he attempts to distinguish motive from intention, as follows:

> The motives with which alone we have any concern, are such as are of a
> nature as to act upon the will. By a motive then, in this sense of the word,
> is to be understood anything whatsoever, which by influencing the will of a
> sensitive being is supposed to serve as a means of determining him to act,
> or voluntarily to forebear to act, upon any occasion.[5]

Motives are the broad psychological factors, such as fear and malice,
that can cause us to form intentions.

On Bentham's account, motives are the causes of intentions. But it
is the intention that "produces the act."[6] Intentions are the immediate
aims of action. Intentions have consequences as their end, and acts as
the means to achieve these consequences. Intentions are aims; motives
are the reasons we have to form aims. Motives also stand in the causal
chain in that they influence an agent to form intentions. Bentham
admits that the line between intentions and motives is sometimes hard
to draw, especially in common discourse. But he insists that we keep
intention and motive analytically separate, especially for the purpose of
assigning blame or guilt. In his account the intention can be innocent

---

3 See John Doris's fascinating critique of the traditional way we think of character, *Lack
   of Character*, New York: Cambridge University Press, 2002.
4 Jeremy Bentham, *Introduction to the Principles of Morals and Legislation* (1789), edited by
   J. H. Burns and H. L. A. Hart, Oxford: Oxford University Press, 1970.
5 Ibid., pp. 96–7.
6 Ibid., p. 89.

even if the motive is bad.[7] I could aim to help my daughter by giving her money, and yet have the motive that I hoped to make her feel bad for forgetting my birthday.

Bentham provides us with a good start but ultimately makes it hard to draw a firm line between motive and intention. To make the distinction clearer, we need to add that intentions and motives are causes, but that intentions are final causes and motives are merely efficient causes. I may join the army out of a spirit of patriotism with the aim of defending my country against its enemies. Defending my country against its enemies is the final cause of my action; whereas patriotism is the efficient cause. In my view, criminal law should concern itself primarily with intentions in interpreting the mental elements of crimes. Motives can enter in, but normally only at the level of mitigating or aggravating conditions rather than as part of the elements of a crime that determine guilt. This is because, as I will next argue, what makes a mind guilty is that it aims to break the law, not that it is moved by malice, patriotism, or some other motive.

One reason why intent rather than motive should be the key to *mens rea* is practical. It is exceedingly hard to determine what motives are, but relatively easy often to read intentions off of actions. If a person does knowingly break the law, it can normally be assumed that he or she intended to break the law unless there are other clear aims of the action. Generally, we don't need to try to climb inside the person's head to ascertain intentions. We can merely infer intent from the behavior that he or she manifests. With motives things are quite different. It is very difficult to tell if one joins the military, for instance, out of the motive of patriotism or malice. Letting the person in question be the final arbiter of what his or her motives are is simply asking for trouble because many people will either lie or misidentify their motives as they seek to get others to think well of themselves. Even if we let folks be the final determiner of their motives, there are significant problems about the reliability of introspection as well.

More significantly, there is a normative reason for focusing on intention rather than motive in the criminal law. What should be the basis of criminal liability is whether a person has freely acted in such a way as to have as his or her aim the breaking of a law. We might want to base punishment on whether there were various extenuating circumstances or excuses available to this person. But criminal liability or guilt is best

[7] Ibid., p. 94.

understood normatively in terms of a choice to do that which is proscribed. Motives sometimes compel us and are not necessarily chosen;
whereas aims are indeed things that people choose. The reason why
guilt should attach to what is chosen has to do with the nature of responsibility in general and liability in particular.

Bentham contends, in addition, that no motive is really a bad one,
even those that can be labeled ill-will or malice, because motives are
ultimately, on his account, merely a response to pleasure and pain. As
he says, "A motive is substantially nothing more than pleasure or pain,
operating in a certain manner."[8] What is good or bad is what the consequences are, and these result from intentions, and vary significantly
because of circumstances.[9] It is true that for Bentham, motives "cause"
intentions in a way that makes it hard to completely disconnect motives
from intentions. I will not follow Bentham in his mechanistic psychology here, because it seems to me that motives do not fully determine
intentions, for it is intentions that bring in some kind of voluntariness
or choice – categories that Bentham did not really recognize as important. But there is a sense in which Bentham's account is useful, for it
focuses on what is the key factor in moral assessment, namely, the intention rather than the motive. This is because motives are only good or
bad derivatively, in terms of the circumstances of the act in question,
whereas intentions seem to involve more than this – what today is called
agency or autonomy.

In the early development of criminal law, the autonomy of the agent
was not as central as was self-protection in the face of evil. *Mens rea* was
equated with having a depraved heart or generally acting from the
motive of malice. Neither of these ways of construing *mens rea* was
based on the free choice of the agent; indeed, depraved hearts were
often born and hence could not have been chosen. What mattered
traditionally was responding to evil in the world. Now, we think of
criminal law in terms of deterrence or retribution for what a person
has chosen to do. We might still mitigate the punishment if the motives
were good or aggravate the punishment if the motives were bad, yet
this is not a matter of guilt but of whether we think that severe punishments should be administered if people seemed to be otherwise
good, or bad, even though they chose to break the law in the case
at bar.

[8] Ibid., p. 100.
[9] Ibid., p. 89.

Focusing on motive is to focus on those things such as character that are generally out of a person's control, instead of intention that is largely a matter of choice. Normatively, respect for people as choosing agents means that criminal law should focus on intention rather than motive, at least in determining guilt. But why can't we allow some considerations of guilt to turn on motive? Why not make the guilt of the worst of crimes involve an additional motive element where the prosecutor needs to show that one acted out of hatred or callousness in addition to showing that one aimed to break the law? Perhaps we could have levels of guilt, where the worst form of guilt required a showing of awful motives as well as intentions. This seems to be what stimulated some of the drafters of the Genocide Convention to try to add motive as an element of the crime of genocide, because they saw genocide as the worst of all crimes, "the crime of crimes."

In a normative division of labor, these drafters seemed to think that they could distinguish the garden-variety crime of persecution from that of genocide by adding to genocide the element of evil motive. But remember Bentham's claim that motives were not really evil in themselves at all. For Bentham, what mattered was what consequences were produced, and it could happen that good would follow from even the basest of motives, depending on the circumstances. Ill-will and even malice is not often under our control the way that our intentions are, in any event. And if motives are not normally under our control, it is not clear what the point is of making them rather than factors that are under our control the subject of determinations of guilt.

As I have argued in previous works, moral and legal responsibility needs to be linked to the choices people make.[10] In this sense I have followed in a long line of philosophers, beginning with Aristotle, in seeing responsibility to be warranted as a response to what a person has chosen to do.[11] Retribution makes sense only as a response to chosen behavior, and even deterrence makes the most sense on the model that we wish to influence the will and hence on the assumption that the will is under the person's control. But it may be that we will want to increase or diminish punishment on the basis of certain motives, perhaps reserving the most condemnatory sanctions to those acts that were not only chosen but also a manifestation of bad or evil character. I will take up this issue in later sections. I wish next to explore why the drafters of

---

[10] See May, *Sharing Responsibility*.
[11] Aristotle, *Nicomachean Ethics*, book III.

the Genocide Convention thought they could accomplish their goals by adding the words "as such" to the definition of the crime of genocide.

II. What Does "As Such" Mean?

If one knew nothing at all about the Genocide Convention's drafting, as I imagine is true of most people, it would seem quite puzzling that anyone would think that adding the words "as such" to the elements of a crime would be taken to mean that a motive element was being added by these words. As a preliminary stab at demystifying this history, let me surmise that the intention to destroy, in whole or in part, a group refers merely to what it says: these words refer to an intent element in the crime of genocide. To add that there must be an intention to destroy the group "as such" seems like one is trying to specify something about the type of destruction. But it may also be that "as such" means that one has animus or hatred toward the group, not merely that one wants to destroy the group.

To intend to destroy a group "as such" is, perhaps, shorthand for not having any other ulterior motives, unrelated to group animus, in acting hostilely toward the group. "As such" would mean that the only reason to intend to destroy the group was that the defendant hated the group and wanted the group destroyed. Of course, it also could be shorthand for saying that there was no motive at all, but only an intention to destroy the group. Indeed, there are already multiple intention elements in the crime of aggression, including the collective intent and several individual intents, as I argued in the previous chapter. If we add a motive element, we might then have the crime of crimes, in that we aim to capture only the worst offenders, but there will be very few cases that will go to conviction with so many mental elements to be proved.

The history of the drafting of the Genocide Convention is quite useful and also puzzling on the question of why the words "as such" were added at the last minute. As William Schabas explains:

> In a search for consensus, Venezuela, which favored the United Kingdom proposal to delete the reference to motive, proposed that the words "as such" should be introduced. Venezuela said its amendment "should meet the views of those who wished to retain a statement of motives; indeed the motives were implicitly included in the words 'as such.'" ... [As] Jean Spiropoulos said, ... "It was decided to include the motives in the definition but not to enumerate them."[12]

[12] Schabas, *Genocide in International Law*, p. 249.

As far as I can tell, the addition of the words "as such" thus was seen as meaning that the crimes were committed against the individuals because they belonged to the group, and that this meant to signify that some sort of vague discriminatory animus motivated the crime.

Could one intend to destroy individuals who are members of a group, as a way to destroy the group as such, and not display a kind of animus toward the group? It seems as if one could. Perhaps the point of an ethnic cleansing campaign was to remove a group that had been an historic enemy of, and constant danger to, one's own people. One might not have animus toward the enemy group, but instead one might simply wish that the group were not posing such a threat. I suppose this is also a kind of motivation, but at this limited level it is also hard to distinguish it from a mere intention not to allow another group to be a danger to one's own group. That the group poses a threat would certainly create a desire, not merely an aim, that it be destroyed. But what is importantly added by requiring that that desire be present? Does it make the crime worse when that desire is present? And should we think that intentions never refer to desires? It is even harder to draw a firm line between desires and aims than between motives and intentions, thus making it unclear whether the drafters quite understood what is the difference between motive and intent. In the end it remains quite puzzling what the drafters of the Genocide Convention meant by adding the "as such" words to the definition of genocide.

Before proceeding further, I wish to note that if the intent of the drafters was to add at least a minimal motive requirement to the elements of the crime of genocide, there were certainly easier ways to do it than to insert the words "as such" into the definition of genocide. Indeed, it is odd that so many members of the drafting group thought that people who read the definition, perhaps generations later, would interpret the words "as such" as referring to motive. The words "as such" do not seem to convey the idea that motive is a part of this crime in any but the most elliptical manner. Also I would note that the very question of the intent of the drafters reminds us of the difficulty of identifying motives and the relative ease of identifying intentions. We do not ask what are the motivations of the drafters except to ascertain how we should regard them. It is their intentions that matter for interpreting what they did.

Schabas says that "Under ordinary circumstances, a motive requirement unnecessarily narrows the offense, and allows individuals who have intentionally committed the prohibited act to escape conviction."[13] Requiring the animus motive will mean that coldly calculated genocidal acts will not be convictable because they will lack the hot-blooded feature that is added with such a motive component. And, yet, it may be that the cold-blooded acts are the ones that are the worst, or at very least the ones we will have the best chance of deterring, instead of those that are based on conditions that are largely out of the defendant's control. Cold-blooded killers are in many ways worse than those who act out of passions that may pass quickly over time. Cold-blooded killers are those who are most likely to repeat their acts. Deterring the cold-blooded rather than the hot-blooded seems to make the most sense, if we have to choose between them.

From a retributive standpoint, convictions for the hot-blooded motive may make some sense, but not if we think that retribution turns on what we have chosen to do when we had other options. Once again, agency and autonomy questions enter into the deliberations. It makes little sense to convict for serious crimes when one was acting on motives that one had not chosen. There is an older tradition of retribution that simply sees conviction as comeuppance for evil done, perhaps even just for being evil. I will not discuss this idea here, but merely will assume that all modern views justify punishment either on grounds of deterrence or on grounds of retribution for what one chose to do. If we wish to return to the older way of thinking of punishment, many other modern ideas of penal justice will have to be changed as well.

From an expressivist point of view, motives may appear to matter as well, although I believe that this is also misguided. Expressivism "transcends retribution and deterrence in claiming as a central goal the crafting of historical narratives, their authentication as truths, and their pedagogical dissemination to the public."[14] Those like David Luban and Mark Drumbl who have defended an expressivist theory of punishment in international criminal law think that there is great value in the sheer dramaturgy of a trial, concerning how the world views the unfolding trial as dramatic expression of the international society's condemnation of what the defendants have done. Here it seems that whether or

---

[13] Ibid., p. 245.
[14] See David Luban, "Beyond Moral Minimalism," *Ethics & International Affairs*, vol. 20, no. 3, 2006, pp. 354–5; and Mark Drumbl, *Atrocity, Punishment, and International Law*, New York: Cambridge University Press, 2007, pp. 173–6 and 187–94.

not one is acting on motives one has not chosen, the world demands that an extreme expression of dislike for what the defendants have done demands severe punishment. If "evil" motives were at play, then the international community demands that a very strong expression of condemnation be elicited.

In my opinion, it is still not clear why even on expressivist grounds motives should count in deciding whether a person is guilty of a crime. Of course, most of the expressivist concerns can mostly be met by addressing motives in the aggravation of punishment category rather than in the guilt category. As I have indicated, I would have only minor worries about doing so. But if the above argument is meant to indicate that motives should function as an element in the crime itself, rather than in the sentencing phase, then I would find that the arguments of expressivists do not support this conclusion. I will have more to say about this topic in later chapters. But at the moment, I would merely indicate that my proposal about not letting motives count as an element in the crime of genocide is not completely engaged by the expressivist arguments in the literature.

There is another problem I wish to address before ending our discussion of the drafters' intentions in adding the words "as such" to the genocide definition. The drafters could have included an additional intent requirement and avoided the difficulties that result when one adds a motive requirement to the definition of a crime. The intention I have in mind is often called "discriminatory intent." By this I mean the aim to discriminate against a particular group by acting in a certain way. Such an intention is often confused with "discriminatory motive." This is the desire to discriminate, which, of course, often is closely aligned with discriminatory intent, perhaps in the way that Bentham suggested, namely, where the discriminatory motive causes the discriminatory intent. But the two should be kept analytically distinct. Discriminatory intent is an aim, not a desire, in the sense that it points to an end state that one wants to accomplish, one in which people are treated unequally, for instance. There need not be any animus or ill will displayed toward the people who are to be treated unequally. I admit, though, that adding this intent requirement may make it even more difficult for lawyers and judges to keep intention and motive separate, but it is better nonetheless than allowing lawyers and judges to interpret things in such a way that they think there is a motive element that must be proved.

III. Should Individual Motive Be an Element in the Collective Crime of Genocide?

If genocide is to be the "crime of crimes," then perhaps there should be an additional element or two that must be proven to establish that what an individual who is accused of the crime of genocide did was truly horrible, not merely a garden variety crime. This is indeed the way that the crime of genocide is normally thought of. Typically the crime is described as having two *mens rea* elements: general and special intent. Yet it is not clear how having two intent requirements links the acts of the individual to the collective crime in such a way that the individual's actions are marked as especially horrible and deserving of the appellation, genocide, that is, as the "crime of crimes." In the previous chapter I suggested a way to make this link. A defender of the motive requirement might think that strategies such as mine that focus only on the relation of collective and individual intentions will not be able to accomplish what adding a motive requirement can do.

Motive could link the individual action to the collective crime in an especially graphic way. Think of the motive of racial hatred. If it could be proven that a defendant not only participated in a genocidal campaign and intended to do so, but did so out of racial hatred, then the oddity of holding him liable for such an enormous and horrific crime as genocide is seemingly lessened. Merely participating in an international crime, even intentionally doing so, could make one liable for very serious offenses. But if the international crime for which one is accused is genocide, and because one's participation may be no different than if the crime were considerably lesser than genocide, one wonders why the mere fact of participation should warrant a conviction for such a serious crime. Yet if the motivation for the individual's participation was itself quite horrible, such as racial hatred, then things seem different. And if the motive is closely related to what it is that makes the collective crime especially horrible, then perhaps we have the beginning of a solution to our problem. In what remains of this section I will sketch this possible solution but also argue that it ultimately does not succeed.

The special horror of genocide is difficult to characterize, but one part is that the destruction of the group, indeed, its annihilation, is the point of the violence that constitutes the crime. If one merely participates in this attempted annihilation, even if intentionally one does so, one may be responsible for the small part that one plays in the genocide, but it is unclear why this means that the participation is worse than participation in other collective crimes. But if one not only participates intentionally but also does so out of a hatred-based desire to destroy the group, not merely to do what others are doing or what one has been told to do, then the action of the individual is itself noxious, and for one of the main reasons that the collective crime is noxious as well.

In general, one of the main conceptual and normative difficulties in international criminal law is to show that individuals should be held liable for what groups do. The way that I have tried to solve this problem is by arguing that individuals often play significant roles in what groups do, thereby allowing groups to commit especially serious atrocities. And so, it is the role or participation of the individual that is an important factor in holding those individuals responsible or liable. The drawback with this strategy is that although it solves the general conceptual problem, it does not really indicate why certain forms of participation should be considered so much worse normatively than other forms, especially when the type of participation looks the same as in lesser collective crimes. Focusing on motive, rather than the more traditional *actus reus* and *mens rea* elements, makes it possible to address this normative difficulty. But we have not yet eliminated all problems.

The chief difficulty with this strategy, as I began to explain in previous sections of this chapter, is that motive is not generally something that people choose and hence an odd basis for responsibility or liability ascriptions. Again, take the case of racial hatred. Although this state of mind is something that can be influenced by the will, it is rare that one has chosen this mental state by explicit acts of will in the first place. Rather, racial hatred arises due to family upbringing and early childhood experiences, all largely out of the control of the person in question. So focusing on motives will not help explain why this person deserves to be found guilty of a collective crime for one's participation more than one otherwise would, on the basis of a motive such as racial hatred. One does not "own" the collective crime more because one's motives were noxious. Hence it is not clear that one should be held to be more guilty, or guilty at all, simply because of acting from the animus.

So we will still be faced with the difficulty of explaining why an individual should be held liable for the enormity of what a group does when it perpetrates genocide, and we will not be any better off in explaining why the individual is especially worthy of conviction for a serious offense here. This is also generally why a consideration of motives has not been thought in recent years to be appropriate in criminal prosecutions for serious offenses for those who contribute to especially horrible consequences. Motives may often make us think much worse of the person in question, but they do not necessarily make the person guilty. Indeed, as I have argued, because motives are not chosen, they are an especially bad basis for the assignment of guilt, unless we return to a time when we based liability and responsibility on character.

One could object that I have too narrow a basis upon which to convict individuals. Bad character of the person who commits an act could indeed make the act in question worse. If one causes harm to another, and does so intentionally, it is still worse yet if the motive was one of hatred. Hatred seems to be bad in itself and will surely add a degree of wrongness to the overall act. On this basis, increasing the sanction or punishment would be justified, and the way to think of this is to hold the individual liable for the collective crime. Focusing on the individual defendant's animus means that we have not merely picked out one among many people who all acted in roughly the same way to facilitate the genocide. Instead, we will be picking out someone who is independently to be condemned.

I would respond in a way that returns us to the account of Bentham's view in earlier sections of this chapter. Motives are not of themselves either good or bad. Patriotism can be very good, as when it moves a person to risk his or her life for the sake of a country's noble goals. But patriotism can be very bad, as when it moves a person to risk his or her life for the sake of a country's ignoble goals. Even animus or hatred is not always bad – consider the case of someone who hates the rapist and is thus more strongly motivated to confront rapists than before. In addition, I would argue that we still do not have a really good basis for linking the acts of the individual to the collective crime. Yes, it is true that the collective crime may be worse if committed by those who have bad motives. But we have not yet explained why the badness of the motive of individuals makes them more responsible for harms caused by collectives. In general, I am not persuaded that interpreting the Genocide Convention to require a motive element in the crime of genocide is indeed justifiable on practical or normative grounds

IV. Motives and Severity of Punishment

Even though I have argued strongly against adding a motive element in the elements of establishing guilt in the crime of genocide, I think that motive can sometimes be relevant in the sentencing phase of a criminal trial. It will turn out that this proposal creates some difficult conceptual problems. I will identify those problems and indicate how they might be solved in this final section of the chapter. From what I indicated above, though, it is not motive alone, but motive in conjunction with circumstance, that will here be the key. Motives are not relevant for determinations of guilt, but motives may sometimes be relevant for determinations of punishment. If we think of punishment in expressivist terms, then it will sometimes matter whether the act was caused by good or bad motives, despite the fact that such motives are not normally under the control of the agent at the time of action.

When thinking about the function of punishment, we can focus on causes of action that are more remote than when thinking about guilt. This is especially true when we are thinking of crimes that involve the participation of individuals in collective enterprises such as genocide. Think of the case of those individuals who are motivated to participate in genocide because of racial hatred. As I argued earlier, racial hatred is not something that is under the control of the agent, at least not normally, at the time of action. But there are often things that the agent could have done differently in one's life that might have diminished the likelihood that he or she would develop racial hatred. In expressivist terms, it certainly would make sense to try to indicate that people should not develop this motivation. Stiffening the punishment is one way that this might be accomplished. Similarly, if the participation in genocide is based on patriotism, we might want to diminish the punishment as a way of sending a message that such behavior is not as disvalued as participation in genocide based on other motives, such as racial hatred.

Expressivism, one theory of punishment, is all about sending messages to those who are potential participants in crimes in the future.[15] One may wish to raise fairness objections to the idea that people should be punished so as to send messages to others than themselves, but this is indeed one of the standard considerations in deciding whether to punish more severely or less. Expressivism can also be aimed at the person who is the accused as well, so that we would send a message to her or him concerning her or his future behavior. Even if it was not possible to change one's motives at the time of action, as long as it is possible to

---

[15] See Mark Drumbl's discussion of the legal theory of expressivism in his book *Atrocity, Punishment, and International Law*, ch. 6. Also see his essay "The Expressive Value of Prosecuting and Punishing Terrorists: *Hamdan*, The Geneva Conventions, and International Criminal Law," *George Washington Law Review*, vol. 75, no. 5/6, August 2007, pp. 1165–99.

do so in the future, and thereby diminish the likelihood that he or she will cause the same wrong in the future, severity of punishment may be justified now to affect that future state, and fairness objections are certainly less relevant now that deterrence is aimed at the accused and not merely at those who might follow. So two types of messages can be sent by means of expressivism that would allow us to count motive in the sentencing phase of the trial even if it is inappropriate to do so in the guilt phase of the trial, namely, concern for future behavior of the defendant as well as concern for the future behavior of others similarly placed to the defendant.

Guilt is a threshold determination of responsibility. Once one has met the conditions of this threshold, then other non-guilt-making considerations can enter into the sentencing of a defendant. For reasons I rehearsed above, motives should not be part of this threshold determination of guilt. But motives may come into the picture after guilt is determined, and we are then trying to decide whether to punish severely or leniently for those guilty acts and states of mind of the defendant. This is what is meant when motive is considered as an aggravating or mitigating factor in punishment.

If the defendant has motives that are normally good, then we also may be justified in diminishing the sentence. Even if we follow Bentham, and think of motives as not good or bad in themselves, we can still talk of motives as more or less likely to lead to good or bad consequences. Mitigation of punishment would be based on the having of motives that are generally likely not to cause bad consequences and likely to cause good consequences. We may justifiably punish less severely in such cases as a way to add another level of motivation to the future behavior of the agent. Justification for punishment thus can be different than justification for guilty verdicts. And it is sometimes reasonable to use different elements in determining punishment rather than guilt. For this reason, motive may be a legitimate element of punishment but not of guilt determinations.

In this respect, think of whether it is the planners and inciters, on the one hand, or those who engage in violent action, on the other hand, as those who should be punished most severely for genocide. In some respects those with the worst motives seem to be the ones who kill or otherwise harm. For these people more clearly resemble the domestic criminals who perform the same acts of murder and harm. As people they appear worse than those who plan and incite, who often are fine upstanding members of their communities, such as politicians and

military leaders. Those who perform the harm are often marginal members of the community whose characters are not upstanding – indeed,
some of these people are straightforwardly vicious. So it appears that if
motive matters, then it is not the planners or inciters, but rather the foot
soldiers, in a genocide who should be most severely punished.

Yet, as I will argue in much more detail in subsequent chapters,
I believe that the planners and inciters should be punished more
severely than the foot soldiers in a genocide. Although the planners and
inciters are not necessarily vicious, their motives often come very close
to that for international crimes. For the crime in question is not merely
the individual act of killing or harming, but rather the mass crime of
intending to destroy a protected group. And here the motive is often
racial or ethnic or religious or national hatred. Such feelings are vicious
in an obvious sense, but even more than this they are like vices in the
international domain in that they so clearly call for harming or even
destroying groups that they are in some sense, even if not strictly vicious,
as close as you can get to being vicious at the international, as opposed
to the domestic, level. Not only, as I will argue later, do the planners
and inciters best instantiate the collective intent of international crimes,
but they also best instantiate vicious behavior as well, and hence should
clearly be the ones who are punished most severely in genocide cases.

I see punishment as primarily involving a partial merging of expressivist and long-term deterrence considerations. One of the main reasons
that a society tries to express condemnation of certain acts is to affect,
at least in the very long run, the harms in that society. Expressivism can,
I suppose, also be merely a value in itself, as the society seeks to identify
what are its most important goals. But, surely, one set of goals, which
intersect with deterrence theory, concerns the reduction of harm in that
society. Expressing condemnation of genocide, for instance, articulates
the values of the society, but it also hopefully diminishes the likelihood
of genocide in the future. By appealing to mitigation and aggravation
factors in sentencing, we try to make the world a place of less rather than
more suffering in the future. This idea draws heavily on a deterrence
model of punishment. Similar results can be had, however, if we draw
on an expressivist model of punishment. For here the idea is to declare
publicly what behavior is to be prized and what is to be condemned.
Punishment is often a very dramatic statement of a community's idea of
how we should regard what its members have done.

In collective crimes, given the severe harms involved, it is especially
important to send an expressivist message so that we are less likely to see

these crimes repeated in the future. Collective crimes do not generally arise overnight. Patterns of behavior develop including strong animus between various social groups. Public expressions of condemnation for such crimes would arguably stand a chance of lessening such animus. This will be more likely to happen if the expressions of condemnation are made through officially recognized channels, such as through courts and their judges' decisions, because such condemnations will then have the weight of collective authority that is generally bestowed upon courts and judges. Of course, when international courts make such pronouncements of condemnation, the effect on various societies will depend on how much moral authority is bestowed on those courts by the members of the society in question. This is one good reason to make sure that international courts and tribunals are established with maximal support, rather than to be resented by the folks back home.

Collective crimes, such as genocide, typically rely on many, many people participating at various levels of involvement. There are significant problems with holding them all guilty, at least to the same degree. But such considerations may not necessarily affect how we view our sentencing options once conviction has been obtained. For if we can avoid the fairness issues I mentioned above, it would be a very good thing indeed to do what we can to make such crimes as genocide less likely in the future. And surely one way to accomplish this objective is to look at the motives of those who have been convicted when we then determine how severely these defendants should be punished.

I remain unconvinced that any good will be done by adding a motive element to the elements of the crime of genocide. Here let me mention two of the issues I discussed above and that would require further argumentation on my part. First, adding a motive element to *mens rea* muddies the water significantly concerning what job *mens rea* is supposed to do in the overall determination of guilt in criminal trials. Second, adding a motive element to *mens rea* will make it much harder to gain convictions in genocide cases, because genocides often occur because of the acts of bureaucrats rather than those who are depraved or otherwise people of bad character.

Much more harm in the world results from collective than from isolated individual behavior, and we would do well to use all of the fair tactics that are available to motivate people not to continue to support mass atrocities. Even if it is unclear what precisely will be the effects of condemnatory acts such as those involved in meting out severe sentences, there is a sense in which it is good for a society to go on record as expressing the view that such practices are not valued, and indeed are strongly disvalued, in the society. Because such mass atrocities as genocide are often fueled by individual motives such as racial or ethnic hatred, it makes sense sometimes to use such elements in sentencing, even though it normally does not make sense to use motive as an element in the initial determination of guilt in criminal prosecutions generally, and prosecutions for genocide in particular.

PART D

RESPONSIBILITY FOR GENOCIDE

9

Complicity and the Rwandan Genocide

We have seen in earlier chapters that the leaders of a genocide are those most clearly guilty of the crime of genocide. But what of those who aid the genocide in various ways? It is estimated that one-third of the population of Rwanda, over one million people, were in some sense complicit in the genocide that occurred there in 1994.[1] A good debate is ensuing about whether all one million of these people should indeed be tried for their varying levels of complicity. In my view, such an outcome might advance the goal of reconciliation, but convictions for all of these people are so unlikely that we should scale back a bit, yet still allow, for many *gacaca*, what Rwandans call "trials in the grass," of low-level participants in genocide. In this chapter I wish to investigate the border between legal and moral complicity in such cases of mass atrocity as genocides.

Complicity is a slippery concept – it is widely used in common parlance, and yet there is little agreement about what precisely it means. In Arusha, Tanzania, major trials have been held for Rwandans in governmental, military, religious, and media leadership positions who had some role in the horrific genocide. At least some of the people who have been successfully tried could count as complicit, as accomplices, rather than principal perpetrators, such as the media executives who ran the radio station that conveyed such a drumbeat of hate mongering in the lead-up to the genocidal campaign. The *gacaca* process, hybrid trials that are held all across Rwanda, have prosecuted many ordinary people who played some role, sometimes fairly minor, in the genocide that swept across their country. It is unclear how many of these Rwandans were complicit in a way that would trigger successful legal prosecution in more normalized criminal proceedings, because it is somewhat unclear how to differentiate legal from moral complicity.

[1] See Drumbl, *Punishment, Atrocity, and International Law.*

I will argue that complicity can be the basis for legal liability, even for criminal liability, if two conditions are met. First, the person's actions or inactions must be causally efficacious at least in the sense that had the person not committed these actions or inactions the harm would have been made significantly less likely to occur. Second, the person must know that his or her actions or inactions risk contributing to a harmful enterprise, and must intend that these actions or inactions risk making this contribution. But it is not part of this analysis that the defendant must intend the harmful result. I explore the boundaries between legal and moral complicity and end with a discussion of how the analysis defended in the chapter affects such questions as how many people in Rwanda should be prosecuted for the genocide, which occurred because of widespread complicity.

In the first section of this chapter, I will present a typology of the various forms of legal complicity, distinguishing these forms from moral complicity. In the second section of the chapter, I analyze several problematic cases of legal complicity, showing how complicity could be extended quite a bit farther than normally recognized. In the third section of the chapter, I will defend my theory of legal complicity against two alternative views, those discussed by Christopher Kutz and K. J. M. Smith. In the fourth section of the chapter I look at the complicity in the Rwandan genocide and ask who should be prosecuted by the wide-ranging *gacaca* process. And in the final section of the chapter, I explain how even those who should not be prosecuted can be nonetheless affected by wide-ranging trials of other people. Because the border between legal complicity and moral complicity is so porous, those who are only morally complicit will often be affected by wide-ranging trials of those who are legally complicit. I end with a discussion of how to view individual criminal complicity in the context of collective crimes.

I. Types of Legal Complicity

Complicity is a vague concept in criminal law as well as in common parlance, but the vagueness of this concept is in my view an important part of its meaning. Loosely, complicity involves responsibility for the commissions and omissions that allow harm to occur but that are not necessarily causally efficacious in a straightforward way. One standard way to understand legal complicity is in terms of holding one person (typically called an accessory or accomplice) criminally responsible for what another person (typically called the principal or perpetrator) has wrongfully done.[2] Another way to think about complicity is to distinguish principals in the first degree (sometimes said to be those with primary responsibility), namely, those with the requisite *mens rea* and *actus reus* who cause a criminal result, and principals in the second degree (sometimes said to be those with secondary or complicit responsibility), namely, those who "aid, counsel, command or encourage the principal in the first degree."[3] A further distinction is often made between aiding and abetting (secondary responsibility for those present at the scene of the crime) and counseling and procuring (tertiary responsibility for those absent from the scene of the crime).[4]

A distinction among those who are present, at least in a constructed way, which is very useful in genocide cases, distinguishes between those who aid or abet, on the one hand, and those who are merely present, on the other. "It is often said that abetting relates to the *mens rea* of the principal offence whereas aiding relates to the *actus reus*."[5] Aiding involves providing material assistance; whereas abetting could involve encouraging, instigating, or inciting. But because the jurisprudence of the crime of genocide distinguishes direct and public incitement in genocide from complicity in genocide, incitement should be treated separately, as I do in another chapter.

Both those who aid or abet are distinguished from those who are merely present when harm occurs. Yet there is controversy about how much assistance one must give to be criminally liable for what the principal does. International prosecutors have argued that "the most marginal act of assistance" can constitute complicity,[6] whereas the international tribunals have so far resisted this suggestion looking instead for "participation that has a direct and substantial effect on the commission of the offence."[7] It has proven to be very difficult to get consensus, though, about what substantial means, and this relates to the built-in vagueness of the concept I mentioned earlier.

Even if complicity is restricted to aiding and abetting, there is still the problem of how far to stretch these concepts. The vagueness of the idea

[2] K. J. M. Smith, *A Modern Treatise on the Law of Criminal Complicity*, Oxford: Oxford University Press, 1991, pp. 1–2.

[3] LaFave and Scott, *Criminal Law*, pp. 496–7.

[4] See Smith, *A Modern Treatise on the Law of Criminal Complicity*, p. 32.

[5] Schabas, *Genocide in International Law*, p. 303.

[6] *Prosecutor v. Dusko Tadic,* International Criminal Tribunal for the Former Yugoslavia, case no. IT-94-1-T, Trial Chamber Judgment, 7 May 1997, para. 666.

[7] William Schabas, *The UN International Criminal Tribunals*, New York: Cambridge University Press, 2006, p. 303.

of complicity concerns just how far the idea sweeps. There is a sense in which any of us "could" have done something to prevent harms that are occurring every day. If aiding includes not preventing, then there is a sense that nearly every person could be said to be complicit for nearly every harm. Legally this would put us in an impossible situation: the law cannot be used to prosecute all members of a society, because then no one could be judge or jury member. So the law makes distinctions between those acts of complicity that are legally actionable and those that call for only moral condemnation, especially when so many are involved.

One of the most significant problems is that complicity can be by commission *or* by omission. But there is common agreement that mere presence at the scene is not sufficient to establish a complicit omission.[8] One way to delimit the concept is to require that it be proven that the defendants had a special duty to intervene before their mere failure to act would constitute a legally complicit omission. On this account, of all the bystanders on the beach who saw the swimmer drowning and did not act to rescue her, only the person who is a lifeguard has clearly engaged in a legally complicit omission. But in cases of genocide it is less clear who has the special duty to intervene to stop the atrocity. Beyond certain military leaders, who do not intervene to stop their troops from committing genocidal atrocities, it is hard to know who is sufficiently like the lifeguard among all of the people who are various sorts of bystanders to a genocide campaign.

One strategy is to ask whether the bystander's presence somehow encouraged the principal to commit the offense. Such encouragement is normally listed under the category of abetting. Abetting comes from the Old French term *a beter,* meaning to bait or excite. So if one's mere presence and inactivity encouraged another, this might be a form of abetting that constituted complicity.[9] One can look for previous association between the agents to see if the current inactivity of one of these agents, where activity in the past had been known and expected, encouraged the principal to commit the crime. Here one of the main questions in Anglo-American law is whether the awareness by the putative abettor that his or her inactivity would likely encourage is sufficient. In this respect the Anglo-American courts generally seem to distinguish between simple cases and so-called public performance cases.

[8] See ibid., p. 304.
[9] See Smith, *A Modern Treatise on the Law of Criminal Complicity,* pp. 35–9.

"Performance cases" include situations where a crowd gathers to watch two men who seem on the verge of fighting. As one 19th-century English judge put it: "spectators really make the fight; without them, and in the absence of any one to look on and encourage, no two men, having no cause of personal quarrel, would meet together in solitude to knock one another about for an hour or two."[10] In this sense some spectators not only encourage but play such an important causal role that they "make the fight" and can perhaps be held liable in ways that even the boxers themselves cannot. In any event, as long as the spectators knew of the effect they were likely to have on the boxers, some courts have ruled that the spectators can be held to be complicit in the harms or wrongs the boxers cause.

In "performance cases," the spectators play a role similar to that of someone who supplies guns to each of two angry people – the resulting fight can be foreseen, and the potential for harm is great. Performance-case complicity looks very much like "setting the stage" that is said to be crucial for "attempt crimes" as well. In addition, having the stage set makes the performance of boxing possible in ways it wouldn't have been without the stage. In these "performance cases," there is a merging of legal and moral complicity, because normally merely standing around when a crime occurs, and doing nothing to prevent it, only triggers moral complicity, yet here at least some commentators also want to say that legal complicity is triggered.

Another interesting set of cases concerns people who are in a position to exercise control and prevent harm but who have no duty to do so. Is the mere fact that they are able to exercise significant control, and that they know they have this ability, sufficient to trigger legal complicity due to failure to exercise that control? Standard domestic cases concern crimes that are committed using another person's car, where the other person could have prevented the use of his car and knew that there was a risk that the car would be used for harmful purposes. Other cases concern employers who have the ability to stop their employees from causing workplace-related harm. There is controversy about how to treat these cases, but there is some agreement that they are at least at the borderline of legal complicity.

K. J. M. Smith has proposed that legal responsibility for failures to act to exercise control should turn on one of two factors being present: "*either* a relationship between the parties, where the 'accessory'

---

[10]   *R v. Coney* (1882) 8 QBD 534 at 564.

is clearly accepted as dominant, and the principal, by virtue of depen-
dency or otherwise, is subordinate; *or* a substantial risk of personal
harm."[11] Smith sets out these factors as a way to alleviate the worry that
too many people will be caught up in the net of those bystanders who
are legally responsible. The idea is that we can expect people to act
reasonably to exercise control over the actions of others, and hold them
legally responsible when they don't, only when there is a special condition satisfied. In what follows, I will partially support Smith's proposal.

So far we have the following categories of legal complicity:

Active Legal Complicity:

Secondary Responsibility – while present at scene
    Aiding – current provision of material assistance
    Abetting – current encouragement
Tertiary Responsibility – while absent from scene
    Counseling – past encouragement
    Procuring – past provision of material assistance

Passive Legal Complicity:

Duty-based Responsibility –
    Failure to fill an assumed role
    Failure to exercise control over subordinate
    Failure to exercise reasonable care concerning situation one initiated
Non-Duty-Based Responsibility –
    Presence in "performance cases"
    (?) Failure to exercise control over nonsubordinate
    (?) Failure to aid person in imminent danger

The final two cases blur into moral complicity, of which there are just as
many, if not more, categories as there are of legal complicity.

One more thing to be said about this typology of legal complicity concerns the idea of "being present" at the scene of the crime. Most legal
authorities seem to allow a fairly wide reading of what "being present"
means. In particular, the idea of "constructed presence" seems to be
widely accepted. Consider a bank robbery. Those who actually enter the
bank are, of course, the principal perpetrators. The driver who waits
outside is arguably still at the scene and has secondary responsibility.
But what of the person who ignites fireworks on the other side of town to

distract the police from the scene? He seems to be just as much providing material assistance as is the get-away driver. This person is normally treated as having secondary responsibility, whereas the person who had stolen the plans for the bank's safe a week before is treated as having tertiary responsibility. Of course, there is a continuum here, and the spatial and temporal dimensions do not always line up neatly.

II. Analyzing Some Difficult Cases

Various forms of bystander complicity involve knowledge that the bystander may be contributing to a harmful enterprise, but the bystander may not be prosecutable. Think again of the bystanders on the beach watching a drowning swimmer. By not going to the rescue of the swimmer, these bystanders would normally recognize that there is a sense in which their inaction contributes to the swimmer's demise. But for various reasons, some good and some bad, the bystanders may nonetheless remain inactive. In the American legal system, although by no means in all other systems of law, there is no legal duty to rescue, and so these inactive bystanders have not done anything legally wrong by failing to act to aid the swimmer. And because there is no duty that the bystanders have, their inactivity does not easily translate into the kind of omission that triggers legal responsibility for the harm to the swimmer.

But there are classic exceptions even in those societies that do not recognize a legal duty to go to the aid of those who are in imminent peril. One standard exception concerns a bystander who is somehow responsible for the swimmer's peril, for instance, by having lured him or her into the water in the first place. Another exception concerns a bystander who starts to go to the swimmer's aid, with others now relying on the person's aiding the swimmer, but who then withdraws his or her aid. A further exception sometimes made concerns bystanders who are the last resort of a person in peril, for instance, the only bystander who is present on the beach when the swimmer starts to drown. In all these cases, many jurisdictions will hold that the apparent unreasonableness of the bystander's inaction outweighs the "right" of the bystander not to get involved in the affairs of others.

There is also a good argument to be made that once these exceptions are recognized, then the very idea behind the no duty to rescue loses its attraction. If especially the last exception, the last resort exception, is taken seriously, it is very hard to see why a bystander would not have a

duty to rescue, rather than merely saying that this duty is weakened insofar as it is distributed across many others similarly situated. Whatever
seems to be the basis of the last resort exception would seemingly also
cover those who were on the beach as a group where the seas were so
rough that the entire group needed to act to save the swimmer and
there were no other groups on the beach at the time. In any event, if it
is unclear whether the others on the beach with you will so act, there is
also a sense in which you are a kind of last resort as well. Yet we rarely
can know what others are thinking and are likely to do. Once the last
resort exception is recognized, the idea that we have a duty to look out
for each other reemerges as significant, and at least as significant as the
right not to have to get involved in others' trouble.

Perhaps the most curious case is the one alluded to above concerning
the bystander who is present in a "performance case." This case has all
of the appearance of a rescue case in that the bystanders do not appear
to have any special duty to stop the fighters, and the bystanders are not
straightforwardly responsible for the fighters' peril. But perhaps this
exceptional category is the one to think about first if the performance
cases are indeed to involve legal complicity. For here it seems, at least
according to a 19th-century British judge, that the bystanders/specta-
tors are in some sense causally responsible for the fighters' peril by making the boxers fight where otherwise they wouldn't.

But in what sense do the spectators "make" the boxers fight? Answering
this question provides us with a good idea of how to deal with one of the
main categories of a case that sits at the border of legal and moral complicity. It seems to me that the judge's words can be seen either as mere
metaphor or as referring to the kind of encouragement, supplied by
the bystanders, which is indeed causally efficacious in ways that would
not normally be recognized. Perhaps, as the judge said, the boxers had
no other reason to fight than that there was a group of spectators to
perform before. Here the performance case might resemble that of an
attractive nuisance case. Just as the unfenced swimming pool draws
youngsters to swim in the pool, so perhaps the group of spectators draws
the boxers to fight in front of these spectators.

If we are to accept the performance case as one involving legal complicity, then the category of legal complicity will have to expand to
include other cases not normally thought to be included under legal as
opposed to moral complicity. Here I am thinking of cases such as occur
in genocides where one's neighbors do not act to prevent a person from
attacking a fellow neighbor. When the first attack occurs, the person

might hesitate, waiting to see if the neighbors will react. As such cases are repeated, there is a sense in which the attacking person might be attracted to more and more violence by the seeming approval of the spectators or neighbors.

The classic case to think of in this context is the Kitty Genovese case. When the initial attack occurred, the perpetrator initially ran away, expecting that the neighbors in the apartment building nearby would react. When they didn't do so, the attacker came back and further attacked, ultimately killing Ms. Genovese. I am not here arguing that the neighbors are as guilty as the perpetrator, but only that there may be a parallel here with the performance cases so that we can talk of legal complicity in this kind of case that is normally only counted as one of moral complicity.

When the attacker came back, it seems that the failure to react on the part of the neighbors contributed to his further harming acts. But in what sense is this true? And why should it trigger legal responsibility on the part of the bystanders that they didn't seem to have before when there was only a single occurrence? I suppose the Kitty Genovese case is actually closer to a performance case where the spectators first don't quite realize the effect they are having, but a second time where they act in the same way could now not be attributed to ignorance, except for culpable ignorance. But even here one could ask why knowledge that people may be encouraged by what others do or don't do should make these others responsible for the harms? The answer, I suppose, based on the original performance case, has to do with the actual effects of one's acts, or failures to act, on others. If the spectators merely being present, and not doing anything active at all, can trigger legal responsibility in the performance case, then there seems no good reason to limit this only to a narrow band of cases, and there is then reason to expand the realm of legal complicity quite broadly, especially in atrocity cases such as genocide.

Of course, one could simply deny that the performance cases generate legal complicity. Or one could try to find an in principle basis for distinguishing the small number of "performance" cases from the large number of "Kitty Genovese" cases. This seems sensible once one realizes how many people would be implicated in atrocities such as genocide if we were to follow the model of the performance cases. Yet we are in need of just such an in principle basis for limiting these cases if the distinction between moral and legal complicity is to be maintained. I attempt to provide this principle in the next section.

One other difficult case to explore briefly is the failure to exercise control over a nonsubordinate. If a person is officially one's subordinate, then one has a duty properly to supervise him or her based on one's role. And if there is no official relationship between one person and another, but in fact the one person is dependent on the other concerning a certain range of action, it is also intuitively plausible that the one who is in the superior position has a duty, although relatively weak, not to contribute to the other's harms by commission or omission. Say I own a car and you are borrowing it. You are dependent on me for transportation. If I learn that you are using my car for the purpose of transporting illegal drugs, and I do nothing to stop you, I participate in your crime – I am legally complicit. Here the knowledge is at least as important as is the relationship that obtains between us.

But if the knowledge is the, or one of the, key factors, then it is not clear why complicity does not also follow when you are not dependent on me, but I know I can nonetheless stop you from engaging in a crime. Think of an intermediary case where you are not strictly dependent on me, but I am one of two people who can supply you with necessary means to your harmful practices. You act while using my resources, rather than the other person's resources. Because you act with my resources, and I know this and could have taken them away, I am seemingly complicit. So why does it matter that you could have, perhaps not quite as easily, gotten what you need from another person? If it is my role as facilitator here that is significant, then it would seem that a similar role of allowing you to act is also something that could ground my complicity. And then it would not seem to matter whether the person is indeed in a subordinate position to me or not.

A consideration of these difficult cases has led us in several productive directions. We have seen that it is often the knowledge rather than the actual relationship between two persons that is crucial for attributing legal complicity. We have also seen that it is hard to come up with an in principle basis for not extending the performance cases to cases where a person's inaction sets the stage for the harmful action of another. And it is not clear how the last resort basis for assigning legal complicity can avoid being extended to many other cases where we simply don't know whether or not we are the last resort. We need a general account of what are the mental and physical elements that constitute legal complicity so that we can begin to adjudicate some of these difficult cases – merely having an intuitively supported list helps a bit, but is in need of theoretical support.

III. A Theory of Legal Complicity

I will defend the view that legal complicity requires two factors across all types of cases described above. First, in terms of *actus reus,* the person's commission or omission must be causally efficacious in the sense that had the person not committed or omitted a certain action a serious harm would have been made significantly less likely to occur. Second, in terms of *mens rea,* the person must know of the risk that his or her commissions or omissions play in that serious harm. One of the central questions of this section will be whether it is also required that the accessory's intention must somehow match that of the principal, or merely intend to contribute to the enterprise that is known to risk harm, in order to be held legally complicit in that harm. I will argue that it is merely required that the defendant intended to contribute to an endeavor that this defendant knew, or should have known, was intended by others to cause harm.[12]

Criminal liability generally requires crossing a higher bar than other forms of legal liability and certainly more than is needed for moral responsibility. In my view, criminal liability for complicity will require that a person exercised some control over the harmful events through commission or omission. Some, such as Christopher Kutz, have argued that control is not required. Instead, what is required is that the person participated in the harmful event, regardless of whether his or her participation was causally efficacious in that it made a difference in the production of the harm.[13] Kutz argues that from the second-person perspective, the perspective of the victim in particular, what matters is only "the fact of suffering."[14]

Given what is at stake for the defendant in a criminal trial, I do not think that the victim's perspective should dominate. In criminal trials generally, and international criminal trials in particular, defendants risk significant loss of liberty. Trials need to operate from a third-person, or impartial, perspective to be fair to the person who has the most to lose from the outcome of the trial. There is a sense in which the victim has very little to lose by the outcome of the trial. Victims certainly hope for closure, and when they do not get it at the end of a trial, some victims experience psychological distress. Impartial trials at least give to those who have most at stake the sense that they have been treated fairly. As

---

[12] See my discussion of this issue in *Crimes Against Humanity,* chs. 7 and 9.

[13] Christopher Kutz, *Complicity,* New York: Cambridge University Press, 2000, p. 122.

[14] Ibid., p. 123.

Kutz admits, the best way to do this is to set a standard for the *actus reus* element of the crime of complicity that stresses the causal properties.

I am willing to admit, though, that the *actus reus* requirement is satisfied by showing that the person could have made a difference if he or she had not committed or omitted a certain action. I do not support the view that it must be proved that harm actually was caused – counterfactual considerations are sufficient. One reason for this is that it is very difficult, and in many cases impossible, to say whether an omission made an actual causal difference. So, unless we want to rule out all complicity on the basis of omissions, we will have to work at least with a counterfactual requirement. It is my view that it would be a serious mistake to rule out omissions from legal complicity. Atrocities are fueled by the omissions of many people, and deterring such atrocities as genocide will require prosecuting those who were complicit in that they failed to act in ways that would have prevented the genocide. Indeed, omissions are now well recognized by the international community as crucially allowing for the genocide to gain steam in Rwanda..

When dealing with a counterfactual test, I do recognize that things are sometimes also quite fuzzy. It is for this reason that I add to the standard way of thinking of the counterfactual causation requirement the idea that the lack of the defendant's commission or omission must have made some difference. It must be shown that the difference was one such that the harm would have been "significantly less likely" if the defendant had not engaged in this commission or omission. Adding this qualification will rule out many cases where the defendant's commission or omission might have made a difference, but it is unclear how much. Only in a small range of cases will it be possible to show that the defendant's complicity met the *actus reus* element of criminal liability. Of course, moral responsibility is another matter altogether, something I will discuss in the final section of this chapter. It may still be possible, though, to prosecute some of those outsiders who did not do enough to prevent or stop the Rwandan genocide.

As far as the *mens rea* requirement goes, I support the view that it must at least be proven that the defendant knew that he or she was participating in an overarching harmful or wrongful enterprise, and intended to participate in this enterprise. The knowledge requirement is meant to rule out strict liability complicity, where all that matters is that one did play a certain causal role, or have certain influence. Strict liability has no place in criminal liability schemes because it fails to treat the defendant as a full moral agent. This is especially true if we are going to allow omissions to count as satisfying the *actus reus* element of this crime. There must be some very serious *mens rea* element, in addition to the *actus reus* component, to avoid the infantilizing of the defendant. And this is significant again given what is at stake in criminal trials.

The salient question is what should be the intention requirement in addition to the knowledge requirement in the *mens rea* of criminal complicity. K. J. M. Smith asks: "Does complicity require anything approaching a 'coincidence of purpose' between principal and accessory?"[15] My view is that this coincidence is not required. All that is required is that the defendant had knowledge of, and intention to participate in, the principal's criminal activity. The defendant need not have the intention to do what the principal also intends. In a sense, what this means is that the defendant need not intend the outcome of the principal's enterprise. But there will need to be a knowledge and intention element proved in any event, it is just that the intention element need not be the intention to do just what the principal intends to do. Yet, given that the defendant knows, or should have known, that by participating he or she will advance whatever intentions the principal has, there is enough *mens rea* for criminal guilt. Of course, there are also *actus reus* requirements that must be met as well.

In my view, recklessly contributing to a collective crime can be sufficient for establishing legal complicity. Recklessness is sometimes considered sufficient for criminal liability. Normally, this is done in those cases where as a matter of public policy a certain kind of result is highly disvalued. In the kind of case I am most interested in, complicity in genocide cases, it should be obvious that preventing such atrocities is of great value. So it would make sense to adopt a slightly lower standard of *mens rea* than is often adopted to mark how important this matter is. But I don't think we should simply employ a strict liability standard or even one that merely requires knowledge. Some intent requirement is needed, but the intent need only be that the defendant intended to participate in a collective effort, not that the defendant intended to do what the principal actors intended. It is enough that the defendant knew, or should have known, that these others intended such harms, and risked also contributing to those harms by his or her commissions and omissions.

One might wonder how one's omissions could have significantly contributed to a given result. I recognize that this will sometimes be difficult

[15] Smith, *A Modern Treatise on the Law of Criminal Complicity*, p. 141.

to establish. But as indicated above, some omissions can be established by reference to one's role or one's relationship to others. For example, if withdrawing one's permission to drive one's car will mean that the perpetrator will not be able to commit the harm, then one's omission to withdraw such permission once one knows of the perpetrator's plans is significant in that not omitting to withdraw permission would have prevented the harm. It is much harder to make such assessments if there is merely a failure of action that does not rise to the level of an omission. But there certainly will be cases where it can be shown that if one did not omit to act a certain way it would have made the ensuing harm much less likely to occur.

My proposal is that legal complicity that leads to criminal prosecution be restricted to those cases where one knows, or should have known, that one is in a sense participating in an enterprise, by one's commission or omission, that risks harm. One must intend to participate but one does not necessarily intend the harm, because one does not necessarily share in the common purpose of the perpetrators. Certain accessories are criminally liable for the harms caused by the perpetrators if they satisfy this *mens rea* requirement. Liability will follow if it is the case that had they not committed or omitted to act as they did the harm would have been significantly less likely to occur. This latter requirement is the *actus reus* condition, and together with the *mens rea* requirement can establish criminal liability for those who are accessories. My proposal limits the number of those who are criminally complicit, but still leaves room for a fair number of prosecutions in cases such as the Rwandan genocide. It is not merely the political and military leaders who should be prosecuted where there is widespread complicity that contributes to significant harms such as genocide. Some who are complicit in the way I have indicated should also be held responsible for crimes such as genocide.

IV. Complicity and Trials in Rwanda

The genocide in Rwanda involved wide-scale complicity. This was true for several reasons. First, most of the killings were perpetrated by civilians, primarily Hutus killing Tutsis. Second, many of the killings were perpetrated against neighbors with machetes in close hand-to-hand assaults. Third, many members of the media, and even many members of the religious ministries, publicized where Tutsis were hiding. Fourth, various groups in Rwanda handed out machetes to Hutus who were already emotionally enflamed. Fifth, neighbors as well as members of the United Nations peace-keeping force, and representatives of various States did nothing to try to stop the killing even after it was well known how extensive the genocide was becoming.

Because of the extensive complicity in the Rwandan genocide, it was thought to be not enough merely to have trials of the leaders who were the most obvious primary perpetrators. As I write, the trials of the leaders are still occurring in Arusha, Tanzania, just across the Rwandan border, by an ad hoc tribunal established by the United Nations Security Council. In addition, approximately ten thousand trials have occurred or are occurring throughout Rwanda where individuals who killed as well as those who were complicit are prosecuted. But the type of trials is highly unorthodox. In this section I briefly describe these so-called *gacaca* proceedings, literally "trials in the grass." I hope to shed some light on how those who are criminally complicit might be dealt with in atrocities such as the genocide in Rwanda.

During the Rwandan genocide, nearly one million victims were killed, many by their machete-wielding neighbors. After the Rwandan genocide in 1994, 120,000 Hutu suspects were arrested and incarcerated while awaiting trial. Because the Rwandan judiciary had been decimated during the genocide, it was not possible to have even preliminary hearings for so many defendants. Indeed, most of these suspects were held in horrible prison conditions for as many as nine years without ever facing a judge. The international tribunal sitting in Arusha couldn't handle even a very small fraction of these cases. In 2003, 20,000 alleged genocide perpetrators were released from prison and sent back to their towns and villages. At this point the local and national leaders had decided to provide some punishment for these individuals as they were also being reintegrated into their former communities. It took several years, but eventually the "genocidaires" began to stand trial. To accomplish this goal, a new form of prosecution was constructed, the *gacaca* process.[16]

The *gacaca* process is indebted to traditional ways of achieving justice in Rwanda, but with significant updating to make the proceedings conform to modern ideas of the rule of law. Historically, the *gacaca* "did not exist as a permanent judicial institution, but rather it was based on unwritten law and functioned as a body assembled whenever conflict arose within or between families, particularly in rural Rwanda."[17]

---

[16] See Phil Clark, "When the Killers Come Home," *Dissent*, Summer 2005, pp. 14–21.

[17] Phil Clark, "Hybridity, Holism and 'Traditional' Justice: The Case of the Gacaca Courts in Post-Genocide Rwanda," *George Washington University Law Review*, September 2007, p. 13.

Today *gacaca* emerges as a hybrid proceedings, between a trial and a truth and reconciliation process, or between a traditional dispute resolution model and a Western-style trial. The *gacaca* judges are elected and receive some advance training (six days for the 250,000 *gacaca* judges elected in 2002). There are significant oversight bodies and appeals procedures designed to protect the rights of the defendant.[18]

Phil Clark gives a very clear and concise statement of how the *gacaca* process works today:

> Judges usually sit once a week before a required quorum of 100 members of the General Assembly [all residents of a local region over 18 years of age]. In Phase 1 of a Gacaca jurisdiction, which ideally should comprise six weekly meetings, the Assembly gathers to determine a schedule of hearings and to begin compiling the four lists (of people in the region who were killed or suffered). ... In Phase 2, which comprises the seventh meeting, the General Assembly gathers to produce a detailed dossier of evidence on each individual accused. ... The accused then have the opportunity to respond to the evidence brought against them during Phase 3 of gacaca, after which in Phase 4 the judges weigh all of the evidence they have heard and pass judgment on the accused.[19]

Clark is right to claim that the *gacaca* process is "unique among post-conflict judicial structures around the world in its mass involvement of the population in the pursuit and carrying out of justice."[20]

Each category of crime that falls within the jurisdiction of the *gacaca*, not including property offense, includes those who assaulted as well as those who were accomplices. I here list the description of what were called "Category 2" crimes falling under the jurisdiction of *gacaca:*

a) The person whose criminal acts or criminal participation place [him or her] among killers or who committed acts of serious attacks against others, causing death, together with his or her accomplices

b) The person who injured or committed other acts of serious attacks with the intention to kill them, but who did not attain their objective, together with his or her accomplices

c) The person who committed or aided to commit other offenses [against] persons, without the intention to kill them, together with his or her accomplices.[21]

---

[18] Ibid., pp. 17–22.
[19] Ibid., p. 26.
[20] Ibid., p. 25.
[21] Ibid., p. 24.

As one can see, the perpetrators were tried along with those who were complicit. Those who were major perpetrators, insofar as what they engaged in was a crime against humanity, and those who were the "ringleaders of the genocide" along with their accomplices, were to be tried by national courts, not by the *gacaca*.

The *gacaca* process sought to provide some modicum of justice but also some reconciliation in the aftermath of the horrible genocide in Rwanda. It was thought to be necessary to go beyond the leaders and those who were the worst of the perpetrators to include those more remotely involved in order better to achieve the goals of justice and of reconciliation. One minister said: "Gacaca should be more than judgments. Punishment was important but it had to give us truth and reconciliation."[22] I agree that this should be the goal of those proceedings that prosecute the complicit, although trying to get the right balance between these two goals of justice and truth, without greatly trampling the rights of the defendants, is a difficult task indeed.

The idea behind the *gacaca* process was that complicity had to be dealt with in a court setting so that a robust reconciliation could occur within this devastated society. It is estimated that three-quarters of a million new suspects will emerge out of the *gacaca* process based on testimony.[23] Never before had such court proceedings attempted to take into account so many of the complicit – tens of thousands of people. Inevitably, problems have been reported from both sides of these proceedings. The lax attitude toward rules of evidence and rule of law considerations has meant that both defendant and victims' families have expressed unhappiness about how the proceedings have been conducted. "Concerns include witness protection, impartiality of proceedings, nature of punishment, getting witnesses to testify in public without fear of reprisal, and the retraumatization of victims."[24]

Despite many problems, there is evidence that the *gacaca* process has indeed advanced reconciliation, although the evidence is by no means uncontested.[25] Augustin Nkusi, chief advisor to the Gacaca Commission of the Rwandan Supreme Court, has said: "At gacaca the truth ultimately

[22] Ibid., p. 17, quoting Protais Musoni, Minister of Local Government, Good Governance, Community Development, and Social Affairs, Kigali, 13 June 2006.
[23] I am grateful to Mark Drumbl for this point.
[24] Mark Drumbl, "Collective Violence and Individual Punishment: The Criminality of Mass Atrocity," *Northwestern University Law Review*, vol. 99, no. 2, Winter 2005, p. 601 note.
[25] See Drumbl, *Atrocity, Punishment, and International Law*, , pp. 85–99.

comes from the population. We know people will tell who is responsible because they saw what [the perpetrators] did. They stood there as it happened and they saw everything with their own eyes. There will be no confusion about who is responsible for such things."[26] Although this may be an overly optimistic assessment, the *gacaca* trials are indeed beginning the process of healing after this horrible atrocity. Whether the right combination of respect for the victims and for the defendants' rights has here been struck is not yet clear. But because the punishments have been relatively light, most not more than five years of jail time, with credit given for time served, the concern about procedural protections is offset by the relative lightness of the sentences given that what is alleged is participation in genocide.[27]

There is an unrecognized goal of trying those who are legally complicit in a genocide, namely, that many others in the society might be caused to reexamine their own role in the genocide and to feel pangs of moral guilt, or at least shame and taint. Such moral feelings might advance the goals of a robust political reconciliation, even if there were few convictions that resulted from *gacaca* and other criminal proceedings. In the next section I explore this issue in much more detail and also try to indicate how these issues relate to the overarching question of how to deal with issues of individual accountability for mass crimes such as genocide.

V. The Boundary between Legal and Moral Complicity

The *gacaca* process provided a way to try to deal with some of those who are complicit without recourse to forms of conspiracy or joint criminal liability, which have become so common and so widely criticized in the jurisprudence of the international tribunals. The people who were tried in the *gacaca* process were tried for their role in the larger genocide, but nonetheless for what they had done. Many were tried for various forms of complicity as I indicated above. But there was no attempt to portray these individual acts as forming a larger *organized* enterprise, whether there was one or not, and here is where complicity is different from conspiracy and other forms of joint enterprise liability. Complicity remains focused on the individual agent, not on the group. It is for this reason that complicity is better suited to criminal trials than is joint enterprise

[26] Quoted in Clark, "When the Killers Go Home," p. 20.
[27] See Clark, "Hybridity, Holism and 'Traditional' Justice."

liability. But there is a sense that a wider group is implicated when an individual is tried for complicity, primarily because of the close connection between moral and legal complicity, as we will see in this final section of the chapter.

One of the potential problems is that those who are found guilty of complicity cannot generally be punished as severely as those who are found guilty as principal perpetrators. The International Criminal Tribunal for the Former Yugoslavia (ICTY), in the Tadic Appeals Chamber judgment, was not satisfied to have such a dual-level characterization of guilt, unlike the *gacaca* founders. Instead, the ICTY declared that it was not enough to hold those who are complicit liable as aiders and abettors because "the moral gravity of such participation is often no less – or indeed no different – from that of those actually carrying out the acts in question." Because of this, the tribunal declared that one should not understate the degree of their criminal responsibility.[28] The Tadic Appeals Chamber provides a classic statement of the inseparable connection between moral and legal guilt, and one that I will challenge in this final section.

In my view it is a mistake to think that legal punishment should be determined by the degree of moral gravity of the defendant's action. There is, of course, a connection between moral and legal guilt – both are forms of guilt and often times they overlap. Murder is wrong both morally and legally in every society, although what counts as murder often differs quite a bit from society to society. Some societies, for instance, have a statute outlawing what is called "felony murder" – the unintentional killing of a person while one is intentionally committing a felony of another sort, such as robbery. Morally speaking, there isn't anything comparable, nor should there be, to felony murder, because, as in a lot of law, felony murder is merely a kind of technical violation.

Even if one thinks that the criminal law is ultimately undergirded by morality, criminal complicity need not track all aspects of moral complicity. For although criminal complicity may be thought to require some form of moral complicity, there is no reason that there still couldn't be some forms of moral complicity that do not trigger criminal complicity. Indeed, the key is the principle of legality, which requires that there be

[28] *Prosecutor v. Dusko Tadic*, International Criminal Tribunal for the Former Yugoslavia, case no. IT-94-1-A, Appeals Chamber Judgment, 15 July 1999, paras. 191–2. See also the discussion of this issue in Shane Darcy, *Collective Responsibility and Accountability under International Law*, Leiden: Transnational Publishers, 2007, pp. 228–9.

a publicly articulated criminal statute in place outlawing a certain form of behavior, before the act in question's occurrence, before the act could be deemed to be criminal. Merely having the act be something immoral does not satisfy the principle of legality, nor should it. It is quite plausible to demand that a putative criminal defendant have been put on notice of what are his or her legal obligations before being held to have acted contrary to those legal obligations. There is generally no such notice requirement in the domain of our moral obligations.

The notice requirement in criminal law is linked to what is at stake in holding someone criminally liable. Jail or prison terms so jeopardize one's liberty that it is plausible to think that a higher threshold of responsibility must be crossed to establish guilt than would be true if only public moral censure were at stake. This is true regardless of whether one holds to an objective or subjective theory of morality. Even objective theories of morality do not necessarily hold that everyone in a society knows or can easily come to know what his or her moral obligations are. Whether or not moral standards are objective is a separate issue from whether or not those standards are plain to everyone in a given society. Objectivity is a matter of justification, not necessarily of public knowability. Of course, even when legal standards are public, some people may not know them. But this issue is different from whether or not it is relatively easy to come to know them, and in this respect, there is nothing comparable in morality to the publicity or promulgation requirement of criminal statutes.

Whether bystanders come to feel legal or moral guilt, a potential is unleashed when bystanders recognize their role in preventing atrocities. Arne Johan Vetlesen has stated the point quite well: "From the viewpoint of an agent of genocide, bystanders are persons possessing a potential...to halt his ongoing actions. The perpetrator will fear the bystander to the extent that he has reason to believe that the bystander will intervene to halt the action already under way and thereby frustrate the perpetrator's goal of eliminating the targeted group."[29] There is more than just this possible deterrent to the perpetrators as well; there is also the way bystanders' recognition of complicity transforms the whole of the society, especially in how the members of society view their moral responsibilities. In a sense I here look more to the future than to the

---

[29] Arne Johan Vetlesen, "Genocide: A Case for the Responsibility of Bystanders," in *Ethics, Nationalism, and Just War,* edited by Henrik Syse and Gregory M. Reichberg, Washington, DC: Catholic University of America Press, 2007, p. 355.

past, more to the deterrence of future atrocities than to the retribution for past atrocities. In this sense, I look more to change and reconciliation than to past offenses, in a way that is also true of the *gacaca* process, which I heartily support.

Criminal trials can play a pedagogic role in getting people better to come to terms with their moral responsibilities, and, in this sense, determinations of legal complicity can also affect how people view their moral complicity. This happens most clearly when people come to identify with the perpetrators, perhaps seeing how easily they could have been in the dock instead of the accused. Indeed, it is an old maxim of criminal law that the person who is an accomplice "may be just as bad, or worse, than the person who actually does the dirty work."[30] There is a sense in which those who are morally complicit may also be just as morally blameworthy as those who are the primary or secondary perpetrators of a given harm. Once the extent of complicity is identified at trial, even those who are not indicted, and arguably could not be indicted, may feel the sting of the condemnation of those who are indicted. I would argue that this is true even if the extent of condemnation will be much less severe in the case of those who are complicit than in the case of those who are the primary perpetrators of a given harm.

Some theorists have talked about the issue of the pedagogy of a trial in terms of the "dramaturgy" of what occurs during the trial.[31] I believe that this metaphor overstates the case by making what occurs in trial look like it is very much of a stage play by focusing too much on the "drama" of the trial's participants, rather than on what is actually conveyed to the public at large about the causes and circumstances of the crime in question. Nonetheless, there is some truth to the dramaturgy account insofar as that account stresses the public educative role of trials. And that role can be moral as well as legal, as I have tried to indicate, even though the moral and legal domains are separate from one another.

I will end this discussion of complicity by indicating how to see the relationships between individual responsibility and collective crimes, and specifically how to view this relationship in the Rwandan genocide. In some of my other writings I have made it clear that there is a potential

---

[30] A. P. Simester and A. T. H. Smith, *Harm and Culpability*, Oxford: Oxford University Press, 1996, p. 200.
[31] See Lawrence Douglas, *The Memory of Judgment: Making Law and History in the Trials of the Holocaust*, New Haven, CT: Yale University Press, 2001. Also see Luban's article "Beyond Moral Minimalism."

disconnect between the individual criminal responsibility of those in the dock and the collective nature of the international crimes with which they are charged by international tribunals. We can make sense of such trials if the defendants are held responsible for their part, but only for their part, in those collective crimes.[32] The difficulty becomes how to characterize what counts as a person's part in a mass atrocity such as genocide. I have tried to provide a framework for such an account in the middle section of this chapter. Only when a principal's or accessory's *actus reus* and *mens rea* can be established should individual criminal liability be assigned.

In the Rwanda case, what this means is that something such as the *gacaca* process is at least potentially justifiable, even though it involves tens of thousands prosecuted for the genocide. As it turns out, the actual *gacaca* process has largely prosecuted those who were minor perpetrators and not as often those who were complicit. But a process such as the *gacaca* could have been used more extensively and even used primarily to target those who were complicit as well. In any event, the *gacaca* process brought together the members of towns and villages in a way that brought to the fore not only what the perpetrators did but also who was complicit, even if many of this latter group were not being prosecuted. What was crucial was that in Rwanda a forum was developed for discussing the important topic of complicity in mass atrocity cases such as genocide.

As I have indicated throughout, there are many forms of legal complicity, and most of them were present in the Rwandan genocide. For instance, the machetes used for many of the killings were not purchased by the perpetrators, but distributed widely by individuals and groups who hoped that just such a killing spree would occur. Many people identified those who were in hiding and urged that some action be taken against them. And many people stood by while their neighbors slaughtered fellow neighbors. Legal complicity was rampant in Rwanda, and it was important that there be a forum that not only acknowledged the complicity, as would have been true in a Truth and Reconciliation process, but also where such complicity was condemned and punished.

Most importantly, having so many trials, especially ones held in the locale where the harms occurred, and held before the community members, many of whom were present when these harms occurred, makes the members of the community, those who were legally complicit and

---

[32] See May, *Crimes Against Humanity.*

those who were only morally complicit, confront their connection to the genocide. In this respect there is certainly nothing wrong with, and much good about, having as many trials as possible in situations of mass atrocity so that the full extent of the roles that various individuals played in the atrocity has a chance of getting aired. The hope is that such an airing of what people did and what they failed to do will lead to changes in their behavior in the future.

10

Incitement to Genocide and the Rwanda
Media Case

Several of the genocide cases in Rwanda have been prosecuted as incitement cases. In this chapter I will look at the difficult case of a group
of three media leaders who were convicted of genocide in Rwanda for
their role in disseminating the message of hatred that seemed to incite
the massacre of Tutsis by Hutus in 1994. This investigation will broaden
our sense of how to understand and assess participation in such massacres. One scholar has said that it is rare that there are prosecutions for
incitement, but the Rwanda case was extreme because "grotesque cari-
catures in racist newspaper and broadcast appeals to participate in such
killings marked the 1994 genocide."[1] Indeed, as the Trial Chamber of
the International Criminal Tribunal for Rwanda (ICTR) said: "RTML
broadcasting was a drumbeat, calling on listeners to take action against
the enemy. ... The nature of radio transmission made RTML particularly dangerous and harmful, as did the breadth of its reach."[2]

In this so-called Media Case, those who incited mass murder and
mutilation against members of the Tutsi ethnic group were prosecuted.
Barayagwiza and Ngeze founded the newspaper *Kangura*, which edito-
rialized in invective terms against the Tutsis.[3] Barayagwiza, along with
Nahimana, also founded a radio station, RTLM, which routinely referred
to Tutsis as "'enemies' or 'traitors' who deserve to die."[4] Both the newspaper and the radio station were used to incite hatred against the Tutsis by
the Hutus and even to target specific Tutsis for attack. In addition, both

---

[1] Schabas, *The UN International Criminal Tribunals*, p. 181.
[2] *Prosecutor v. Ferdinand Nahimana, Jean-Bosco Barayagwiza, and Hassan Ngeze*, Trial
Chamber Judgment, para. 1031 [hereinafter "Media Case Trial Chamber"].
[3] *Prosecutor v. Jean-Bosco Barayagwiza*, International Criminal Tribunal for Rwanda,
Amended Indictment, 4 April 2000, para. 5.3.
[4] Ibid., para. 5.10.

media companies purchased weapons from 1992 through 1994 for the Hutu militias that eventually carried out the mass killings of Tutsis.[5] All three defendants were convicted, yet there was no evidence that any of the three committed any killings.

In this chapter I will examine in detail the case of the journalists and broadcasters in Rwanda, and I will do so as a vehicle for saying something about the idea of incitement, an often overlooked basis of individual criminal liability. As an initial take on the idea of incitement, the ICTR urges that we think of it as it has been conceptualized in Common Law systems, namely, "as encouraging or persuading another to commit an offence" and not merely by "vague or indirect suggestion." Incitement is thus associated with provoking, which involves both causation and intent, namely, "the intent to directly prompt or provoke another to commit genocide."[6] In Rwanda the ICTR said that the actions of the Media Case defendants constituted the kind of "direct incitement" that is prosecutable under the crime of genocide.[7]

Specifically, I will begin with an examination of the facts of the Media Case. Second, I will look at the jurisprudence in previous cases involving incitement in international law. Third, I will examine the idea of incitement as an inchoate crime, especially in Common Law systems. Fourth, I will discuss the idea of superior responsibility as it relates to individual responsibility for incitement. Fifth, I will summarize my view of incitement and apply it to the Media Case. Throughout, I am guided by a remark of the USSR's delegate to the 1948 Convention on Genocide that seems especially apt to Rwanda: "It was impossible that hundreds of thousands of people should commit so many crimes unless they had been incited to do so."[8] I will also discuss how incitement is related to complicity, the subject of the previous chapter.

I. The Facts of the Media Case

The case against Nahimana, Barayagwiza, and Ngeze turned on the roles they played in running a newspaper, *Kangura*, a radio station, RTLM, and a political party, the CDR. Through these sources a steady stream of hate propaganda was produced preceding and during the Rwandan

---

[5] Ibid., paras. 5.16 and 5.14.
[6] Ibid., para. 560.
[7] *Prosecutor v. Jean-Paul Akayesu*, Trial Chamber Judgment, paras. 555–7 [hereinafter "Akayesu Trial Chamber"].
[8] Quoted at ibid., para. 551.

genocide. In Chapter 1 I discussed some of the most graphic examples of the way that these media leaders are said to have played an important role in the Rwanda genocide in terms of incitement. In considering such facts, the International Criminal Tribunal for Rwanda's Trial Chamber was at pains to examine the content of the speech to see if indeed it goes beyond the bounds of otherwise protected freedoms.

The first example I discussed concerned the cover of the November 1991 issue, no. 26, of *Kangura*. The newspaper published vitriolic articles urging Hutus to take up arms against Tutsis. The second example was from the radio station founded by two of the defendants. In the middle of the killing spree that left 800,000 Tutsi dead, many RTLM broadcasts identified individuals by name and urged that they be killed.

Here is a third example concerning the workings of the political party run by the defendants. The defendants, especially Ngeze and Barayagwiza, were instrumental in setting up, and running, a political party, the CDR, which distributed weapons, organized demonstrations and roadblocks, and sometimes was even directly involved in killing. Here is the summary of a prosecution witness's testimony about Ngeze's activities:

> When the CDR was set up, Ngeze became an influential member of that party...they looted and threatened the Tutsi. ... Weapons were distributed by Ngeze and Barayagwiza. Training sessions were also arranged during these years on the use of these weapons. ... [I]n February 1994...a fax sent by Barayagwiza...was addressed to the Youth Wing of the CDR Party and the MRND Party, and it stated that now that the *Inyezi* had killed the CDR President, all Hutus were requested to be vigilant to closely follow up the Tutsis wherever they were hiding. It said that even if they were in churches, they should be pursued and killed. Ngeze then went around the town in his Toyota Hilus, on which he had mounted a megaphone, saying that that was it for the Tutsis. ... From April until June 1994, CDR and *Interhamwe* groups held meetings every evening to report on the number of Tutsi killed. These meetings were attended by the leaders, including Barayagwiza and Ngeze.[9]

Concerning one specific incident at the very beginning of the genocidal killings, on April 6 1994, the Trial Chamber concludes: "Although there is no evidence that [Ngeze] was present during these killings, this attack was ordered by Hassan Ngeze, communicated through a loudspeaker from his vehicle."[10] The use of a loudspeaker directly to incite is surely

---

[9] Ibid., paras. 784–5.
[10] Ibid., para. 825.

one of the clearest examples of incitement, but the other examples are also thought to be significant incitement as well.

The newspaper *Kangura*, the radio station RTLM, and the CDR party disseminated much hate propaganda against the Tutsis – what the Trial Chamber called a "drumbeat" leading up to and contributing to the genocide. In response to this charge, one of the defendants said that it was the shooting down of the president's plane that fueled the genocide. The Trial Chamber responded:

> But if the downing of the plane was the trigger, then RTLM, Kangura, and CDR were the bullets in the gun. The trigger had such a deadly impact because the gun was loaded. The Chamber therefore considers that the killing of the Tutsi civilians can be said to have resulted, at least in part, from the message of ethnic targeting for death that was clearly and effectively disseminated through RTLM, Kangura, and CDR, before and after 6 April 1994.[11]

The main way that the three defendants are said to be involved is in inciting people to kill, through the dissemination of propaganda and instructions in print media, radio broadcasts, and megaphone speeches.

Incitement to genocide, through the printed and spoken word, can be accomplished in the variety of ways illustrated above. The Trial Chamber assigns individual criminal responsibility for this incitement to genocide on the basis of what it calls "superior responsibility" of the defendants for failing to act to prevent the genocidal harm that they should have predicted would result from their publications, broadcasts, and speeches. The ICTR Trial Chamber ruled that Nahimana and Barayagwiza had superior responsibility for RTLM broadcasts and for publishing issues of *Kangura*. And Barayagwiza and Ngeze had superior responsibility for CDR. This is an additional reason why Nahimana, Barayagwiza, and Ngeze were convicted of incitement to genocide.

II. The Jurisprudence of Incitement

Incitement means "encouraging or persuading another to commit an offence."[12] There are two ways that incitement tends to be treated in criminal law. As the Akayesu Trial Chamber said, "Under Common law systems, incitement tends to be viewed as a particular form of criminal

---

[11] Ibid., para. 953.
[12] Andrew Ashworth, *Principles of Criminal Law*, Oxford: Clarendon Press, 1995, p. 462, quoted in Akayesu Trial Chamber, para. 555.

participation, punishable as such," whereas "in most Civil law systems, incitement is most often treated as a form of complicity."[13] If incitement is treated as merely a form of complicity, then it may not be charged and punished in its own right. Under the Genocide Convention, and also under the Rwanda Tribunal Statute, "direct and public incitement is expressly defined as a specific crime, punishable as such."[14] To be direct incitement, there must be "more than mere vague or indirect suggestion."[15] In this section I will examine several cases before the Media Case, namely, two cases from Nuremberg and an earlier case from Rwanda, to get a sense of the extant jurisprudence about incitement in international criminal law.

As in most matters of criminal law, the hardest element to establish for the crime of incitement to genocide is *mens rea*. The ICTR's Akayesu Trial Chamber is forthright in recognizing that the intent of two different people must be proved: "It implies a desire on the part of the perpetrator to create by his actions a particular state of mind necessary to commit such a crime in the minds of the person(s) he is so engaging."[16] There is a desire to create in others a desire to commit a crime. And because of this odd type of *mens rea,* the crime of incitement to genocide is especially hard to prove, because in effect we must peer into the mind of two different people, or infer from their behavior what the mental states for two different people are.

The element of causation is also fraught with problems. The most important case to take up this issue was the case of Julius Streicher at the Nuremberg trial. As the ICTR Trial Chamber says, "Known widely as 'Jew-Baiter Number One,' Julius Streicher was the publisher of *Der Stürmer* from 1923–1945" where he often called "for the extermination of Jews."[17] Although this was the conclusion of the Nuremberg prosecutors, Streicher's defense counsel tried to show that Streicher was mainly arguing for removing Jews from Germany, perhaps to Madagascar, rather than for the killing of all Jews in Germany.[18] So the defense argued for a lesser charge than would be true if Streicher had urged the extermination of the Jews. Most importantly, the defense made an

[13] Akayesu Trial Chamber Judgment, para. 552.
[14] Ibid., para. 554.
[15] Ibid., para. 557.
[16] Ibid., para. 560.
[17] Media Case Trial Chamber Judgment, para. 981.
[18] *The Trial of the Major War Criminals before the International Military Commission,* Secretariat of the Tribunal, Nuremberg, 1948, vol. 18, p. 197.

unusual admission during its attempt to defend Streicher against the charge of incitement.

Streicher's defense counsel, Dr. Marx, said that it could not be denied that Streicher "continually wrote articles in *Der Stürmer* and also made speeches in public which were strongly anti-Jewish and at least aimed at the elimination of Jewish influence in Germany."[19] Indeed, the defense counsel went out of its way to paint Streicher in the most unflattering terms. "It cannot be denied that by writing ad nauseum on the same subject for years in a clumsy, crude, and violent manner, the Defendant Streicher has brought upon himself the hatred of the world" for which "absolutely no excuse exists."[20]

Streicher's defense counsel nonetheless raised the issue of causation as a part of the defense to the charge of incitement:

> But criminal action can only be seen here – and this is presumably the opinion of the Prosecution also – if this type of literary and oral activity led to criminal results. ... The prosecution ... has not produced actual proof. ... If, however, the defendant Streicher is to be made legally responsible for this, then not only must it be proved that the incitement as such was actually carried through and results achieved in this direction; but – and this is the decisive point – conclusive proof must be produced that the deeds which were done can be traced back to that incitement.[21]

The Nuremberg judges did not agree with the defense counsel on this issue, and convicted Streicher even though the evidence of causation was indeed not conclusive.

The ICTR Media Case Trial Chamber notes that another defendant at Nuremberg, Hans Fritzsche, who was head of the Radio Section of the Nazis' Propaganda Ministry, was acquitted because he did not have "control over the formulation of propaganda policies," being merely "a conduit of the press directives passed down to him."[22] There was no conclusive evidence to show that Fritzsche deliberately falsified any of the information he conveyed, or that he knew it to be false. Unlike Streicher, there was no evidence that Fritzsche intended that his published views would inspire genocide or even the removal of Jews from Germany. Indeed, the Nuremberg judges seemed to agree with the defense that Fritzsche intended only to convey information that was not significantly

---

[19] Ibid., p. 198.
[20] Ibid., p. 217.
[21] Ibid., p. 199.
[22] Media Case Trial Chamber Judgment, para. 982.

different from other information that journalists in many other societies conveyed to their readers.

While not claiming to be an opponent of Nazism, a plausible case is nonetheless made that Fritzsche "opposed abuses insofar as he could recognize them."[23] Fritzsche's defense counsel claimed that in order for his client to be convicted as an inciter, it must be shown that Fritzsche actually instigated specific individuals to do a criminal act, or at least that he had the intention to do so. Here is the conclusion of the defense:

> The evidence has not furnished the slightest proof in the Fritzsche case that he has committed an individual crime as instigator through his transmission of news; there is not the slightest evidence to show that he has instigated a single person to murder, cruelties, deportations, killings of hostages, massacres of Jews, or other crimes mentioned in the Charter, or had as instigator, caused a single crime by his speeches to the public. Not a single passage from his nearly 1,000 wireless speeches to the public could be produced from which individual responsibility could be deduced. That was not possible from his speeches, anyway. The crimes that were committed were carried out by people completely indifferent to Fritzsche's propaganda. They received their impulses or instructions from altogether different sources.[24]

Underlying this defense is the defense counsel's reading of German law concerning incitement: "An attempt at instigation presupposes that the person to be incited is not already determined to commit a criminal act of his own accord or under the influence of others."[25]

The Streicher and Fritzsche cases set the stage well for the defendants on trial in Rwanda. In one of those cases, decided by the ICTR before its decision in the Media Case, the ICTR said that there must be a connection between the dissemination of propaganda and someone's commission of crime. The ICTR's Akayesu Trial Chamber says: "The prosecution must prove a definite causation between the act characterized as incitement…and a specific offence."[26] Jean-Paul Akayesu, a bourgemestre of a commune, that is, a kind of mayor, was convicted on this standard.

The Media Case Trial Chamber of the ICTR takes a somewhat different line, however, not requiring the prosecution to find a nexus between what the defendants said or wrote and some specific crimes of others. Indeed, when quoting the Akayesu opinion, the Media Trial Chamber

---

[23] *Trial of the Major War Criminals*, vol. 19, pp. 319–51.
[24] Ibid., p. 346.
[25] Ibid.
[26] Akayesu Trial Chamber Judgment, para. 557.

does not cite the passage just quoted above but starts quoting just after that passage: "[T]he Chamber is of the opinion that the direct element of incitement should be viewed in the light of its cultural and linguistic content."[27] Focusing on this dimension of the judgment, namely, the variable meaning of causation, puts things in a very different light than seemed to be true for the "definite causation" required by the Akayesu Trial Chamber. Indeed, if a judgment of causation were open to cultural variation, then it would not easily admit of direct proof and may allow indirect forms of proof such as that provided by anthropologists or linguists.

Despite the other parts of the Akayesu analysis, the ICTR Media Case Trial Chamber concluded "that this causal relationship is not requisite to a finding of incitement. It is the *potential* of the communication to cause genocide that makes it incitement."[28] The Media Case Trial Chamber acted somewhat differently from both the Akayesu Trial Chamber and the Nuremberg tribunal by seemingly diminishing the importance of the causation element, thereby perhaps emphasizing the inchoate nature of the crime of incitement to genocide, that is, that the crime does not require a successful instigation for prosecution.

The Appeals Chamber of the ICTR added quite a bit of clarity to these jurisprudential issues when it issued its opinion in the Media Case on November 28th of 2007:

> The Appeals Chamber considers that there is a difference between hate speech in general (or inciting discrimination or violence) and direct and public incitement to commit genocide. Direct incitement to commit genocide assumes that the speech is a direct appeal to commit an act referred to in Article 2(2) of the Statute; it has to be more than a mere vague or indirect suggestion.[29]

A defendant "cannot be held accountable for hate speech that does not directly call for the commission of genocide."[30] In this regard the context in which the speech is made is relevant, at very least, in determining whether the speech can indeed be interpreted as having made a direct appeal to commit killing and other acts of genocide.[31]

---

[27] Media Case Trial Chamber Judgment, para. 1011.
[28] Ibid., para. 1015, italics added.
[29] *Prosecutor v. Fernando Nahimana, Jean-Bosco Barayagwiza, and Hassan Ngeze,* International Criminal Tribunal for Rwanda, case no. ICTR-99–52-A, Appeals Chamber Judgment, 28 November 2007, para. 692 [hereinafter "Media Case Appeals Chamber"].
[30] Ibid., para. 693.
[31] Ibid., para. 697.

In this ruling the Court was following the drafters of the Genocide Convention. Nehemiah Robinson wrote an influential report that discusses the Ad Hoc Committee's draft genocide convention authorized by the UN Secretary General. Much of what was in the draft eventually became part of the Genocide Convention. In particular, Robinson reports that "the draft explicitly makes incitement punishable 'whether such incitement is successful or not.'" The present wording of Article III of the Convention "restricts 'incitement' to cases of 'direct' action, i.e., incitement which *calls* for the commission of acts of genocide, not such which *may* result in such commission ... [but] does not preclude the punishment of acts calling for the commission of Genocide which did not result in its commission."[32]

In determining the meaning of a given speech, the cultural context must be taken into account. The ICTR Appeals Chamber ruled:

> The principal consideration is thus the meaning of the words used in the specific context: it does not matter that the message may appear ambiguous to another audience or in another context. On the other hand, if the discourse is still ambiguous even when considered in its context, it cannot be found beyond a reasonable doubt to constitute direct and public incitement to commit genocide.[33]

The crime of incitement to commit genocide normally does involve speech, but not merely hate speech.

In addition, the Appeals Chamber qualified the nature of the crime of direct and public incitement to commit genocide, reaffirming that the crime "is an inchoate offense, punishable even if no act of genocide has resulted therefrom."[34] But the Appeals Chamber also recognized a significant problem with such inchoate crimes. A defendant could be convicted merely for "programming" in some general way without showing that there were specific speeches that were likely to have specific effects, even if those effects did not result. Here is how the Appeals Chamber characterized the challenge from one of the Media Case defendants, Nahimana:

> He submits that the Trial Chamber improperly extended criminalization to 'the collective and continuing programming of speeches, which in themselves were not criminal and were by different authors,' thereby implying a form of collective responsibility that is impermissible in international

---

[32] Robinson, "The Genocide Convention: Its Origins and Interpretation," pp. 19–20.
[33] Media Case Appeals Chamber Judgment, para. 701.
[34] Ibid., para. 678.

law, and setting 'no clear criteria' whereby a journalist can be aware, at the time when he is speaking, of the extent of his right to free speech.[35]

The ICTR Appeals Chamber agrees with Nahimana on the general jurisprudential point about the nature of incitement, and concludes that the ICTR Trial Chamber needed to clearly identify the specific broadcasts that constituted incitement, and not rely on the entirety of broadcasts or newspaper articles.[36] In the next section I will focus attention on what it means to say of incitement to genocide that it is merely an inchoate crime.

III. Incitement as an Inchoate Crime

Inchoate crimes are crimes, such as attempted murder, that do not require the completion of a harmful act in order for criminal liability to be assigned. The standard list of inchoate crimes includes attempt, conspiracy, solicitation, and incitement. There are three main reasons why it makes sense to punish people when it is not proved they have caused harm. One reason is that some acts risk such horrible results that for deterrence sake it might make sense to punish the attempt to do the act even when the act is not completed. A second reason is that there may be very good grounds to think that the defendant did commit an act that caused harm, but not quite enough evidence to prove it conclusively. In such cases, punishing for a lesser crime, such as an inchoate crime, may be justified. Third, the defendant could have clearly committed an act that would normally lead to harms, but because of the defendant's good luck harm did not result. It may make sense to punish for having started a causal chain even though unbeknownst to the defendant the chain was not in fact completed. But it certainly doesn't make sense to hold people criminally liable for consequences they couldn't have foreseen. It also does not make sense to hold people criminally liable for contributing to events that only much later are understood to be genocide, but that at the time looked innocent. There has to be an anticipated harm that is foreseen.[37]

---

[35] Ibid. para. 718.

[36] Ibid., paras. 726–7.

[37] I am grateful to Virginia Held for discussions of this issue. On a similar issue concerning how to understand the causation dimension of hate speech, see L. Wayne Sumner, "Incitement and the Regulation of Hate Speech," 2008, unpublished manuscript in the possession of the author.

Antony Duff lists incitement as one of three forms of inchoate crime that he calls "offenses of intention," which "involve an intention to commit (or secure the commission of) a substantive offense, or to cause some primary harm, but need not involve the actual commission of that offense or the actual occurrence of that harm."[38] He contrasts incitement and other "offenses of intention" with "offenses of explicit endangerment," which do not involve intention to harm, but merely negligence or recklessness. This way of understanding incitement makes the causal element quite closely related to the intent element. My sense is that incitement may fall between these two categories of inchoate crime, not so closely linked to causation, but still linked in some fashion nonetheless, and also involving explicit endangerment.

If incitement does not involve endangerment, and if it is not clear that incitement actually causes harm, then from a retributive standpoint it is hard to see why incitement should be punished severely. I have already discussed some of the problems of causation in incitement cases. In the Streicher case, and even more in the Fritzsche case, although there was some evidence that people may have been inspired to act violently by the hate speech propagated by these Nazi defendants, the defendants did not appear to intend that their words would have this violent effect. Streicher claimed that he intended only to have Jews removed from Germany (perhaps to Madagascar) and Fritzsche seems to have quite explicitly condemned violence in his speeches, despite how hate-filled they were. In these cases what was called incitement was really a kind of reckless endangerment. Yet there was also more to it than this, because there was still some kind of link between what the defendants said and the violence that ensued.

In the ICTR's Akayesu and Media Cases there is a closer link between the defendants' actions and violence, but still the link need not be as close as the "offenses of intention" definition seems to involve. Did Barayagwiza have the intention to cause violence? Of course, he denied that he had such an intention. Yet his actions certainly could be reasonably said to risk such an outcome. In this sense it might make more sense to describe what he did in terms of recklessness rather than intentional causing of harm, and to punish him on that basis. As we will see, the ICTR felt that it has to add a doctrine of superior responsibility to hold Barayagwiza liable for what others said and did under his watch, not being able to hold him directly responsible. Nonetheless, what he

---

[38] Antony Duff, *Criminal Attempts*, Oxford: Clarendon Press, 1996, p. 129.

did, or rather didn't do, was so clearly reckless that this seems to be the better way to conceptualize his crime. A somewhat different case is that of Ngeze, who drove around with a bullhorn telling Hutus to attack Tutsis. What Ngeze did went beyond recklessness.

Punishing inchoate crimes is normally often hard to justify, and incitement is a particular case in point. An act that excites, or entices, another to act is often thought to be like an offer – something that another person can take up or leave be, but when taken up is now wholly the responsibility of the one who takes it up. It could be claimed that, unlike acts of compulsion and coercion, incitement exerts such small pressure that when acted on should not be the responsibility of the one who incites rather than solely the one who is enticed or excited. Indeed, one Court has said that "There is perhaps a no more unsatisfactory branch of our criminal law than the law relating to attempt, and there is not the slightest prospect that with the passage of time it will become less satisfactory."[39]

There is a sense in which incitement is integral to the participation of a number of people in the commission of a mass crime or other crime that requires multiple participants. But the question is at what point incitement, as an inchoate crime, blends into instigation, as a full participation in the crime. One way to think about it is that when a person incites he or she often also instigates, but not always. The way that incitement does lead to instigation may involve a significant temporal or spatial gap. For this reason, if for no other, it makes sense to distinguish incitement to genocide from instigation or some other direct participation in genocide. But it also makes sense to treat it as a separately punishable offence. In the case of participation, success is a necessary element. Yet incitement is so potentially dangerous an activity that perhaps it should be treated as punishable in itself, just as "attempted murder" is punishable independently of whether the defendant murdered. Indeed, as we will see, incitement to genocide plays such a crucial role in setting the stage for genocide that punishing it is absolutely crucial to the deterrence of genocide.

As I have been suggesting, incitement sometimes looks more like recklessness than like a straightforward intent crime. Yet, even in cases of recklessness, it remains problematic to punish incitement severely, especially in those cases when the incitement does not lead to the commission of a crime. Of course, this is true of all inchoate crimes, and so we

[39] *State v. Kudangirana* 1976(3) SA 565 AT 566 PER Macdonald JP (AD).

should consider some of the standard justifications of punishing severely these inchoate crimes, that is, crimes that do not necessarily lead to the completion of a harmful result. Antony Duff and others speak of both the deterrent as well as retributive effects of punishing inchoate crimes. People may be deterred even though they do not worry about violating inchoate crimes, because they may be deterred by the realization that their actions might cause harm and be punished. Nonetheless, it is cleaner to deter by reference to the inchoate act than to expect people to make the calculations of the likelihood that their acts might result in direct harm that could then be punished.

In retributive terms, as Duff says, "it is also (and not much less) wrong to attempt to cause such a harm, or to take an unreasonable risk of causing such a harm."[40] I would add that the relevant point seems to be that we should not diminish the retribution merely because of the "good luck" of the defendant in not seeing that his or her actions would result in harm to others. Retribution does not make sense of distinctions based on luck, because luck is normally out of the control of the agent. The only thing that is in the control of the defendant is initiating the causal chain, not of the luck of the chain ending in harm. And because retribution is mainly about responding to what agents voluntarily do, it makes sense to punish on that basis, that is, to punish on the basis of what the defendant deserves based on his or her choices.

But there are reasons to wonder whether it does indeed make sense to punish severely such crimes as incitement, especially where there is no harm produced. For it may turn out that the inciter runs a risk of harm but that the risk is fairly small. At very least, on both deterrence and retributive grounds, the inchoate crime should be punished severely only when there was a high likelihood that harm might result from the act of incitement. We need to keep in mind the principle that the punishment must in some sense "fit the crime." Promulgation of racial hate speech runs the risk of causing violence, but the extent of the risk is determined by the time, place, and manner of the dissemination. If one makes a racist speech to a group of people already predisposed toward acting violently, there will be quite a different likelihood of causing harm than if the speech is delivered to a group that is not so predisposed.

In my view, it is very hard to justify severe punishment, merely in terms of the deterrent effect, for inciters who have a low likelihood of producing harm. If the harm has only a low probability of occurring, then only

---

[40] Duff, *Criminal Attempts*, p. 134.

fairly mild punishment is justified – that is, deterrent punishment should be commensurate with likelihood of producing harm. Similarly, severe punishment is very hard to justify, in terms of retribution, if the harm had only a low probability of occurring – retributive punishment should also be commensurate with likelihood of producing harm. In addition, punishment for inchoate crimes should not be the same as punishment for the crime that is being incited. I believe that there should be punishment for incitement to genocide, but that punishment should generally be less than for genocide by direct perpetration. The inciters, unlike the direct perpetrators, merely risk great harm, and this fact should make at least some difference in terms of severity of punishment.

Incitement derives from the Latin word *citare*, which means to set in rapid motion. One of the most pressing conceptual problems with the category of incitement to genocide is that there is a significant lag time between when the racist hate speech is broadcast or printed and when violence ensues – thus undermining the core idea of setting in *rapid* motion. The speeches surely did heat up the emotions of people in Rwandan society, but to say that they were moved rapidly to engage in violence is not clearly seen in the Media Case with the exception of some of the acts of Ngeze, such as when he broadcast from his truck to crowds of people who were already primed to engage in violence. Incitement remains an inchoate crime in several senses of that term, but it is also true that punishable instances of incitement do not, but should, clearly resemble the core idea behind the Latin root of the term.

The Appeals Chamber recognized some of these points in its rejection of Trial Chamber arguments about sentencing in the Media Case. In particular the Appeals Chamber ruled that it was not enough that certain RTLM broadcasts were proved to be examples of "inflammatory speech." Instead, the journalists were shown to be engaging in such speech "to mobilize anger against the Tutsis" but not to incite people to commit genocide.[41] The Appeals Chamber also distinguished between evidence that proved incitement to ethnic hatred from that which proved incitement to commit genocide. In many cases only the former and not the latter was proven by reference to vitriolic broadcasts on RTLM. Things were different, though, in the articles published in *Kangura*. The Appeals Chamber found that "Kangura articles published in 1994 directly and publicly incited the commission of genocide."[42]

---

[41] Media Case Appeals Chamber Judgment, para. 742.
[42] Ibid., para. 775.

IV. Incitement and Superior Responsibility

Another problem with the idea of incitement to genocide concerns uncertainty about what the general theory of individual responsibility is that would allow for the inciters to be held criminally liable. This is especially problematic in the Media Case because two of the defendants are primarily media executives rather than the ones who published or broadcast the hate speech. One intriguing way that the Media Case Trial Chamber tries to finesse the individual responsibility of those accused of incitement to genocide is by reference to superior responsibility, that is, by reference to the idea that those media executives accused of incitement can be convicted based on how their subordinates excited readers and listeners to commit acts of genocide. But one of the main problems with this approach is that it runs against the grain of how superior responsibility tends to be understood, and, I would argue, can plausibly be understood. I will examine this idea in this section. It should be remembered throughout, however, that the superior responsibility route is only one of the routes to criminal conviction in this case.

Here is how the Media Case Trial Chamber characterizes the superior responsibility of the defendants:

> The Chamber has considered the individual criminal responsibility of Ferdinand Nahimana and Jean-Bosco Barayagwiza for RTLM broadcasts, by virtue of their respective roles in the creation and control of RTLM ... [they] were, respectively, "number one" and "number two" in the top management of the radio. ... While the Chamber recognizes that Nahimana and Barayagwiza did not make decisions in the first instance with regard to each particular broadcast of RTLM, these decisions reflected an editorial policy for which they were responsible. ... Nahimana and Barayagwiza knew what was happening at RTLM and failed to exercise the authority vested in them as office-holding members of the governing body of RTLM to prevent the genocidal harm that was caused by RTLM programming. ... For these reasons, the Chamber finds that Nahimana and Barayagwiza had superior responsibility for the broadcasts of RTLM.[43]

The Media Case Trial Chamber acknowledged that it was somewhat extending the normal usage of the idea of superior responsibility, but noted that such an extension to nonmilitary settings had already been recognized by an earlier ICTR Trial Chamber (namely, in the Musema case).[44]

---

[43] Media Case Trial Chamber Judgment, paras. 970–3.
[44] Ibid., para. 976.

The Trial Chamber also held Barayagwiza responsible for what members of the CDR party did, largely because he was said to be in a superior position to these members as the founder of the party and played an active role in the meetings and discussions about what the party's members should do. As the tribunal recognized, the members of a political party are not like the members of a corporation or army. Yet the Trial Chamber nonetheless thought that Barayagwiza exercised enough control over the party's members to make him responsible for their actions.[45] Notice that it then becomes possible to hold Barayagwiza responsible not only for his own acts of incitement but also for the acts of incitement of these party members.

I wish to offer several criticisms of the Trial Chamber's use of the theory of superior responsibility in the Media Case. Here is how LaFave and Scott describe one basis of what has been called "superior responsibility" in criminal law:

> The Model Penal Code provision is generally consistent with those cases adopting the so-called "superior agent" rule. Under this rule, corporate criminal liability (except for strict liability offenses) is limited to situations in which the criminal conduct is performed or participated in by corporate agents sufficiently high in the hierarchy to make it reasonable to assume that their acts reflect the policy of the corporate body.[46]

In the Media Case, there does not appear to be straightforward criminal conduct by high-ranking members of the newspaper or radio corporations.

Another possibility is merely to lift the tort idea of *respondeat superior,* namely, the idea that a master is responsible for his servant, and adapt it for the criminal law. It certainly is true that in some cases "the tort principle of respondeat superior is applied without question so that the crimes of any employee – no matter what his position in the corporate hierarchy – become the crimes of the corporation."[47] But this model is also not well suited to situations where there is a very loosely organized group such as a political party, as I shall next try to show.

When the concept of *respondeat superior* is used in the law of corporations, the master is the corporation and the servant is the employee. It is unclear who is in a relevant position to master or corporation in the context of political parties. The leader of the party does not normally have

[45] Ibid.
[46] LaFave and Scott, *Criminal Law,* pp. 233–4.
[47] Ibid., p. 232.

the kind of control over the members of the party that exists in either of the two paradigm contexts of superior responsibility, the army or the corporation. The leader of a party certainly can shape the policies of the party, and those policies can strongly influence the members of the party. But the relationship between party leader and party member is not of the sort that has been characterized as one of superior responsibility where one party is made to stand liable for what another does.

It makes more sense to talk of superior responsibility in the case of the radio station directors and their employees, as well as the similar relationship for a newspaper's directors and their employees, than in the case of the CDR party. Importantly, the radio station and newspaper can exercise enormous control over their employees because the employees are partially dependant on the directors for their livelihood. Party leaders do not employ party members, except in unusual circumstances, and the kind of directions that party leaders give to party members does not have the same force as the directives that employing directors give to their employees. So, although I question the use of the concept of superior responsibility for Barayagwiza concerning the actions of the members of the political party that he led, it makes more sense for the actions of the radio station and newspaper where he was a director. The clearest case concerns Ngeze, who literally instructed people to take up weapons and kill particular Tutsis. But when the charge against him, like that against Barayagwiza, is for superior responsibility for running the CDR party, this is a much more difficult case to prove.

Even in the cases of the superior responsibility for running the radio station and newspaper, more needed to be shown than merely that Barayagwiza and Nahimana failed to stop those who worked at the radio station and newspaper from inciting others. For it is important how much influence the directors of the radio station and the newspaper had over those who were broadcasting or writing in a way that vilified the Tutsis and called for their elimination. Here the prosecution and the Trial Chamber did not supply enough evidence, in my opinion, to make the charge of superior responsibility plausible for Barayagwiza and the other defendants.

The Appeals Chamber considered some of the arguments that I have advanced and by and large sided with the Trial Chamber's judgment. The Appeals Chamber focused on whether the defendants did indeed have "effective control" over the employees who were under them at RTLM and at Kangura. In particular, the Appeals Chamber concluded that "Nahimana was a superior and had the material capacity to prevent or punish the broadcasting of criminal discourse by RTLM staff." The arguments advanced by the Appeals Chamber are not significantly different from those advanced by the Trial Chamber, and that I found lacking in my discussion in this section. In the final section I will resume discussion of the more plausible charge that Barayagwiza and the other defendants are responsible for their own actions that constituted incitement to genocide. I will also provide what I regard as a plausible revised account of incitement as well.

V. Incitement to Genocide through the Media

In my view, incitement makes the most conceptual sense when it is linked with its Latin root, namely, where a person's actions begin a causal chain, and soon thereafter there is, or would normally be, a certain harmful result. In the case of incitement to genocide, the result, of course, is a series of genocidal harms. Incitement is not best understood as preparing the ground for harm, but rather as initiating a causal process. It is also to do so intentionally, although as we will see the intention is only to take a risk, not to do that which is risked. And here is where the inchoate nature of the crime arises, for if one were to start such a causal chain by one's words, spoken or written, and to intend that these words would have a certain result, then this is enough for incitement, as long as the so-called proximity condition is met, namely, the condition that stipulates that the act must involve causation that is more than mere preparation.

In my view, incitement should be understood to involve a "close connection between the conduct engaged in by the accused, and the (kind of) offense which she or he is alleged to have" incited.[48] But there is a sense in which incitement crimes do not fit the standard definition of inchoate crimes because there really isn't any preparation to do something else involved in incitement. What makes the connection is more direct than mere preparation, hence the idea of setting in rapid motion. But incitement does fit with other inchoate crimes in the sense that what is done to start the causal chain, even though it is of a different sort than preparation, does not necessarily have to lead to completion in a harmful outcome. Recall that Duff places incitement in a class with attempt and conspiracy. Yet in these cases, preparation is crucial to satisfy the

---

[48] Jeremy Horder, "Crimes of Ulterior Intent," in *Harm and Culpability*, edited by A. P. Simester and A. T. H. Smith, Oxford: Clarendon Press, 1996, p. 160.

proximity condition. It seems to me that incitement is significantly different from other inchoate crimes in that there is a more direct link between what the defendant is alleged to have done and the result that is harmful.[49] Once again, this will move our understanding of incitement closer to its Latin root.

As I indicated above, I also think that incitement falls between the stools of some inchoate crimes such as attempts that involve intentional acts to do harm, and other inchoate crimes that merely involve recklessness. For this reason, incitement should be defined in terms of only one, not two, intention elements, although there is a second mental element that should be required. Incitement should be understood as the intention to do a certain act, where the act is known to be highly likely to produce harm, but where it may not be intended that those harms occur. In that sense incitement is at minimum a crime of recklessness, not necessarily a crime of intention, to use Duff's terminology, because only knowledge of the risk of, not also intention to cause, serious harm is required.

Putting all of these pieces together, here is my proposed way to understand incitement. Incitement involves the intention to take certain actions that initiate a causal chain that is known to risk serious harm, but where the harm need not be intended, and in addition the harm need not be effected. Incitement is thus an inchoate crime in that harm need not result from the inciters' action, but incitement is not like most other inchoate crimes in how the proximity test is to be met. There is a very limited sense in which preparation must be taken, in that the inciter must in fact do those things that, by strongly affecting others, risks causing these others to engage in harms. But this is not best thought of in terms of preparation because it is not as if the inciter need be planning to do the things that those who are likely to be affected by his or her actions may cause, nor that he or she intends there to be a plan to produce these harms.

There will be degrees of incitement, and more severe penalties should be set for those who know and intend the risk than those who merely know of the risk and are hence reckless. The severity of the punishment turns not on the initial intent, but on a secondary mental element, namely, whether the specific harm is intended or merely the result of recklessness or negligence. Incitement is thus what is often called a crime of specific or special *mens rea*. Incitement to genocide is thus to be

---

[49] Duff, *Criminal Attempts*, p. 128.

understood as the kind of crime where there must be both the intent to do an act of broadcasting or publishing or public speaking in a highly prejudicial way about a social group's members, and where the risk of harm so created is at least known by the inciter.

Finally, let me say just a few words about how the defendants in the Media Case should be treated given my revised understanding of incitement. All three defendants acted in various ways that incited genocidal violence by publishing and broadcasting articles and speeches. There is still incitement even if it may be true that the defendants did not intend that harmful results would occur, just as seems to be true in the Fritzsche case before the Nuremberg tribunal. How exactly the responsibility of the defendants should be characterized has remained a bit of a difficulty, as I will now indicate in the ending paragraphs of this section.

In the case of Nahimana, if he claims that he did not intend to make, or allow to have made, prejudicial remarks that he knew would risk harm to Tutsis, and the prosecution cannot prove otherwise, then he should not be subject to conviction at all. Yet some of the statements and actions attributed to Nahimana certainly seem to me to be reckless, and insofar as the prosecution could prove that they are, then Nahimana would be subject to conviction and punishment, although not as severe punishment as if he intended to fuel genocidal violence. In this context we might also wonder about the purchase and distribution of machetes on the part of these defendants. Such acts, along with the speeches Nahimana made, might make him guilty of complicity by participating in genocide although perhaps still not as an inciter.

Barayagwiza cannot avoid successful prosecution by claiming that he merely knew about the risk that his remarks would fuel genocidal action, but that he did not intend to fuel the genocide. He seems to me to be clearly guilty of incitement to genocide based on his own admissions about his knowledge of the risk he caused. His admitted recklessness might count in favor of a less severe sentence than if he had intended these results. In neither case will it matter that the genocidal violence did not occur as a result of these actions. Unless there was evidence presented that Barayagwiza intended that his actions would incite and also intended that such incitement would fuel the genocidal violence, he should not be sentenced severely for what he did.

Ngeze is the one who should be most severely punished for having intended to incite genocide given that he also intended that his inciting actions would cause harm, especially when he stood in his truck and while speaking through a megaphone urged Hutus to kill specific Tutsis. So, according to the model I have set up, Ngeze is the one who should be punished most severely because his actions were so much more clearly and directly connected to the genocidal violence that swept Rwanda than were those other defendants in the Media case. Of course, one might also wonder whether the Hutus were not already primed to respond as they did, in which case Ngeze might have his sentence diminished because there would be evidence that the violence may have occurred without his actions.

In the actual sentencing, the Trial Chamber of the ICTR gave life sentences to all three defendants, reducing the sentence for Barayagwiza slightly only because of due process violations concerning his case. I have given reasons to think that only Ngeze should have been sentenced so severely. Although I have admitted that if the prosecution could show that all three defendants intended to fuel the genocide by their inciting actions, then they could all be subject to the same severe punishment. By giving all three defendants the same sentence, the ICTR made a major mistake in not recognizing the importance of a second intent element.

I have not embraced the ICTR's use of the doctrine of superior responsibility for the case of party leaders and the members of their parties, but I might support this theory for heads of corporations. The question in the Media Case is whether newspapers and radio stations are run like normal corporations where those executives in charge really do have the power to monitor and change the views of those who do the broadcasts and write the editorials. I do not have a firm view of this and suspect that it will vary quite a bit from newspaper to newspaper and radio station to radio station. But it is clear that the editorial policy would have to be known to be risking violence for the newspaper or radio station executives to be held responsible as inciters to genocide. In the cases we have been examining, I do not think this was indeed clear. So Nahimana, Barayagwiza, and Ngeze would have to be found guilty on the basis of their own acts of incitement, not for superior responsibility for failing to stop others from being inciters.

In this chapter I have attempted to assess the Rwanda Media Case and to amend the general account of incitement that exists concerning liability in international criminal law. In my account incitement is not best seen as a form of complicity. In general I have supported the idea that people can be held criminally liable for incitement, even in those cases where violence does not follow from their actions and even if the violence is not intended. Incitement can be one of the inchoate crimes that is part of the general crime of genocide, just as was indicated in the Genocide Convention of 1948. But as I have argued, the jurisprudential understanding of incitement to genocide should be altered to make the idea more plausible. In the next section I will continue investigating the special acts that trigger criminal liability in the case of genocide. I shall discuss the relationship among instigation, incitement, and complicity in the crime of genocide. I am especially interested in who among all of those who played a role in the crime of genocide should be punished most severely. I will argue that when both intention dimensions of incitement can be proven, the inciters can justifiably be punished severely.

11

Instigating, Planning, and Intending
Genocide in Rwanda

In this concluding chapter to the fourth part of the book, I will argue, perhaps counterintuitively, that in the Rwandan genocide the most significant actions that should be punished were by some of those who were not merely reckless but intended to incite rather than those who killed or were merely complicit. If we think of genocides on the model of the Holocaust, responsibility is primarily assigned to those who planned or participated in the planning of the genocide against Jews in Nazi Germany and elsewhere in Europe. The "intent to destroy a group" is seen in the explicit and quite elaborate plans that were drafted by, or administered under the direction of, Hitler. But, then, when we think about genocides such as that in Rwanda, conceptual puzzles arise. There seems to have been no central plan to destroy Tutsis in Rwanda. Rather, there was a tinder box of ethnic hatred in Rwanda that various individuals ignited. Mostly these individuals did not communicate with each other and did not follow a single script. Nonetheless, if there was genocide occurring in Rwanda, as seems evident to most legal theorists and practitioners alike, then there must have been something like instigation even if there was no planning. In this chapter I will try to shed some light on this difficult conceptual puzzle.

The specific conceptual and normative questions I address in this chapter concern who should be held criminally liable for the crime of genocide that occurred in Rwanda, and who should be punished most severely. I argue that, at least as a matter of international criminal liability, those who killed are more like accomplices who are complicit, than like those who instigate the crime. Those who seem to be most like those who directly instigated, in that they did something like planning and initiating genocide, were those who intended to incite it. And in this respect, certain acts of Jean-Paul Akayeshu are key. Akayeshu didn't merely exploit an already volatile situation, as would be true in cases of indirect instigation like some of the cases examined in the previous chapter. Rather, he created the combustible situation and then in effect lit the match to ignite genocide. He is then worse even than those who did the killing, who become more like those who were complicit as aiders or abettors of the genocide. This thesis is highly controversial, but in defending it I try to understand better the nature of prosecutions at the international level.

In the first part of the chapter I discuss varieties of genocide and culpability for genocide in Rwanda, looking at how it was that the Rwandan genocide differed from that of the Holocaust. In the second part of the chapter, I will survey various forms of instigation that have been recognized in criminal law. I will focus on instigation through the means of igniting already inflamed hatred among the population. Even though many have previously put straw on the camel's back, the back does not break until the last straw, yet we do not need a master plan for the placing of the straw. In the third part of the chapter, I will set out a theoretical account of instigation without planning that can give rise to criminal liability even for such group crimes as genocide. In the fourth part of the chapter I look specifically at the Akayesu case before the International Tribunal for Rwanda, where omissions and some commissions by a bourgmestre were claimed to be enough of an initiation to trigger international criminal liability. And in the fifth section of the chapter, I will set out my account of the general idea of instigation without planning, and its specific application in the Akayesu case, and defend my view against a series of objections. Throughout this chapter I remain focused on the genocide in Rwanda, although I also try to generalize a bit, pointing out how the Rwandan genocide differs from and is similar to other genocides.

I. Types of Genocide and Culpability

In this chapter I will be trying to determine who is principally responsible for genocide, and among these people who should be most severely punished. In highly organized atrocities, the question often can be easily answered, because there is a general consensus that the political and military leaders who planned and orchestrated the atrocity are clearly the most responsible for it and should be most severely punished. So, at Nuremberg, the 22 leading political and military leaders of the Third Reich were tried, with only a handful of them escaping death sentences.

There were other trials for lesser figures spanning several decades after the Holocaust, and some of these people also received stiff sentences. But the high-profile first trial after the end of World War II in Nuremberg clearly was meant to mark the culpability of those judged most responsible, namely, Nazi Germany's political and military leaders.

In Rwanda, on the other hand, things were more complicated. Initially, government and military leaders instigated the killing of Tutsis after a Tutsi militia allegedly shot down the plane of the president of Rwanda, who was a Hutu. After the first week or two, the killing spread to the countryside, with Hutus killing their Tutsi neighbors. The ensuing atrocity resulted in the deaths of 800,000 people, mainly Tutsis, over a three-month period. There were also Hutus who were killed, especially those who were trying to aid or were otherwise sympathetic to the Tutsis, but the killing was primarily directed at the Tutsis. Who should be considered principally responsible in such cases? I use this case as an occasion to say something more about three categories of potentially culpable parties: those who instigate, those who incite, and those who are complicit. As in most genocides, there were all three types of actors who together brought about the Rwandan genocide.

In the early stages of the massacre, there is evidence that the government was actively involved in some planned killings. Samantha Power states: "From April 7 onward, the Hutu-controlled army, the gendarmerie, and the militias worked together to wipe out Rwanda's Tutsi. Many of the early Tutsi victims found themselves specifically, not spontaneously pursued."[1] Power continues her description of the Rwandan genocide noting that after the first week or so, the character of the massacre changed: "In Kigali in the early days, the killers were well equipped government soldiers and militia. ... In the countryside, where the slaughter gradually spread, the killing was done at first with firearms, but as more Hutu joined in the weapons became increasingly unsophisticated – knives, machetes, spears."[2] The change in the character of the weapons indicates that if there was a plan at all, it had shifted significantly.

The International Criminal Tribunal for Rwanda (ICTR) quotes one expert witness, the anthropologist Dr. Alison Desforges, who said that there were "centrally organized and supervised massacres." The tribunal indicates that some evidence supports this view, although the main

[1] Power, *A Problem from Hell*, p. 333.
[2] Ibid., p. 334.

evidence seems to be that "the psychological preparation of the population to attack the Tutsis, which preparation was masterminded by some
news media, with the [radio station] RTLM at the forefront." The tribunal concludes that there was genocide occurring, but does not contend
that it was centrally organized.[3]

What seems most plausible is that there was an initial plan to seek
revenge against the Tutsi for its alleged complicity in the murder of the
president of Rwanda, but that there was no blueprint of how the revenge
should be carried out, and there was no master plan that extended from
the initial killings by police and members of the military into the countryside where neighbors killed neighbors. Various individuals, some of
whom were political and military leaders, and some of whom were in the
media, did things that initiated violence and increased the likelihood
that individual Tutsis would be killed. But these acts were not part of an
organized, central plan and do not seem to have been organized on the
level and scale of that perpetrated in the Holocaust.

Article II of the Convention on Genocide defines genocide as "any
of the following acts committed with the intent to destroy, in whole
or in part, a national, ethnical, religious, racial or religious group, as
such." The acts that follow include killing, and causing serious bodily
harm. Article III of the Convention on Genocide lists five acts punishable by the Convention: (a) Genocide; (b) Conspiracy to commit genocide; (c) Direct and public incitement to commit genocide; (d) Attempt
to commit genocide; (e) Complicity in genocide. Acts (b) and (d) have
been rarely charged recently, so I will focus on (a), (c), and (e).[4]

The problem I wish to address concerns both the *actus reus* and the
mens rea of criminal liability in cases such as genocide. Certainly a group
can be destroyed without central planning, especially if the group is
not very large. And, given that each act that resulted in the destruction
of the group could be intentional, then a group can be destroyed by
intentional acts. But it seems initially quite odd to say that there was an
intent to destroy the group without some kind of collective decision to
destroy the group. The *actus reus* of the crime of genocide may involve
many individual acts, but it seems they must be coordinated somehow.
And the *mens rea* of the crime of genocide may also involve many guilty
minds, but seemingly there must be a sense in which they were directed

[3] Akayesu Trial Chamber Judgment, para. 126.
[4] Convention on the Prevention and Punishment of Genocide; Rome Statute of the ICC
(1998).

as well. For without the coordination and direction, it looks like what we have is merely killing based on persecution. Persecution is a crime against humanity where acts of killing, rape, and so on are based on hatred of the group, not an overarching intent to destroy the group. This problem then calls into question whether there really was genocide in Rwanda, rather than merely persecution as a crime against humanity, at least as genocide is defined in international law.

I believe that genocide occurred in Rwanda, but that it was of a very different sort than that which occurred in the Holocaust, and which is much more conceptually problematic, because the genocide in Rwanda was decentralized. Yet there are not especially difficult questions about who should be held responsible for this type of genocide. We need not spend time wondering whether the big fish or small fry should be prosecuted, because most of the main players are small fry. Nonetheless the individual acts performed at a pretty low level in the leadership chain can be seen as guilty acts, and even as acts that were guilty as international crimes. This is because an individual's intent can have a collective component, as we saw in Chapter 7. Individuals can intend to destroy a protected group, although normally without planning or without many others having the same intent, the group intention is empty.

But, as we will see, there is a special case of how a genocide could be "organized" concerning situations where only a few intentional acts are needed to ignite ethnic hatred and to be the principal acts of the group crime of genocide. Some kinds of incitement look very much like a kind of direct instigation, even though the incitement does not come to be full-fledged planning as one would have in paradigmatic cases of direct instigation. Nonetheless, incitement is not merely indirect instigation. I now proceed to a discussion of these two forms of instigation.

II. Two Forms of Instigation

The category of acts that is normally the most significant, instigation of genocide, is what the Genocide Convention simply calls genocide simpliciter. There is an initial conceptual and normative puzzle about this category. Those who instigated are rarely those who killed. And yet there is common acceptance of the idea that the instigators are more responsible than the ones who killed in genocide cases. The reason for this is that the crime of genocide is a collective crime even though individuals are the ones who are prosecuted for the international crime of genocide. Individual killing is not genocide; genocide is group killing or harming aimed at the destruction of a protected group. And those held most responsible are those who played the greatest role in creating the collective harm.

There are two kinds of instigation, direct and indirect. The classic cases of direct instigation involve those who plan a large-scale campaign of violence and then start the implementation of the campaign but do not themselves carry out the violence. Without the plan, the individual acts that constituted the group crime would not have occurred, or would not have occurred in a concerted way that led to, or at least could have led to, the collective crime. What is not often noted is that the setting up of a plan, without any action aimed at starting the implementation of the plan, does not count as direct instigation. So, even in the paradigm case of direct instigation, such as Hitler instigating the Holocaust, there are two parts: planning plus initiating. The question I raise in this section is: what are the other forms of instigation, or instigation-like activity, that would not involve planning? I argue for a variety of such cases, where something replaces planning. In some cases it is something under the agent's control and in other cases not under his or her control.

Let us begin with cases where something like planning has occurred by the instigator, and then there is also initiation. Think of the case where a person sets the stage for others to act, and then in effect pushes these others onto the stage. Perhaps we can begin with a literal case of this sort, and then proceed to the situations where the stage is only metaphor. So let us say that I build a platform, arrange for an audience to be observing what goes on, and then push you out onto the stage. If what you then do is perform, it is fair to say that I have directly instigated your performance. On the assumption that engaging in a performance is illegal, then I as well as you have committed a crime. Am I more criminally culpable than you?

In the literal stage-setting case, my actions are necessary for the performance, and for that reason my culpability seems clear-cut. Of course, your actions are also necessary for the performance, or at least for this performance. But the difference between us lies in our mental states. I have a guilty mind and you do not, or at least not necessarily so. If you lack *mens rea*, then you won't be criminally culpable at all. If you know that performances of this sort are illegal, and yet you perform, you will manifest some mental state that might trigger criminal culpability, but surely not as much as my mental state that involves an intention to break the law. Planning is often described as a kind of stage setting, and we can now hopefully see why this is. Those who plan a crime have the *mens rea* of intentional wrongdoing, often in just the way that the stage setter does.

There are other acts that do not literally set up a stage but resemble stage setting sufficiently to make us think that the "stage setter" should be the one primarily to be held criminally culpable. Think of a military commander who wants not only to destroy the enemy but to "make them pay" for what they have done. He therefore trains his troops to use the most aggressive tactics, and also trains these troops to come to hate the enemy. The commander then tells his troops that there is a hamlet where it has been reported that the enemy has been sighted. The commander then does not supervise his soldiers, and they commit atrocities against the people in the hamlet. Here we have planning that is not stage setting but sufficiently like it for it to be treated as if it were stage setting on the part of the commander. This is still sufficiently like the paradigm case of direct instigation also to be called direct instigation.

Now consider a variation on the previous case. Suppose that the commander does not want to "make the enemy pay" but does all of the acts described in the previous paragraph. He seems to have done something like setting the stage for the attacks even if it was not intentional on his part. We might somewhat mitigate his punishment because he acted recklessly or negligently rather than intentionally, but he has nonetheless done something like setting the stage for these attacks, and it may be fair to say that he initiated these attacks by his actions. Whether or not we think that this commander initiated the attacks, and is a direct instigator, will depend on whether or not we think that initiation requires intent, or is primarily a causal term.

Finally, consider a case where the commander knows that his troops are using highly aggressive tactics, knows that they have come to hate the enemy, tells the soldiers about having sighted the enemy, and intends that his soldiers are thereby moved to attack. The commander here exploits a situation where it can be said that the stage was set for an atrocity, even though the situation was not of his own making. Here is a form of initiation by means of indirect instigation, where an agent exploits a situation where the stage is already set for violence. Now we have a situation that might resemble the one in Rwanda where the genocide did not result from some kind of central planning but where we can still say that some people initiated the genocide by exploiting the already existing hate-filled and tense situation between ethnic groups. Yet, if there was someone who set the stage in some other way, for instance, by inciting as a type of stage setting, then that person might more resemble the direct instigator, and be more culpable, than the person who indirectly instigated by exploiting the tense situation.

Initiation does not require advanced central planning, but there must be something that replaces the planning aspect if criminal culpability is to follow from initiation. I have proposed one such condition, namely, the exploitation of an already existing volatile situation. One cannot initiate without something like the stage already being set. This is a well-known idea that has been most clearly articulated in the literature about attempt crimes – for it makes no sense to say that one is attempting to do the impossible, as in the case where one is said to attempt to kill someone who is already dead.

Intentional rather than reckless incitement is the creation of a situation where others are sufficiently inflamed to be ready to cause harm. Similarly, initiation through exploitation of a given situation is the striking of the spark that actually ignites the flames. Whereas indirect instigation through exploitation of a given situation is the striking of the spark that actually ignites the flames, intentional incitement seems to be the creation of a situation where others are sufficiently inflamed to be ready to cause harm. Instigation and incitement are clearly different from each other, and can meaningfully be charged as separate crimes. And because incitement is more like planning than indirect instigation here, incitement can be the more important action in the crime.

One question is: who were the individuals principally responsible in the Rwandan genocide? Is it the person who did the killing, or who exploited an already combustible situation, or is it the intentional inciter? I am inclined to say that it is the inciter, because the inciter more closely resembles the direct instigator than those who are merely indirect instigators. In some cases incitement appears to be very close to a form of complicity as encouragement where there is no significant time lag. In other respects, however, incitement looks like direct instigation, because there is intentional stage setting and then initiation, and is not best seen as mere complicity. But if incitement does not involve intent, but only recklessness, to cause harm, incitement will not then be as culpable as direct instigation.

III. Lack of Planning and the Intent Elements in Genocide

The key in all forms of culpability for genocide is the link between the individual's action and the larger crime. And here is the main problem for atrocities such as that in Rwanda. If there is no central planning, how can there be a larger intent that goes beyond what is the intent of each person who participates in the atrocity? One answer is that if there are individuals who incite to provide the spark that ignites a genocide, then there is something like planning that has occurred. An individual's intentional act of incitement can in effect unite the intents of other individuals into the larger intent, the intent to destroy the protected group, which is necessary to satisfy the intent definition of genocide.

There are several intent requirements of the international crime of genocide, as we saw in Chapter 7. There is the normal *mens rea* requirement of any crime, namely, that the defendant had the aim of committing a criminal offense by performing a certain act. And there is the specific requirement that the defendant have the aim of destroying a social group. Some crimes have both a general and special intent requirement, although I indicated earlier that I didn't think this was the best way to think about intent. In murder cases there is both a general intent to do something illegal, and there is also the special intent to do the illegal act by bringing about the death of this person. If one merely intends to act illegally and kills thereby, one is guilty of manslaughter. But to be guilty of murder, one must intend both to act illegally and also to kill this person.

In addition, as in most international crimes, there is the element that what the defendant participates in is genocide. Genocide is a mass crime that has as its intent the destruction of a protected group. This element is different from, although related to, the other intent elements. And this is where something like collective planning is important for the international crime of genocide. For without something that intentionally "organizes" or "coordinates" the acts of many people, there won't be a collective of the sort that is normally required for successful prosecution of genocide as an international crime.

In other international crimes, it must be proved that there was an international crime occurring for the defendant to be convicted of having participated in an international crime. For example, to be proven guilty of the international crime of aggression, it has to be proven that there is aggression occurring that the individuals participated in. Aggression is mainly defined in terms of acts that violate political sovereignty or territorial integrity, so the main thing that needs to be shown is that there were the acts that constituted aggression, normally committed by a State against another State. Similarly, with crimes against humanity there is a requirement of proving that there were widespread and systematic assaults against a population. This is normally done by showing either State involvement or that the killing ranged over a certain territory.

Today in international law, genocide is different from crimes of aggression or crimes against humanity in that the larger crime that the individual participates in is mainly defined in terms of intent. It isn't just that the crime involves acts that ranged widely, or that crossed State borders. And it isn't even enough that the acts were motivated by racial or ethnic hatred – for this is only persecution as a crime against humanity. There is the requirement that the attacks be aimed at destroying a protected group. Individual acts of violence become an international crime normally by the extent of the violence, whereas in genocide individual acts of violence become an international crime because of what those acts aim at. When there is no central planning in the atrocity, it is difficult, at least initially, to figure out whether or not that intent requirement has been satisfied. The International Criminal Tribunal for the Former Yugoslavia (ICTY) Appeals Chamber recognized that a plan is not required for genocide: "While the existence of such a plan may help establish that the accused possessed the requisite genocidal intent, it remains only evidence supporting the inference of intent, and does not become a legal ingredient in the offence."[5]

I have been suggesting that incitement may play a role similar to that of planning that could help us out of this difficulty; but it will be only a partial help. The difficulty is that incitement is not necessarily intentional itself, or at least not in the right way. Incitement may be merely reckless rather than intentional. In those situations, incitement will not play the role of "organizing" the acts of various individuals into a collective act with a single intent, namely, to destroy a protected group. The group may indeed be destroyed by the widespread individual acts that were ignited by the inciting media sources, for instance. But it may not be that there was a prior intent to destroy that group. Indeed, the group may have been destroyed by widespread persecution at the individual level that did not rise to the level of being an intentionally collective crime such as genocide.

Understanding the crime of persecution will help in identifying what more is needed in genocide cases. The requirement that persecution, as with all crimes against humanity, be widespread or systematic is in effect to say that the intent can all be at the level of alleged individual perpetrators. In the case of widespreadness, the collective nature of the crime

---

[5] *Prosecutor v. Radislav Krstic,* Appeals Chamber Judgment, para. 225.

may be based only on sufficient aggregation of the individual acts. Many people acting out of hatred of a group can be said to engage in persecution of the members of the group without there being any overarching intent to persecute the group, or even an overarching intent to persecute the group's members. Rather, all that is required is that a certain threshold number of individual acts of intentional violence is reached. There is no additional requirement that these acts together have the intent to harm the group, even though this might turn out to be the result of the accumulated acts in any event. Genocide requires just this collective intent, and planning satisfies the requirement, but the question is whether certain forms of incitement do so as well.

Genocide's collective intent requirement could be met by a single intentional act of incitement if the idea behind the act of incitement was to aim at just the destruction of the group that would otherwise require a coordinated plan. In some cases the incitement both engages in stage setting and also initiates the campaign of violence. It might also be possible to satisfy the collective intent requirement if there is only some stage setting and only some initiation, so that this form of incitement looked like indirect instigation. In either case it is possible that incitement could function like instigation to supply the collective intent element that would be necessary to prove genocide. In the Rwandan genocide, some members of the media engaged in incitement that seemingly had the aim of creating a genocide, just as if those individuals had planned and initiated the genocide. In this case incitement is not mere complicity but a basis to hold the inciters primarily responsible for the genocide.

Complicity is secondary responsibility. But what interests me in this section are the various forms of primary responsibility, for without some primary responsibility there will not be any secondary responsibility in terms of complicity. If there is a putative genocide and no planning, or other basis of collective intent, then there won't be anyone to hold primarily liable for the mass harms, and there won't then be anyone to hold secondarily liable, because secondary responsibility such as complicity does not kick in until the first hurdle has been crossed, namely, that there was someone who could be held primarily liable, even if that person is not in fact held liable. So it matters quite a lot whether the intent element of incitement can instantiate the collective intent, for without it then there will not be anyone, in cases such as Rwanda where it seems there was no central planning, who will be responsible for the atrocity or at least not under the description of a genocide.

Perhaps counterintuitively I think that those who harm or kill should be treated like aiders and abettors, as secondarily responsible, rather than as those who instigate genocide and are primarily responsible. This is at least in part because of the collective nature of the crime of genocide. It may appear that in genocides such as that in Rwanda, the small fish who carry out the violence are aptly named the principals, because there are no true principals who plan the genocide. But although it does indeed make sense to prosecute small fish, some of those who incited are more like the principals than are those who carry out the violence. Severity of punishment should reflect this fact. There may be other crimes that people can be charged with associated with the atrocity in Rwanda, such as various forms of crimes against humanity as persecution, but the so-called crime of crimes, genocide, will not be one of these crimes. In the next section I discuss an example of how the genocide charge could have been substantiated in Rwanda even without central planning.

IV. The Akayesu Case before the ICTR

In previous sections I have indicated why it matters whether or not there is central planning, or something like it, in cases of mass atrocities. In the current section I will look closer at the Rwanda case, especially at one particular court case from the International Criminal Tribunal for Rwanda. The ICTR Trial Chamber considered many issues in the Akayesu case. Akayesu was charged with genocide simpliciter (instigation), complicity, and incitement. This section will speak to these charges and to the main evidence offered to support the charges. I will argue that Akayesu is a very good example of an inciter who should be viewed as primarily responsible for the genocide that ensued. But some of the specific acts that supposedly warrant his conviction for direct instigation are not as plausible as the tribunal seemed to think.

Akayesu was bourgmestre of Taba commune, making him effectively the town mayor and chief of police of this region of Rwanda. He is accused of having ordered various killings, especially of "intellectual and influential people."[6] But for this to be a crime of genocide, there must be evidence that Akayesu ordered these killings as part of a plan to destroy a protected group, the Tutsis. The evidence here is not as clear as it is for some of the other acts that he took. Akayesu's failure

[6] Akayesu Trial Chamber Judgment, para. 20.

214   *Responsibility for Genocide*

to stop the genocide from occurring, when he could have ordered the police under his command to do so, is one such act that makes him culpable for the genocide, but not yet as someone who is principally responsible and deserving of severe punishment. His acts of ordering people killed needs to be connected to the collective intent of genocide. And his acts of failing to stop the genocide also need to be part of an intentional effort on his part at least to contribute to the genocide.

In my view, the acts that most directly linked Akayesu to genocide are the acts that are listed as the evidence to support the charge of incitement, not direct instigation or complicity. Here is the tribunal's summary of that evidence:

> The Morning of April 19, 1994, following the murder of Sylvere Karera, Jean-Paul Akayesu led a meeting in Gishyeshye sector at which he sanctioned the death of Sylvere Karera and urged the population to eliminate accomplices of the RPF, which was understood by those present to mean Tutsis. Over 100 people were present at the meeting. The killing of Tutsis in Taba began shortly thereafter.

> At the same meeting in Gishyeshye sector on April 19, 1994, Jean Paul Akayesu named at least three prominent Tutsis, Ephrem Karangwa, Juvenal Rukundakuvuga, and Emanuel Sempabwa – who had to be killed because of their relationships with the RPF. Later that day, Juvenal Rukundakuvuga was killed in Kanyinya. Within the next few days, Emanuel Sempabwa was clubbed to death in front of the Taba bureau communal.[7]

Here we have a more explicit linking between what Akayesu did and genocidal intent than even in those cases where he more directly ordered that killings take place.

Once again, my view is that those who are the killers or harmers are not those who are most responsible for international crimes like genocide. The people who are most responsible are those whose intentions most connect with the collective intention that is definitive of the international crime. Akayesu does not necessarily connect with the genocidal intent requirement merely by targeting Tutsis. Such acts could easily be seen as acts of persecution, but not yet genocide, because insofar as the acts are isolated they are at least not straightforwardly aimed at the destruction of a protected group. They may be, but in most cases prosecutions will not proceed because it is so hard to prove that this was the person's intent.

7 Ibid., paras. 14–15.

In the case of Akayesu's incitement, in the description above, there is a much more straightforward way to link Akayesu's actions to genocidal intent. When Akayesu "urged the population to eliminate accomplices of the RPF, which was understood by those present to mean Tutsis,"[8] he was clearly displaying genocidal intent, and also setting the stage for mass killings that would be part of the genocide. By inciting people to kill Tutsis, just because they were Tutsis, there is a sense in which Akayesu was urging the destruction of the protected group, the Tutsis, or at least a significant part of that group. And in urging that people take such action he was displaying the genocidal intent that is required for the international crime of genocide.

It is not enough that someone such as Akayesu urged that Tutsis be killed, even in large numbers. The crime of genocide is not merely a mass atrocity, but one that has a certain character. As I have emphasized several times, the crime of genocide requires a showing that the defendant had the intent to destroy a protected group. Merely urging that various members of a protected group be killed does not establish this intent. There must be a link between the urging that members of the protected group be killed and the aim of destroying, not merely persecuting, the group. The urging was not just to kill specific people, but to kill them as members of a group with the clear implication that other members of the protected group should also be killed. Of course, an even better case would be one where the inciter explicitly urged that killings or other harms occur as a way to destroy the group. But it is rare that there is evidence of this additional fact. It is my view that there can be a direct inference to such a state of mind nonetheless and that certain aspects of the Akayesu case well illustrate this point.

The Akayesu case should have focused even more than it did on Akayesu's acts of incitement, because, in my view, these are the acts that establish most clearly that Akayesu could be held responsible, and punished severely, for the collective crime of genocide. This is especially true because Akayesu, unlike those who ran the radio station and newspaper that delivered the steady drumbeat of vitriol, was a public official with specific duties toward the entire population within his jurisdiction. Akayesu did not just participate in the early stages of the genocide but continued to incite the Hutus in his town throughout the genocide. On this ground, he is appropriately convicted of incitement to genocide and

---

[8] Ibid.

should be punished more severely than the more minor players in the Rwandan genocide.

In this section I have tried to advance our understanding of who should be held most responsible for genocide by looking at a concrete case. Jean-Paul Akayesu's case illustrates how one kind of incitement could link the inciter to an international crime such as genocide, and make the inciter one of those who is principally responsible for that genocide, and deserving of correspondingly severe punishment. Along the way I have also indicated which type of case would not warrant prosecution for genocide, but may nonetheless warrant prosecution for persecution as a crime against humanity. It should be remembered that genocide is not the only international crime, and that some cases that fail to meet genocide's high evidentiary standard may still be successfully prosecuted as international crimes other than genocide nonetheless. In the next section I will try to respond to some objections to the general view I have set out in the previous sections as well as the application of the view to the Akayesu case, one of the first cases to result in a conviction of an individual for genocide.

V. Objections

One of the most important objections to my view concerns my claim that those who kill or harm are not those who are most responsible and most deserving of severe punishment in genocide cases. The obvious objection is that surely it is those who actually choose to do the killing who are primarily responsible for the deaths of those who are killed by the direct and intentional actions of the killers. To make others primarily responsible infantilizes the killers, treating them as if they are children or automatons, rather than the responsible agents that they are. To diminish their responsibility sets the stage for more irresponsible behavior in the future in such cases.

My response to this important objection is that the small fish, who nonetheless do awful things, should be punished, but they normally lack the connection to the mass crime in terms of *mens rea* to be justifiably punished severely for genocide by an international court or tribunal. I have been addressing retributive reasons to punish rather than deterrence reasons in this chapter. I could agree that punishing the small fish, even punishing them severely, will help achieve deterrence, but still defend my view on grounds of retribution. But one could wonder nonetheless what to make of retribution in the context of international, collective crimes rather than individual ones.

There is a serious question of why individual perpetrators should be prosecuted at all in international courts, and this question is even harder to answer for those individuals who engaged in harmful conduct merely to seek revenge for a long-standing grievance against a neighbor. International courts should prosecute individuals for international crimes, and those crimes are limited in number. My view concerns only the crime of genocide, not the crime of murder – and it is both of these crimes that are on the table and should not be confused in such cases. Murder is a violation of international law if it is part of a widespread and systematic attack on a population, perpetrated by a soldier against a civilian during armed interventions, or part of a campaign of genocide. Isolated acts of murder do not violate international law. One can raise questions about whether this is the right way to think of international crime, and there are certainly other proposals out there about how to define such crimes, but at the moment it would not be fair to individual defendants to treat them according to standards that were not in place at the time they allegedly acted wrongly.

The second objection is related to the first. Don't we infantilize those who choose to kill and harm by treating them less severely than those who planned but also decided not to kill or harm themselves? People should be treated as fully responsible for what they choose to do, and their responsibility should not be diminished merely because others encouraged or incited them to choose to act the way they did. In any event there is something odd about treating those who were the killers and assaulters as mere accomplices, as if they only drove the get-away car instead of actually robbing the bank. Surely these individuals are not merely complicit, but principals, and to treat them as less than this fails to treat them as the agents they are.

I agree that individuals should be treated as fully responsible agents when they choose to act wrongly. Those who kill should be held fully liable for what they do. But there is a difference between how this should be understood domestically as opposed to internationally. Domestically, those who intentionally kill should be held responsible as murderers. Domestically, it would indeed be odd to think of intentional killers as mere accomplices, and as only secondarily rather than primarily responsible. But internationally, murder is not a crime unless it occurs in a collective context. In the international domain, it is not odd to think of individuals who kill as accomplices in the larger atrocity, if the part that they play in that atrocity is considerably less significant than that played by others. It is only odd to think about those who kill as merely accomplices in domestic legal settings, not international ones. We do not infantilize people by treating them as mere accomplices when that status fits their actual role in an international crime.

Third, it could be objected that some of those who do the killing and harming directly may indeed manifest the collective intent, and I have neither acknowledged this important fact nor provided the kind of theoretical framework of genocide that could include such individual defendants. In stressing the leaders or higher profile defendants I have misidentified how genocide occurs. In the trials subsequent to Nuremberg, camp guards and others were proved to have the requisite guilty intent to advance the Holocaust. Not only do the minor players do most of the acts that could be called *actus reus,* but some of these so-called minor players also manifest the *mens rea* of the crime of genocide and should be seen as properly the principals in the crime as well as those who are punished severely for their roles in this crime.

My response is to admit that there certainly could be such cases, and that there have been a few such cases recorded in the trials concerning the Holocaust, and more such cases could occur. The crucial question is whether there are many such cases and what the prevalence of such cases would tell us about the nature of, and accountability for, genocide. I don't think anything I have argued is strongly affected if it turns out that I am wrong about the frequency of having minor players manifest genocidal intent. All that I have claimed is that comparing those who do not have such intent and who kill or harm to those who do have the genocidal intent and incite, we should hold the latter group more responsible and punish them more severely than the former group. If we find minor players who manifest the collective intent, then they should certainly be punished severely as well.

The fourth objection is to wonder whether inciters should indeed be singled out for the most severe punishment given that they often play an unclear causal role in the crime. Unlike those who explicitly plan and initiate a genocide, it is often very hard to determine what the role of inciters is in the perpetuation of a genocide. Think of those who write hate-filled newspaper articles several years before violence actually breaks out. These people are inciters, but there is only a tenuous connection between what they did and the violence that ensued. This case is like a putative direct instigator who formulates a plan but whose initiation act is so weak that it is unclear if anyone will indeed follow the plan. Inciters are often not sufficiently like direct perpetrators to make them the most responsible for the crime of genocide.

I agree with this objection, at least up to a point, as well. Some inciters are indeed only tenuously related causally to the violent acts. We could call these people indirect inciters. But there are other inciters, call them direct inciters, such as Akayesu, whose acts of incitement can be clearly seen as causally contributing to the spread of violence. If Akayesu is proven to have made public statements urging that Tutsis in general, and named Tutsis in particular, be killed, and then very shortly thereafter these people were killed, little reasonable doubt remains about the causal efficacy of Akayesu's remarks. This is why I said earlier that I found Akayesu's case to be a paradigm example of the kind of incitement that should make him principally responsible and also subject to severe punishment.

The final objection concerns the collective intent requirement. The objection is that I have made too much of this requirement. Surely it is enough that the individuals involved in the harming and killing did so out of malice or hatred toward Tutsis. Why should there also be the requirement that the acts of these individuals be linked under an intent to destroy the group of Tutsis? And if this is not truly required, then there would be no reason to think that the inciters were more responsible for the genocide than those who did the killing and harming. There would certainly be no good reason to punish the inciters more severely than those who actually killed and harmed Tutsis.

My response is to point out that if genocide is one of the worst of all crimes, what makes it so is that a person not only acts wrongly toward individuals but also toward groups. I have elsewhere wondered whether harming groups, or intending to do so, really does make things worse, but suffice it here to note that that is the state of international law. For this final objection to be persuasive it would have to be not about who is most responsible under the current regime of international law but who should be so considered independently of such considerations of international legal practice.

Of course, one could also object to my characterization of the facts of the Rwandan genocide, and even about whether it is indeed to be thought of as a genocide on the same order as the Holocaust. Such considerations are important, but well beyond the scope of this chapter. All I have tried to do here, working within the framework of existing international law categories, is to argue that in some cases certain inciters should be punished more severely than those who killed or harmed members of a protected group. To make the case for this position, I have tried to show that these inciters perform a similar role to that of direct instigators who plan and initiate a genocidal campaign of violence. The key similarity is that something like the stage is set for massive violence. Those who set the stage and initiate violence are most responsible for that violence, and are also those who should be most severely punished.

PART E

SPECIAL PROBLEMS OF GENOCIDE

12

Genocide and Humanitarian Intervention

Even among those who are strong critics of humanitarian intervention, exceptions are often made for cases of genocide. Michael Walzer, for instance, puts genocide at the top of a very short list of exceptions to his general condemnation of humanitarian intervention for having violated the rights of a people to manage their own affairs.[1] In this chapter I will try to explain why genocide is seen as so important that it can justify wars that otherwise would be roundly condemned. Indeed, genocide is often the example that is appealed to when one wishes to justify almost any strategy that might have hope of success, and this is true even for those who are not generally sympathetic to consequentialist strategies of justification. I will provide a limited defense of humanitarian intervention, but only a limited one.

When the term "genocide" is used popularly, it is often indistinguishable from mass atrocities in which thousands of people are killed. But the term genocide also has several specialized meanings that separate it from other atrocities, even from those that necessarily involve mass slaughter. I will continue to employ the term genocide as it is used in international law, namely, as the intent to destroy certain protected groups. When critics of humanitarian intervention make an exception for genocide, they typically have the more technical meaning in mind. Yet, as we have seen and will find again, it is not as easy as one might think to explain the harm of genocide that would justify resort to humanitarian wars.

Many international theorists and practitioners have argued in favor of humanitarian intervention in cases of genocide. Walzer, for example, said that humanitarian interventions "can be justified whenever a

---

[1] Michael Walzer, "The Moral Standing of States: A Response to Four Critics," *Philosophy & Public Affairs*, vol. 3, no. 3, 1980, pp. 209–29.

government is engaged in a massacre or enslavement of its own people."[2] Jeff McMahan, and many others, argue that genocide can provide just cause for States to go to war.[3] And the recent United Nations World Outcome Document calls for decisive collective action to stop or prevent genocide in its characterization of the responsibility to protect populations.[4] Indeed, the burgeoning responsibility to protect literature typically uses genocide as the prime example of a situation where the world community has a strong responsibility to intervene, and to do so militarily if necessary.

Humanitarian intervention is a form of war, and for this reason the justification of this practice is not as easy as one might think, even in cases where it is waged to stop genocide. In the first section of this chapter I give an account of humanitarian intervention that stresses some of the conceptual and normative problems with this recourse to war. In the second section, I discuss the controversy about whether humanitarian intervention should have occurred in the Rwandan genocide. In the third section of this chapter I will give a very limited justification of humanitarian intervention to stop genocide, considering whether it is legitimate to use tactics that one knows to be immoral in order to satisfy a duty to go to the aid of those who are in distress. In the final section of the chapter I discuss some objections to my limited defense of humanitarian intervention to stop a genocide.

I. Problems in Humanitarian Intervention

As I argued in previous chapters, the most easily defensible basis for the claim that genocide is one of the worst, if not the worst, of all crimes has to do with the loss of group identity and status that the members face. Identity loss is not normally as significant as loss of life, which of course also happens in many genocides, but which also happens in other atrocities as well. In trying to find the unique moral harm of genocide, loss of life will not be sufficient, although it may indeed play a huge role in the quite substantial harm that occurs in many genocides. In genocides, unlike other atrocities involving massive loss of life, there is a loss of group identity and status. Such a loss can have particularly devastating

---

[2] Ibid., p. 217.

[3] Jeff McMahan, "Just Cause for War," *Ethics & International Affairs*, vol. 19, no. 3, 2005, pp. 55–75.

[4] United Nations General Assembly World Outcome Document, G.A. Res. A/RES/60/1, para. 139, U.N. Doc. A/RES/60/1 (Oct. 24, 2005).

effects on many people, although people will differ in this respect, and some people will find it easier than others to recover from this loss. But as we have seen, the other candidates for genocide's unique, or even its strongly condemnatory, moral status generally will not succeed.

If we accept the social death thesis discussed in Chapter 5, then it seems to be easier to justify humanitarian intervention than before. And even if instead we accept my preferred account of the harm of genocide, the loss of group identity and status thesis, it will be easier to justify humanitarian intervention as well. Loss of group identity and status is very harmful to individuals, and it seems that it must be stopped at nearly any cost. Wars waged to stop genocides thus may become the new paradigmatically justified wars, even replacing self-defensive war in this sense. I agree that wars waged for humanitarian reasons, especially to stop a genocide as in the case of Darfur, seem to be good examples of wars waged for a just cause.[5] But there are proportionality worries as well as other worries that make such wars not good candidates for the label of paradigmatically justified wars, all things considered. Let me first begin by rehearsing why stopping genocide does indeed look like the kind of thing that might make war justified, if anything does.

Humanitarian intervention does not look like most other forms of war. In international law the standard for what counts as aggressive war is whether there is a violation of territorial integrity or sovereignty. There is quite a bit of controversy about whether humanitarian intervention meets these conditions for unjustified use of force. But the motivation behind humanitarian intervention is clearly not to invade another State to conquer it, but rather merely a humanitarian motivation to stop the attacks. And typically after the attacks have ceased, the humanitarian intervention, in the form of use of force, generally stops as well. Humanitarian intervention looks more like the acts of a "Good Samaritan" than the acts of a belligerent, aggressive invading army.

Humanitarian intervention also is not like normal recourse to war because there are often no clear military objectives, as Henry Shue has argued convincingly.[6] Instead, often the point of a humanitarian war is merely to put pressure on a government, perhaps by motivating the populace to rise up against the government, to stop oppressing a minority

---

[5] See chapter 5 of May, *Aggression and Crimes Against Peace.*

[6] Henry Shue, "Bombing to Rescue: NATO'S 1999 Bombing of Serbia," in *Ethics and Foreign Intervention,* edited by Dean Chatterjee and Don Sheid, New York: Cambridge University Press, 2003, pp. 97–117.

within the State. Indeed, recently humanitarian wars have been waged without putting many troops on the ground at all. Rather, these wars, like NATO's war against Serbia, are waged primarily from the air. And the targets are civilian infrastructure rather than the more standard supply depots of wars in the past. If one meant to launch an invasion, one wouldn't target civilian infrastructure, for this will not win the hearts and minds of the people one will eventually look to for cooperation in a new regime. Humanitarian wars are today fought in such a way that it would make the conquering of a people nearly impossible in the aftermath of the sorts of tactics that are employed, namely, tactics that have a fairly clear short-term goal, merely the ending of attacks on a protected group.

Another approach is to see humanitarian war undertaken to stop genocide as a singular exception to the general prohibition on use of force by one State against another that is not based on self-defense. Jack Donnelly has written about humanitarian intervention for genocide in just such terms.[7] Those who support this view are very cautious because of a concern about mixed motives and overreaching on the part of States that begin intervention for humanitarian reasons but then continue those wars for other reasons. But these cautious theorists have indeed seen genocide as providing possibly the only clear case of justified humanitarian intervention. I am inclined to a similar view, although several significant considerations need to be addressed on the other side of this issue as well.

The problem is that when States use force typically people die, and often those that die from a State's use of force are the innocent, the very class of people who are the intended beneficiaries of the humanitarian intervention. When States launch humanitarian wars by targeting civilian infrastructure, or even population centers, so as to motivate the populace to pressure its government to stop the genocide, significant loss of civilian lives is risked. There are two problems here, and both have been major concerns of wars for hundreds of years. First, there is a deontological concern with the targeting of civilians or of nonmilitary targets. The Just War tradition talks about such tactics under the label of the principle of discrimination (or as it is called in law, "the principle of distinction"). The idea here is that it is normally unjustified to target civilians or civilian facilities. Instead, justifiable tactics in war are

---

[7] Jack Donnelly, *Universal Human Rights in Theory and Practice,* Ithaca, NY: Cornell University Press, 2nd edition, 2003, ch. 14.

supposed to target combatants and other military installations. Justice demands that wars be fought only in such a way that civilian casualties be minimized and certainly not in a way that targets civilians, for war to be justified at all.[8]

There is a sense in which we could see this dispute as involving two nonconsequentialist principles: the principle that requires aiding others when in distress, and the principle that requires that wars be waged only by the use of tactics that do not target civilian populations and infrastructure. I have previously suggested that this dispute could be resolved by postulating a revised normative principle, first proposed by Emir de Vattel in the 18th century. That principle is that we are only entitled to go to the aid of those who are in distress if we do not risk more harm to self and others by so acting than by refraining to act.[9]

There is secondly a consequentialist concern that also emanates from the Just War tradition as well as from contemporary standards of international humanitarian law. The principle of proportionality stipulates that force be used only if the amount of good to be done is not outweighed by the amount of harm caused by the use of the tactics in question. And yet humanitarian wars, with their use of civilian targets and use of bombing that virtually guarantees large-scale civilian infrastructure damage, will be hard pressed to meet this condition. All wars risk significant harm to civilians, but wars waged from high altitudes where there are no clear military targets, as is the norm in humanitarian wars today, risk very significant loss of civilian life for what are often very uncertain gains. For although the hope is to stop a genocidal campaign, that hope must be discounted against the likelihood of success, which is often low or at least hard to calculate in humanitarian wars.[10]

Humanitarian war to stop a genocidal campaign is indeed one of the most seductive reasons to go to war, but there are realities here that should give us pause. And if humanitarian wars to stop a genocidal campaign are not clearly justified, then it is not at all clear when such humanitarian wars would ever be clearly justified. In the next section I will discuss the specific efforts that were taken as well as other things that could have been done to stop the genocide in Rwanda. I will then

---

[8] See May, *War Crimes and Just War*, , for more on this point.
[9] Emer de Vattel, *Le Droit des Gens, ou Principes de la Loi Naturelle* (The Laws of Nations or the Principles of Natural Law; 1758), Washington, DC: Carnegie Institute, 1916, p. 130.
[10] See ch. 13, "Humanitarian Intervention: Problems of Collective Responsibility," in May, *Aggression and Crimes Against Peace*.

take up the challenge of providing a limited justification of such wars. For we cannot sit idly by while another Holocaust occurs. It would be a failure of monumental proportions if the international community felt that it was powerless to go to the aid of an oppressed people that was facing annihilation at the hands of a tyrannical government of the sort that Nazi Germany epitomized.

And yet the facts of contemporary genocides are sometimes not as clear-cut as were those in the Holocaust. As I have argued throughout the book, genocides today do not fit the mold of the Holocaust. Incitement is often as important as central planning, and the individuals who are most responsible may be private citizens rather than heads of State or other political and military leaders. Indeed, if the genocide is perpetrated not by soldiers but by neighbors, armed response by foreign States will not have as clear an effect as would be true when soldiers are carrying out the genocide.

II. The Rwandan Genocide and Intervention

The failure of the international community to intervene in Rwanda had at least two devastating consequences. First, and most obviously, the genocide was allowed to occur and to spread rapidly from village to village until 800,000 people were killed. Second, the ensuing genocide in Rwanda greatly destabilized the region. But there were also grave costs in intervening. Here is how a theorist of international relations has put it:

> In fact, the powder train ignited by the Rwandan genocide helped blow what was then left of the Congolese state virtually out of operational existence. Unfortunately, fear of anarchic conditions might just as easily inspire support for brutish governments and, in the case of civil conflicts, for a quick and decisive victory by the initially more powerful faction, whatever the humanitarian costs.[11]

It is noteworthy that even some of those who favored intervention in Rwanda on humanitarian grounds saw that such intervention could also cause humanitarian problems as well.

Fernando Teson has been one of the most important legal theorists to accept the conflict that tends to ensue when humanitarian intervention

---

[11] Tom J. Farer, "Humanitarian Intervention before and after 9/11," in *Humanitarian Intervention: Ethical, Legal, and Political Dilemmas,* edited by J. L. Holzgrefe and Robert O. Keohane, New York: Cambridge University Press, 2003, p. 86.

is used even in cases of extreme emergency as in the Rwandan genocide. He writes: "So if we think that it is sometimes permissible to allow the deaths of innocent persons in order to save others where the beneficiaries suffer no injustice, a fortiori it should be permissible to allow (regrettably) the deaths of innocent persons in cases where the agent is attempting to rescue persons from ongoing and serious acts of injustice."[12] But, of course, to avail oneself of this type of rationale for intervening in Rwanda, there must be some reasonably good likelihood of success.

Based on the Rwandan genocide and other atrocities in the last decade, the United Nations sponsored a World Summit in 2005 on the responsibility that States have to protect populations. The key clause of the document drafted at the Summit is this:

> The international community, through the United Nations, also has the responsibility to use appropriate diplomatic, humanitarian and other peaceful means, in accordance with Chapters VI and VIII of the Charter, to help protect populations from genocide, war crimes, ethnic cleansing, and crimes against humanity.

If peaceful means fail, the Summit signers committed themselves to use instruments of war as well:

> In this context we are prepared to take collective action, in a timely and decisive manner, through the Security Council, in accordance with the Charter, including Chapter VII...should peaceful means be inadequate.[13]

The Rwandan genocide, and the failure of the international community to intervene, seemingly raised the bar and made many States see the need to recommit themselves to going to the aid of those who were subjected to genocide and other horrible atrocities.

For intervention to have made sense in the Rwandan genocide there must have been both a clear military plan to stop the genocide and a diplomatic plan to make it unlikely that the genocide would take up again after the foreign troops were withdrawn.[14] In Rwanda this was an especially vexing set of problems. Militarily, it would have taken many

---

[12] Fernando Teson, "The Liberal Case for Humanitarian Intervention," in *Humanitarian Intervention: Ethical, Legal, and Political Dilemmas*, edited by J. L. Holzgrefe and Robert O. Keohane, New York: Cambridge University Press, 2003, p. 120.

[13] United Nations General Assembly World Outcome Document.

[14] See Jane Stromseth, "Rethinking Humanitarian Intervention," in *Humanitarian Intervention: Ethical, Legal, and Political Dilemmas*, edited by J. L. Holzgrefe and Robert O. Keohane, New York: Cambridge University Press, 2003, p. 69.

troops on the ground to make a difference given the pervasiveness of the genocide throughout the country. Diplomatically, the hatred was also already so persuasive that it was unclear how to change things in Rwanda so that it was less likely that the genocide would recur after troops were withdrawn. I will take up each of these issues in the following paragraphs.

Militarily, as in most instances of humanitarian intervention, massive troop deployments would have been needed because there were no clear military targets that could have been the subject of aerial bombardment. In addition, as we have seen in Somalia and Sudan, interventions into the center of Africa are not easy for foreign troops. When the genocide is carried out in house-to-house killing of one neighbor by another, it is not possible to stop the genocide by interposing an army between the warring parties. Moving heavily armored vehicles into a jungle region is also fraught with peril. And yet the peril to the troops is even greater if they cannot be supported by such armored units, making it less likely that foreign States will be willing to go into places such as Rwanda for humanitarian reasons. So, although it is true that putting large numbers of foreign troops on the ground in Rwanda probably would have had the initial effect of at least slowing down the genocidal campaign, the military solution to even a slightly more than short-term solution remained deeply problematic. Of course, this is not to say that it was not worth trying, but only that likelihood of success should be factored into any discussion of what should have been done to stop the Rwandan genocide.

Diplomatically and politically, there are special problems because societies where genocide has occurred are typically not robust democracies, but are instead "troubled societies," where there are rarely easy answers about how to reform the authority structure.[15] In Rwanda, things were especially troublesome given the recent history of colonialism and the worry that the Rwandans would reject any intervention that smacked of a return to colonialism and racist regimes. Indeed, as the long Iraq war in the first decade of the 21st century has shown, it is rare that even a very powerful State can remake another State into a regime that will be stable and respect human rights. Although the short-term solution was somewhat problematic, the long-term solution to the Rwandan genocide was deeply problematic.

---

[15] See Robert O. Keohane, "Political Authority after Intervention," in *Humanitarian Intervention: Ethical, Legal, and Political Dilemmas,* edited by J. L. Holzgrefe and Robert O. Keohane, New York: Cambridge University Press, 2003, pp. 278–82.

In considering what should have been done in Rwanda from a humanitarian point of view, it is also worth considering the fact that the Hutus and Tutsis were constructed as different from one another by the Belgian colonial power early in the twentieth century. One might think that this would make it easier to get the ethnic groups to stop killing each other, because there were not centuries or millennia of animosity to deal with. But as in other ethnic animosity, the fact that the ethnic groups shared many things in common did not necessarily make it easier for them to stop hating each other. Psychologically, hatred and states of denial do not seem to be greatly affected by how groups came to the present situation of hating each other. And the response to atrocities is much easier if one keeps abreast of situations where violence is beginning to flare up. Stanley Cohen coins the term "bystander states" to refer to those States that claim not to notice that preparations are occurring that could be prevented.[16]

It is far easier to figure out what sort of humanitarian intervention would make a difference when genocide is still in the preparations stage. In Rwanda it was relatively plain that ethnic hatred was being intensified by radio and newspaper stories, which were transmitted throughout the world for all to hear and see. If only States would have taken their responsibilities seriously and intervened before hostilities got out of control, the genocide could have been significantly lessened. But having said this, it is also much harder to get States to intervene, especially in a military way, if there has not yet been much violence occurring. And we have not yet addressed the question that we began with, namely, what sort of military, or diplomatic, means, could have been employed to stop the genocide.

In the early days of the Rwandan genocide, Hutu troops took an active role, under the direction of the leaders of the presidential guard. In these days it was estimated that a force of 5,000 foreign troops could have made a significant difference in controlling the violence. Samantha Power has documented that the United States government rejected a request that it send those troops to Rwanda in late 1993. Indeed, the United States even refused to fund a United Nations force of 2,500 troops to police the mounting violence.[17] The United States

---

[16] See Stanley Cohen, *States of Denial: Knowing About Atrocities and Suffering,* Cambridge: Polity Press, 2001. See also Fred Grunfeld and Anke Huijboom, *The Failure to Prevent Genocide in Rwanda: The Role of Bystanders,* Leiden: Martinus Nijhoff, 2007.

[17] Power, *A Problem from Hell,* pp. 340–1.

thus became a "bystander state," standing by when it could have acted probably to stop the emerging violence in Rwanda. In my view, after the violence spread to the countryside, it was no longer an easy question of putting foreign troops on the ground in Rwanda, but initially this may very well have been effective.

Given my analysis of who is most responsible for the genocide when it moved into the countryside, those who intentionally incited the genocide played a key role. Something else that could have been done, and was discussed, was stopping the hate-filled radio transmissions of RTML. The radio station's tower could have been destroyed, the broadcasts could have been jammed, or there could have been "counter-broadcasts" transmitted through the auspices of foreign States. Here, according to Samantha Power, the United States was best placed to act. A Pentagon analysis concluded that the jamming would be too difficult and costly and instead urged that resources be devoted "to use air to assist in Rwanda in the [food] relief effort."[18] This analysis is in keeping with the view that a civil war was occurring because of conflict over scarce food resources, rather than an ethnic conflict that turned into a genocide.

In addition, foreign States could have tried to block the vitriolic editorials from the newspaper *Kangura*. But this would have been very difficult indeed, especially because there was an underground effort to reprint and disseminate these editorials long after they first appeared in print. To do something about this source of incitement, action would have been necessary several years before the genocide. Also, the role of the CDR party should not be underestimated in the incitement to genocide effort. Yet, again, it is not clear what a foreign State could have done to curtail a political party within Rwanda that would not have risked a backlash internally or at the very least the establishment of a precedent of interfering with the seemingly democratic process of a sovereign State.

Not only did foreign States, or the United Nations, fail to take any action to stop the RTLM broadcasts or *Kangura* editorials, but most foreign States followed the lead of the United States in never admitting that genocide was occurring in Rwanda until most of the slaughter had ended. This last point is very significant because it meant that the United States was part of a movement to deny the normal international legal obligations that would be triggered when genocide occurs. A small

---

[18] Ibid., pp. 371–2, quoting a May 5, 1994, memo from Frank Wisner, under secretary of defense for policy.

United Nations peacekeeping force was sent to Rwanda, which was later replaced by a force that was given more firepower and authority to act to stop violence. But these forces were very small and never really amounted to a significant effort at humanitarian intervention to stop the Rwandan genocide. At least in part this was because the world community was very slow to acknowledge that genocide was occurring in Rwanda, and in part because it was unclear what efforts would have been successful, especially after the violence spread to the countryside.

As mentioned earlier, since the Rwandan genocide the world community has been spurred to set up principles and procedures that would make it more likely that intervention would occur in future genocides. The UN 2005 World Outcome declaration on the Responsibility to Protect (R2P) makes reference to situations such as that of the Rwandan genocide when it says: "Each individual State has the responsibility to protect its population from genocide, war crimes, ethnic cleansing, and crimes against humanity. This responsibility entails the prevention of such crimes, including their incitement, through appropriate and necessary means."[19] The reference to incitement, as we have seen, is especially important for situations like those in Rwanda.

The change in emphasis from humanitarian intervention to responsibility to protect is perhaps one of the most significant in recent years. As Williams and Stewart say: "In the face of the tension between the emerging norm of human security and sovereignty, the debate on a legal basis for intervention has now shifted...from the right to intervene to one about the responsibility of states to protect innocent lives and the duties inherent in sovereignty."[20] But significant challenges remain to the emerging new norm. In an especially astute comment, Williams and Stewart indicate the source of the potential problems:

> Despite broad acceptance of the Responsibility to Protect, the international community has failed to find a legal basis in which to seat the concept. The Responsibility to Protect argument essentially adopted the moral approach of just war theory, but not the legal framework. Interestingly, as the historical advocates of the just war approach placed right authority with the Pope, those who advocate for a "responsibility to protect" place that authority with the United Nations.[21]

[19] United Nations General Assembly World Outcome Document.
[20] Paul R. Williams and Meghan E. Stewart, "Humanitarian Intervention: The New Missing Link in the Fight to Prevent Crimes against Humanity and Genocide?" *Case Western Reserve Journal of International Law*, vol. 40, nos. 1 & 2, 2007–8, p. 105.
[21] Ibid., p. 106.

Other theorists have been more hopeful, even as many of the optimists have admitted that "There is an awkward structure in the U.N.'s mandate for R2P."[22]

The United Nations and the world community have made a clear and profound statement of the need to think of humanitarian intervention not merely as a right but as a responsibility of States. What will be the outcome of such a change in wording and resolve is unclear. Grunfeld and Huijboom ask the relevant question for this chapter: "The final question to be raised in this context is whether the genocide in Rwanda would have been prevented or halted, had the "responsibility to protect" been in place in 1994. Both decisionmakers and scholars are rather pessimistic in their answers to this question." They end their book on the complicity of the world community, as bystanders, for the genocide in Rwanda on a hopeful note. Things are better now than in 1994, they argue. Even if such genocides will not now be prevented, nonetheless there is now greater awareness of the responsibility of the world community for such atrocities as the Rwandan genocide and such "awareness is a necessary condition for any policy in this field."[23]

III. Humanitarian Intervention to Stop Genocide: A Limited Defense

If we follow in line with the earlier sections of this book, we will ask whether focusing on loss of group identity and status also makes it any easier to justify the use of humanitarian wars to stop genocides. The first point is that if we are interested in proportionality issues, it might be that we will be forced to think of more than merely the possible deaths in a genocidal campaign to be balanced against the lives lost by the waging of the humanitarian war. We will also have to take into account the harms to those who survive the genocide, harms that may end up being nearly as harmful as if the people had died. The loss of status and social rootedness, in addition to the loss of significant identity-conferring group memberships, puts more in the balance than would be true if we were focusing only on the deaths that occur in genocide.

Second, the harms, short of death, that befall people because of genocide cannot be measured merely in the short run if the "loss of group

[22] David Scheffer, "Atrocity Crimes Framing the Responsibility to Protect," *Case Western Reserve Journal of International Law*, vol. 40, nos. 1 & 2, 2007–8, p. 134.

[23] Grunfeld and Huijboom, *The Failure to Prevent Genocide in Rwanda*, pp. 246–7.

identity" thesis is true. There will be long-term repercussions, many of which will be at least as significant as the short-term harms that are the more obvious results of a genocidal campaign. Think of those who are Holocaust survivors, and who have spent their lives since the 1940s racked with emotional distress over what happened to themselves as well as to their friends and loved ones. Such considerations affect the proportionality assessments and also the assessment of how nonconsequentialist factors might be part of a full understanding of why it is so important to confront genocide even with tactics that we might otherwise be reluctant to employ.

Third, focusing on loss of group identity forces us out of seeing the harm of atrocities not only in terms of deaths. Indeed, as in the case of torture, the "loss of group identity and status" thesis contemplates the possibility that there might be something nearly as bad as death itself. This fact helped us see how genocide, which need not involve any deaths at all, could nonetheless be one of the worst atrocities. We are here given a reason to think that even if humanitarian intervention is not justified in other atrocity cases, it may be justified in the case of genocide nonetheless. We have not said, however, how such a justification might go through. I turn to that task in the final few pages of this section. But so far we have identified a kind of atrocity that seems in many respects to be one of the worst and one for which it might make sense to employ nearly whatever tactics are at our disposal to stop or prevent it.

The defense of humanitarian intervention that I now offer is a limited one, in that it is offered for genocide or genocide-like cases, and only for some of those cases. Some humanitarian intervention can be justified on rather straightforward consequentialist grounds if it turns out that the loss of civilian life and civilian infrastructure that often accompanies humanitarian war can be outweighed by the prevention of significant loss of life or inroads into the quality of life of those who would be victims of genocide. The focus on loss of group identity and status has allowed us to see the full weight of these losses in genocidal campaigns. It is not the sheer number of deaths that is so important, for, as we have seen, if this were the most important thing, genocides would not be the worst, or even one of the worst, of crimes, because genocide can occur without any such deaths. Rather, it is what genocide does to the quality of life, and death, that might offset the loss of civilian life and infrastructure of some wars to stop genocides.

But it will not be possible to condemn all genocides and similarly justify all humanitarian intervention to stop or prevent genocide. The main reason for this is that the consequences of fighting humanitarian wars are often themselves so horrible that they sometimes override the good that these wars will obviously do. This is to say that extremely bad consequences may override even very important and laudable goals that may be required on nonconsequentialist grounds. There is a difficult normative issue lying in the background here, namely, how to assess considerations that arise from different approaches to moral principles. Should consequentialist considerations be seen to outweigh strong duties in the moral domain? My tentative answer is that consequentialist considerations are always on the table, especially in emergency or extreme situations.

One could argue that although the tactics necessary to stop a genocide may themselves be deeply unjust, yet the result of morally generated hesitation in stopping genocide is that there will be a horrible precedent established. States will learn that they can pursue genocidal campaigns, or allow them to exist in their territories, without major challenge from other States that will worry about the morality of the tactics they would need to employ to stop the genocide. Indeed, this problem is like the problem of the civilian shields that have been employed on the battlefield for hundreds of years to stop conscientious army leaders from destroying military targets. It is also true that if we think of our strong moral obligations as matters that we can avoid when the situation is such that meeting our duties may cause harm, even extreme harm, then our duties don't really amount to much in any event.

Thomas Nagel has argued that it may be necessary to support illegal and unjust institutions in the short run to accomplish a more just global environment in the long run (perhaps the very long run).[24] Especially because of concerns about State sovereignty, it will be very hard to establish anything like a global system of justice without engaging in some forms of injustice. For any given new international institution that has any teeth to it, sovereign States will claim that their rights have been trampled. This is most serious when wars are waged against those States, clearly violating the States' territorial integrity or political independence. Perhaps one such institution is the humanitarian war. I am sympathetic to such a suggestion, but I wish to voice some continuing concerns that also need to be addressed.

It may seem odd to think of humanitarian war as a kind of institution that might promote global justice, but this is indeed the insight that has

---

[24]   Thomas Nagel, "The Problem of Global Justice," *Philosophy & Public Affairs,* vol. 33, no. 2, Spring 2005, pp. 113–47.

led many people to support such wars as the new example of paradigmatically justified wars, and is clearly the impetus behind the Responsibility
to Protect movement. When States see themselves as bound to go to
the aid of not only other States but also of peoples in any part of the
world, then we will have a truly cosmopolitan moral and political order.
Indeed, this is just what is countenanced when each of the new multi-
lateral treaties has a clause at the end that calls on all States to do what
they can to enforce the terms of the treaty.[25] So we should be concerned
if the worries I have expressed about humanitarian intervention would
set back the attempt to create such a cosmopolitan order by institutions
such as those encouraging humanitarian responses to the world's worst
atrocities.

Yet there is another kind of precedent that is nearly as worrisome as
the precedent of not responding to humanitarian crises in the world.
I worry about the precedent of letting good intentions, and humanitarian intentions are extremely good, override what are clearly known
to be the terrible consequences of war on civilian populations. Among
other problems, good intentions are often also accompanied by mixed
motives. We can see this most clearly in the recent war on terror that
the United States claims to be waging. Even if we grant that the political
leaders in the United States have the best of intentions in waging this
war, it is also quite clear that they are sometimes motivated to take the
steps they take on grounds that are not laudable at all, such as the selfish
desire to control the world's oil reserves. Indeed, it is very easy for a State
to declare that it is entering a war for humanitarian goals even as that
State also is pursuing the war for other reasons. Nazi Germany claimed
to be pursuing humanitarian goals in the Sudetenland, namely, to stop
the oppression of native Germans in that region, even as it clearly sought
to bring Czechoslovakia into its sphere of influence for other reasons.[26]

Given the possible abuse of the rationale of humanitarian intervention, we should be especially critical of such humanitarian rationales
even in the face of stopping or preventing genocide. I make this final
claim with much ambivalence because I recognize that this could mean
that States will be more reluctant than they already are to intervene
in cases of genocide such as that in Darfur. As I said at the beginning
of this chapter, I do not wish to be seen as having provided one more

[25] See M. Cherif Bassiouni and Edward M. Wise, *Aut Dedere Aut Judicare: The Duty to Extradite or Prosecute in International Law,* Dordrecht: Martinus Nijhoff, 1995.
[26] I discuss this issue in greater detail in chapter 8 of May, *Aggression and Crimes Against Peace.*

theoretical exposition of genocide that utterly fails to speak to those
who are the victims and their families. Yet I have come to a similar position out of respect for those others who will be victims, and their families, when even very well-intentioned humanitarian intervention occurs
in such places as Darfur. As the old saying goes, we cannot do just one
thing, for with each thing we do, there are new consequences. In waging humanitarian war to end genocide we will also be risking the lives
of many civilians. Perhaps someday we will live in a world where the
consequences of intervention are less worrisome than the harm to be
prevented by humanitarian intervention.

IV. Objections

One of the most serious objections to my limited defense of humanitarian intervention is that I have not given sufficient weight to the fact
that the victims of genocides are completely innocent and hence even
more deserving than people normally are of being rescued by humanitarian intervention. In other respects I myself have strongly defended
the idea that there is an obligation of the international community to
act in defense of others, especially innocent others. This has been recognized in the just war tradition at least as long ago as Augustine in the
fourth century A.D., who thought that the defense of others was even a
more serious justification to go to war than was self-defense, because the
former was more selfless than the latter.

My response is that I am quite sympathetic to this objection, and have
struggled with it ever since embarking on this book project on genocide. I agree that the international community has a heightened duty
to go to the rescue of those who are innocent. But there is a serious
question of what is the best way to rescue those who are innocent in a
genocide. Using the blunt instrument of war is a very risky way to try
to rescue the innocent, and should always be a last resort, rather than
a first resort, even given what is at stake in genocide. Also, as I argued
earlier, in Chapter 9, there are situations where there is no unambigu-
ous group of victims, because of the very widespread complicity that
exists in many genocides. So it is not as clear-cut as one might expect
that showing respect for the innocent will lead to a robust defense of
humanitarian intervention.

A second objection is that I have relied too heavily throughout this
chapter on what are admittedly consequentialist considerations, giving insufficient consideration to deontological considerations that are

especially apt in cases that involve serious and sustained violations of the right to life of the victims. Consequentialist considerations are almost always significant, but when they abut claims of rights, especially rights of the most fundamental sort, consequentialist considerations need at very least to be shown to be of overriding importance, and this is hardly ever the case, and surely not merely because there are some risks involved.

Once again, I am not unconcerned with such an objection. Indeed, the model I have sketched has not been weighted to either consequentialist or deontological considerations. In general I support a mixed model where we follow certain rules and where exceptions are made to those rules in situations where there are extreme emergency situations. Genocide is certainly such an extreme emergency, but this doesn't mean that we should abandon consideration of rules. In fact, I am concerned with the application of a rule such as the one respecting the right to life in its relevance to both the need for humanitarian intervention and in the restraint that we should show in its use. I have argued that humanitarian intervention is justified in some cases, and that in those cases the urgency is the reason for its justification. I do not wish to undervalue the importance of the rights of the victims in genocide cases – but only to point out that there are other rights involved as well.

The third objection I wish to consider concerns the nature of humanitarian intervention in genocide cases. Throughout this book I have been suggesting that it is hard to explain the unique moral harm of genocide, and that humanitarian intervention is likewise harder to justify than people might otherwise think. But, it might be objected, even if the harm of genocide is somewhat more difficult to capture than people think, genocide is still very bad, in fact, it is certainly one of the very worst things that can be perpetrated on a people. It needs to be stopped at nearly any cost, and I have muddied the waters in ways that will make it harder for well-meaning people to do what they think needs to be done in the light of such extreme crises as that of genocide.

In response, I do not wish to discourage well-meaning people from acting to stop genocides. At most, it is true, I wish to slow them down if they are contemplating using war as a means to stop genocide. But I do not wish to diminish the idea that genocide remains one of the very worst of things that can be perpetrated. And at least in part this is because there are nearly always other less violent means available for halting genocide and especially for preventing it in the first place. Indeed, the prevention of genocide is hardly ever secured through war.

It is the prevention of genocide that needs to be given far more consideration than it is normally given. In the final chapter I will discuss some of the aspects of the deterrence of genocide, namely, those having to do with the punishment of those who are responsible for genocides at the moment. I will argue that criminal trials that aim at such deterrence also have an important role to play in reconciliation as well, and it is reconciliation in societies that have a history of cycles of violence that is a key factor in the prevention of genocides in the future.

Finally, let me consider the objection that I have placed too much emphasis on just one kind of humanitarian response to genocide, namely, use of violent force through war. Surely there are other means that also can be employed that would count as humanitarian response on the part of foreign States to genocide. When we take away the stigma of war, the consequentialist considerations do not weigh so heavily against intervention. Indeed, if the response is taken on multiple levels, where recourse to violent force is only one of several strategies undertaken simultaneously, the adverse consequences will not normally be overridden by the clear good that comes from stopping a genocide.

As I indicated earlier in this chapter when discussing possible responses to the Rwandan genocide, I am not unsympathetic to this point. Surely, nonviolent means should be employed first to try to stop genocide, and a mixture of nonviolent and violent means can sometimes be effective at stopping genocide. When measures must be started well in advance of the worst of the genocidal violence, it is very hard to get the world community to interfere with a sovereign State. Of course, we might be considerably better off some day if we have a more cosmopolitan world community than the one we now have that is dominated by such concerns about sovereignty. I have elsewhere suggested that eliminating or even weakening States is not necessarily something that will better protect human rights.[27] Suffice it here to say that we do not live in such a cosmopolitan world, and from the perspective of nonideal theory we must deal with the situations that exist or that can reasonably be expected to occur in the not too distant future.

In this chapter I have discussed one of the seemingly least controversial topics related to genocide, namely, whether war should be waged to stop it. I have argued that this issue is much more problematic than is often thought today. I began by casting doubt on the unique moral wrong of genocide but suggesting that, as we saw in previous chapters,

---

[27] See my treatment of this topic in ibid., especially chs. 3 and 10.

there was still a very serious wrong that genocide embodied. I then argued that humanitarian intervention to stop genocide has many attendant risks, some of which are as important, or nearly so, as what the wars of humanitarian intervention aim to stop. Nonetheless, I then provided a limited defense of humanitarian intervention in genocide cases, largely drawn in terms of the comparing of the risks of engaging versus not engaging in humanitarian intervention in such cases. Finally, I considered four objections to my proposal that forced me to admit how ambivalent I am about urging caution by those contemplating humanitarian intervention in genocide cases. Humanitarian intervention, even in cases of genocide, should be a live option, but one that people are slow to use, especially when diplomatic and other avenues have not been exhausted. I now turn to the use of criminal trials in the aftermath of genocide, in part, as a way to deter future genocides.

13

Reconciliation, Criminal Trials, and Genocide

In this final chapter I will draw on themes from previous chapters to discuss some of the main criticisms of having international criminal trials for genocide. The main objection is that trials obscure and may impede other important goals, such as reconciliation. Indeed, the International Criminal Tribunal for Rwanda has defended itself against critics by claiming that "The Chamber recalls that its fundamental purpose of holding individuals accountable for their conduct is intended to "contribute to the process of national reconciliation and to the restoration and maintenance of peace."[1] Thus, the tribunals themselves are aware of the need for international trials to advance multiple goals.

It is often thought that genocide is the easy case in international law. Genocide is so horrific and "evil" that its confrontation through criminal prosecutions of the monsters who perpetrate it is uncontroversial. Yet, many theorists, such as Martha Minow, have argued that criminal trials retard reconciliation in the aftermath of genocide. Minnow has said that "reconciliation is not a goal of trials, except in the most abstract sense."[2] I will argue that in genocide cases certain kinds of criminal trials can advance rather than retard reconciliation. There are many uses of the term reconciliation, including the idea that any tensions and attendant ill-will between parties is diminished. Instead, I will be discussing what I will call robust political reconciliation, which requires a long-term solution that focuses on reducing complicity.

I will argue that the key to robust political reconciliation is that the underlying causes of violence and tension are diminished significantly,

---

[1] *Prosecutor v. Ferdinand Nahimana, Jean-Bosco Barayagwiza, and Hassan Ngeze,* Trial Chamber Judgment, para 109, quoting S. C. Res. 955, S/RES/955 (1994), 8 November 1994.

[2] Martha Minow, *Between Vengeance and Forgiveness,* Boston: Beacon Press, 1998, p. 26.

along with the development of a reasonable degree of trust among the previously conflicting parties. I will then explain why reconciliation may be especially problematic if trials for genocide proceed as they have in the recent past, also suggesting how criminal trials, in modified form, could nonetheless advance the goals of reconciliation in the future. I use the debate on whether to hold criminal trials for those responsible for genocide as an occasion to get clearer about political reconciliation in war ravaged societies.

Several reasons are typically given for why criminal trials make matters worse rather than better for reconciling a society ravaged by these atrocities:

a) Criminal trials excite and inflame both sides to a conflict because of the combative nature of trials, and obscure the truth about the atrocity.[3]

b) Criminal trials demonize the perpetrators, thereby further inflaming the group from which the perpetrators come.[4]

c) Criminal trials seek retribution and deterrence, goals that are at odds with the goal of reconciliation.[5]

d) International criminal trials render invisible the crucial role of bystanders, thereby making long-term reconciliation very difficult.[6]

I will attempt to rebut each of these arguments. In what follows, I argue:

a) Criminal trials need not inflame

b) Only "show trials" demonize in this way

c) Retribution and deterrence are not incompatible with reconciliation

d) An international criminal regime can focus on bystanders, and can do so best by providing strong support for defendants' rights.

In this chapter I argue that criminal trials can play an important role in facilitating reconciliation. Especially when there is vigorous defense,

---

[3] See Martha Minow, Between *Vengeance and Forgiveness,* Boston: Beacon Press, 1998.
[4] See Martti Koskenniemi, "Between Impunity and Show Trials," *Max Planck Yearbook of United Nations Law,* vol. 6, 2002, pp. 1–35.
[5] See the essays in Robert I. Rotberg and Dennis Thompson, editors, *Truth v. Justice,* Princeton: Princeton University Press, 2000.
[6] See Laurel Fletcher, "From Indifference to Engagement: Bystanders and International Criminal Justice," *Michigan Journal of International Law,* vol. 26, Summer 2005, pp. 1013–95.

the role played by many people, including bystanders, can become known and accepted. To support this view, I will first provide a sketch of the problem that includes a discussion of the definition of genocide in international law along with some of the conceptual and normative problems with this definition. I will also consider several cases that will help us see what actions of individuals have triggered the charge of genocide in international criminal trials. Second, I consider what effects the trials seem to have had on the goal of reconciliation. Some of the features of genocide make reconciliation considerably harder if there is a criminal trial for the genocidal acts; yet trials are especially well suited to deal with crimes like genocide, that is, crimes where complicity and intention play such a large role. Third, I reassess the meaning of reconciliation in the context of genocide. Fourth, I ask how the role of bystanders, so crucial to understanding genocide, can be accommodated in criminal trials as a means toward reconciling the goals of justice and reconciliation in these trials. Fifth, I discuss how the *gacaca* process in Rwanda has expanded the use of criminal trials better to deal with bystanders in genocide cases. Finally, I discuss how the expressivist normative goals of criminal trials can be consistent with reconciliation when we focus on the role played by bystanders in genocide and other mass atrocities.

I. Genocide Trials

Throughout I will argue for the seemingly counterintuitive view that reconciliation is made easier the more defendants' rights are respected in international trials for genocide. This thesis will become plausible when we view the goals of trials against the backdrop of the rule of law. In the current section, I briefly raise the question of what makes those who commit genocide the worst of all criminal offenders, especially given that those who commit genocide do not appear to be all that different from normal members of the community.

Recent international criminal trials for genocide seem to be a significant advance in the movement toward a global recognition of human rights and the international rule of law. Yet such trials are not necessarily an advance in reconciling parties of ethnic wars. It has seemed to certain theorists that criminal trials are able to do only one of two tasks: either to provide retribution or deterrence for the perpetrators or to teach about the truth of the atrocity as a way toward healing.[7] When

---

[7] See Rotberg and Thompson, *Truth v. Justice.*

criminal trials are structured to provide the fairest result for defendants, it seems that it is difficult to get to the larger truth of a genocidal campaign. In part, this is because individual defendants normally stand accused of only playing a small role in the genocide, and to let in evidence about the larger genocidal campaign will seemingly prejudice the case against the individual defendant. Even the Nuremberg trial could be accused of failing to give the individual defendants their due because 22 defendants were tried together, surely making it hard for the judges to sort out who did what.

Consider a recent case that was tried as genocide case, and an atrocity case about to go to trial, in international criminal law. The first case concerns the atrocity in Srebrenica, where units of the Bosnian Serb army launched an attack against Muslims in what the United Nations had declared to be a "safe area" in Bosnia. Over the course of nine days, 25,000 Muslims attempted to flee from the attacks. But their attempts were largely futile as 7,000 were systematically slaughtered and the rest left homeless.

Here is how the International Criminal Tribunal for the Former Yugoslavia (ICTY) described this atrocity:

> Military aged Bosnian Muslim men from Srebrenica...were taken prisoner, detained in brutal conditions and then executed. More than 7,000 people were never seen again. The events of the nine days from July 10–19, 1995, in Srebrenica defy description in their horror and their implications for humankind's capacity to revert to acts of brutality under the stresses of conflict.[8]

One of the trials concerned Radislav Krstic, a Bosnian Serb general who commanded a unit called the Drina Corps, which had responsibility for security in the area surrounding Srebrenica.[9] Despite his claims to the contrary, the tribunal held that "forensic evidence supports the Prosecution's claim that, following the take-over of Srebrenica, thousands of Bosnian Muslim men were summarily executed and consigned to mass graves."[10]

The problem with this case was that although Krstic and the unit he commanded had responsibility for the area where the alleged genocide occurred, it was very unclear what role if any Krstic played in the

---

[8]   *Prosecutor v. Radislav Krstic,* International Criminal Tribunal for the Former Yugoslavia, case no. IT-98–33-T, Trial Chamber Judgment, 2 August 2001, paras. 1–2.
[9]   Ibid., para. 3.
[10]   Ibid., para. 73.

genocide. At most it appeared that he knew about the executions and did not order his unit to try to stop them. The executions appear to have been ordered by Krstic's superior commander who controlled a different unit. That commander, General Mladic, has not yet been captured. The ICTY Trial Chamber admitted that the evidence was "conflicting."[11] General Krstic "generally supervised the transportation operation"[12] but did not order that any of the Muslims in Srebrenica be killed.[13] Krstic was not even present at the sites where the killings took place.[14] And Krstic was heard, by more than one witness, to say that no harm should befall those who were being transported out of the safe haven.[15] But there was also evidence that General Krstic must have known that mistreatment[16] if not killing was taking place,[17] and did not take action to stop the killings or to punish the perpetrators. Krstic was convicted of being a direct perpetrator of genocide.

The Appeals Chamber of the ICTY took up the Krstic case and reversed his conviction as a direct perpetrator of genocide.[18] The court found that the prosecution had not established that General Krstic had the requisite genocidal intent for direct perpetration of genocide.[19] Instead the Appeals Chamber ruled that the evidence established only that Krstic was guilty of aiding and abetting the genocide. Because there was not conclusive evidence that Krstic did any killing on his own, or that he had a genocidal intent, he could not be a direct perpetrator.

In the Krstic case, although the atrocities were some of the worst since the Holocaust, in my view there was significant reason to doubt what role these individuals played. One of the reasons why this has proved such a difficult subject, and one about which there was considerable disagreement in the subsequent appeals of these convictions, was that these defendants seemed to be responsible for not doing more to stop the killing, rather than for any explicit acts of killing. It is also true that these defendants were successful and admired professionals who seemed not to fit the picture of a mass killer or even of one who would facilitate mass atrocity. When they were tried for the crime of genocide,

---

[11] Ibid., para. 328.
[12] Ibid., para. 347.
[13] Ibid., para. 361.
[14] Ibid., para. 357.
[15] Ibid., para. 358.
[16] Ibid., para. 367.
[17] Ibid., paras. 379 and 385.
[18] *Prosecutor v. Radislav Krstic*, Appeals Chamber Judgment, paras. 137–8.
[19] Ibid., paras. 98 and 137.

the people back home did not vilify, but often applauded, them and instead vilified the courts that convicted them. In genocides there is typically widespread complicity, and singling out just a few as guilty may seem both unfair and to tar the rest of the population with the same brush. Indeed, if the main case against Krstic was that he did nothing to stop the genocide, similar charges could have been lodged against many others, including Croats and Muslims as well as Serbs.

Second, let me say just a few words about the current Darfur atrocity. In Sudan, 400,000 people have perished in the Darfur genocide, and over a million have become refugees. The newly constituted International Criminal Court (ICC) was given the Darfur case in March 2005 by the Security Council of the UN. No trials have yet been held, but some critics of the ICC have argued that the impending trials have complicated an already difficult political situation in Sudan. Even if it is possible to pick out a few of the worst participants in the atrocity, there are reasons to think that holding trials in which such individuals are convicted and sentenced does not advance other important goals in the aftermath of war.

Here is how one critic, Stephen Rademaker, makes the case against the use of trials in such cases.

> War crimes prosecutors didn't stop the genocide in Yugoslavia, and they haven't stopped it in Darfur either. To the contrary, the example of the Balkans, where peacekeepers in Bosnia and Kosovo have tracked down and arrested war crimes indictees, appears to have hardened the opposition of Sudanese officials to a U.N. force. Quite predictably, those officials are saying they're not interested in a U.N. peacekeeping force in Darfur if, as in the Balkans, it would offer them a one-way trip in handcuffs to the Hague.[20]

Such critics of international criminal trials see these trials as impediments to reconciliation.

The complaint against the Darfur trials is somewhat different from that concerning the Krstic case. Here the problem is that even indicting the political or military leaders can cause destabilization and undermine efforts to stop genocides. The idea here is similar to the other case in another respect though. For there is a risk of inflaming already heightened passions when well-respected figures in a society are accused

---

[20] Stephen Rademaker, "Unwitting Party to Genocide: The International Criminal Court Is Complicating Efforts to Save Darfur," *Washington Post*, January 11, 2007, p. A25.

of such horrendous crimes as genocide even though their roles in the
genocide are not crystal clear.

II. Justice, Truth, or Reconciliation

The trial tactics of international tribunals and courts often mimic those
in advanced Western democracies, along with their attendant problems.
In U.S. domestic criminal trials, especially very high-profile capital murder trials, prosecutors and defense lawyers seem incapable of resisting
the transformation of the trial into an emotional appeal to the jurors
that clouds any possibility of objective judgment. In the sentencing
phase of such trials, prosecutors and defense lawyers often provide duel-
ing films that provide "a day in the life" of the victim or of the defendant
as a way to emotionally manipulate the jury to reach a certain verdict.
Sometimes the use of these films ends up being worse than the most
manipulative funeral orations in Roman times. In high-profile international trials, especially that of Milosevic and Saddam Hussein, similar emotional appeals were seen in these trials to that of high-profile
American trials.

The problem is that ethics requirements of lawyers seemingly demand
that they do all that they can, with only a few restraints, to get the best
result for the parties they represent. The best result is not likely to be a
pedagogic spectacle of the truth, but rather whatever portrays their side
of the case in the best possible light. The U.S. Supreme Court, in *Payne
v. Tennessee,* recognized this fact when it mandated that both defense
lawyers and prosecutors had to be allowed to use incredibly partialistic
tactics in capital trials.[21] In addition, there is the further problem of
allowing the high-profile defendant to defend himself or herself and
indict the tribunal for the benefit of his supporters back home. As long
as lawyers work within a certain kind of adversary system of law, one that
does not restrain them much at all, and at the moment all international
criminal trials proceed in this way, it will be very difficult indeed for
lawyers to meet their duties to the parties they represent and still make
it possible that the world will be taught who really were the perpetrators
in an atrocity like a genocide.

---

[21] See *Payne v. Tennessee,* 501 U.S. 808 (1990), where the United States Supreme Court
ruled that prosecutors were allowed to introduce "victim impact" evidence to establish the loss to the victim or the victim's family, including testimony from loved ones
about how much they have emotionally suffered.

Yet there is no necessity that lawyers in international courts abuse the system in the way that occurs in U.S. capital murder cases. There are two things to say about combative trials, one negative and one positive. First, part of the difficulty is that standard rule of law issues seem to prohibit interference with trial tactics of prosecutors and defense attorneys. Yet there are many restrictions on trial tactics already recognized as legitimate, such as are captured in the U.S. Federal Rules of Evidence concerning hearsay testimony and references to the previous similar acts of defendants. And there is no reason why restrictions on emotional appeals cannot pass rule of law standards if the restrictions are applied to both sides of the lawsuit. Indeed, I would have thought that the U.S. Supreme Court in *Payne v. Tennessee* would have done better to restrict both sides from displaying impact evidence rather than allowing both sides to do so.

Second, aggressively, although not emotionally, defending and prosecuting makes truth more likely to emerge. One doesn't have to support John Stuart Mill's free market place of ideas to see that vigorous telling of two or more sides of a story can lead to the truth. Indeed, a vigorous defense often means enlarging the scope of people who can be held responsible for a crime. So my proposal is that both sides in an international criminal trial be restricted to very minimal emotional appeals, even when it may appear to be deserved because of either the horrific character of the crime or the "patently" innocent nature of the defendants. The rule of law is not impeded when both sides to a lawsuit have to operate by the same standards.

The current genocide cases point to the further problem that the truth of what one defendant did is often very hard to connect to the truth of the larger atrocity. Criminal trials for genocide generally focus on the specific role that individuals played, not on the larger genocidal campaign. And it will not normally be clear-cut what role these individuals played, causing most of the trial to focus on the specific acts and intentions of the defendant. If there are really going to be fair international criminal trials, rather than mere "show trials," then it seems that there should be a focus on what the defendant did, and the evidence should not go much beyond this – for then we would risk convicting the defendant for what others did.[22] And yet, it is also true that without paying attention to the larger circumstances of the defendant's crime, it will

[22] See Douglas, *The Memory of Judgment.*

be hard to make sense out of what the defendant did and even harder to understand the causes of the larger atrocity.[23]

As the trial takes into account all of the subtleties of the defendant's role in the crime, we seemingly move further from the kind of truth of the atrocity that the larger population might be seeking. Indeed, reconciliation might also be hampered if what the populace wants, or thinks it wants, in order to bring the horrific events of the past to a close is for there to be a telling of the complete story that makes sense of the causes and harms of the genocide. In addition, reconciliation might be stymied because the truth of the defendant's role may be so ambiguous as to diminish the significance of the larger atrocity. If it turned out that the perpetrators of the genocide who stand trial were merely following orders or thought they were doing what was right at the time, the victims of genocide will be puzzled and not able to express their resentment and recrimination as they had hoped.

Trials have played a significant role in reconciliation since their inception. The main idea here is that what community members most want, in many cases, is that perpetrators be identified and appropriately punished for what they have done.[24] Such an understanding turns on the fact that the perpetrator gets his or her comeuppance and is no longer seen as having committed harms with no cost. In addition, criminal trials have to a certain extent provided a kind of closure, although this is not necessarily consistent with reconciliation because it depends on whether the community is indeed ready for such a closing act. Once the defendant is brought to answer for his or her crimes, one chapter is brought to an end. Yet it is also true that the kind of closure effected here may not be the best for achieving true reconciliation.

There are several things that can be done to make international criminal trials more helpful in reconciliation than they often are. One practical proposal is to have the trial separated into two parts: one concerning the larger genocide, and the second the role played by the defendant.[25] Some international criminal trials now proceed in just this manner, although not formally partitioned. This was true in the first of the ICTY cases, *Prosecutor v. Tadic*, where hundreds of pages of the

---

[23] See May, "Act and Circumstance in the Crime of Aggression."
[24] The work of Antony Duff can be cited here as providing an especially clear idea of how punishment has played an important role in trials and also in reconciliation.
[25] In the United States, capital murder cases are formally divided, with the first part concerning the defendant's guilt, and with the second, typically held at least a day later, concerning the defendant's sentencing.

final judgment were devoted to the larger context of Tadic's crime. Of course, without actual partitioning, it will be too easy for the defendant to be linked with all aspects of the atrocity not merely to that part for which he or she is accused. But there is nothing in principle wrong with having criminal trials play two roles. This is especially true of crimes such as aggression and genocide where the individual is being tried for a role played in a large atrocity, and where it is relevant whether or not that atrocity occurred and what precisely were its features; indeed, this is part of what needs to be proved. This can be accomplished in other ways than through a trial, but trials can be effective here.

Criminal trials can help deal with the idea that genocide is not primarily wrong because of the killing that is involved. This can be accomplished by the focus on the intentions of the defendant that also matches the focus on the intending to destroy a group that is the cornerstone of the crime of genocide in international law. For the crime of genocide is largely aimed at the destruction of a protected group, which can be accomplished by various means as I indicated above. In many ways it is the intention of the defendant that is most important. And although it is true that all crimes involve intention elements, genocide has two and possibly three different mental elements. Trials can be especially good at getting at these special *mens rea* crimes, as we saw in Chapter 7. The *mens rea* requirements of the crime of genocide are especially apt for the goals of reconciliation.

For centuries criminal trials have focused on the intentions of defendants – where the guilty mind of that defendant is absolutely crucial for conviction. And here, although it is not well recognized, the key consideration is not motive, but intent, not one's desires, but what one aimed at. Thus, the prosecution does not have to prove that the genocide defendant acted out of evil motives, but only that the genocide defendant aimed at destroying a protected group. The defendant may have had the best of motives, namely, compassion or patriotism, and yet could still be convicted of genocide if the defendant's aim was to destroy a group. Often intent is inferred from behavior, and this will also surely be true in genocide cases as well.[26] Yet the behavior need not be the killing of people, as we indicated above. Rather, often it is other methods, aimed at destroying a group, which are the key ones.

Trials are an especially good mechanism for getting at the guilty intentions of individuals, indeed, that is what virtually all criminal trials

---

[26] See Schabas, *Genocide in International Law*, pp. 222–5.

must do, since *mens rea* is the *sine qua non* of criminal liability. And given the centrality of intent to the crime of genocide, criminal trials will be well suited to this task. But it is also true that the pursuit of intentions will also potentially help in reconciliatory efforts in societies that have been ravaged by genocide. For although it may be that a large portion of the population was complicit in the genocide by their actions, there will be only a few individuals in most cases who had the genocidal intent that was displayed by various planning activities. Closure may very well be achieved when it is discovered who had the intent to initiate the genocide, and closure will often occur after that person is tried, convicted, and sentenced for his or her crime.

I agree with the critics that demonization of the defendant retards reconciliation. But accepting this point also has two sides. First, only one kind of criminal trial, a "show trial," really does demonize in a way that retards reconciliation. This is where the defendant is vilified and portrayed as a deranged and demonic figure, rather than a fellow member of a community who has done wrong. There is a second sense of show trial, though, where the trial's purpose is to show the world what really happened, which does not retard reconciliation because it can provide a sense of closure for the victims as well as a public comeuppance for the perpetrators. Second, criminal trials are not the only means by which demonization occurs. Truth and Reconciliation Commissions, and even Amnesty Plans, can also demonize.

Demonization should be shunned, but not only in criminal trials. Dehumanizing does two things: it makes those who are primarily responsible for atrocities look not at all like anyone we would recognize in our societies; and it makes the rest of us "humans" not think of ourselves as capable of contributing to atrocities such as genocide. Demonization is a major impediment to reconciliation, because parties who do not recognize each other as humans are not very likely to feel the need to reconcile. Instead, they will regard themselves as morally superior people who should not compromise their principles. But criminal trials can be structured so that this effect is minimized and where there are no greater risks of demonization in trials than in other ways to treat atrocities.

Getting closure for the victims is consistent with reconciliation; indeed, it is crucial. One way to do this is by deterrence, a task that criminal law is well suited for. Another way is through the retributive goals of trials, which provide closure and allow people to attempt to regain some nonhostile feelings toward those who had attacked them.

More than scapegoating is required. Sometimes reconciliation can be achieved only through a criminal trial, where a guilty party is identified. In these cases the mutual recriminations will not stop until there is such a determination of guilt.[27]

Criminal trials also are especially good at pointing out that there were others who played significant roles as well, and recognition of this fact may help the reconciliation process, as will be argued later in this chapter.[28] Reconciliation is not always consonant with criminal trials, but there is good reason to think that some criminal trials for genocide will indeed promote rather than hinder reconciliation, and this has to do with the special nature and harm of genocide. It should be admitted, though, that trials by themselves are not likely to achieve full reconciliation. This should lead us also to think harder about the nature of reconciliation, a subject to which I now turn.

III. Rethinking Reconciliation

After a genocide has occurred, what can reasonably be hoped for in terms of reconciliation? And what are the contours of reconciliation in general? The term "reconciliation" etymologically refers to the return to a time when people were not hostile toward each other. If people are going to live with one another without further hostilities, they must reconcile with each other. Indeed, much of the literature on political reconciliation employs the analogy with marital reconciliation. Just as a husband and wife reconcile by reestablishing friendly feelings and harmony toward each other, so it is thought that the two sides to a political conflict need to do the same.

The dictionary definitions of the noun "reconciliation" are influenced by the two-person model. So *Roget's Thesaurus* defines reconciliation as "A reestablishment of friendship or harmony" and lists rapprochement as its synonym. *West's Encyclopedia of American Law* also follows this model: "The restoration of peaceful or amicable relations between two individuals who were previously in conflict with one another...often implying forgiveness for injuries on either or both sides." Here, as with

---

[27] See May, "Reconciliation and Amnesty Programs," in *Crimes Against Humanity*, especially pp. 236–9.

[28] Of course, this is true primarily in those cases where other factors that could further divide the society, such as by the use of inflammatory rhetoric during trial, are dampened, not always an easy task.

the use of the term reconciliation in the South African Truth and Reconciliation Commission, there is a heavy influence of the theological idea that confession and penance are key. Indeed, since I was a youth the Roman Catholic Church has renamed the sacrament of "Confession" as "Reconciliation," presumably seeing the parties that need to reconcile by forgiveness as the sinner and God.

The two-person model of marital reconciliation, where the focus is exclusively on getting the husband and wife to stop fighting with each other, is not a good model for robust reconciliation because it does not address the conditions that would make for lasting harmony. Such conditions may have to do with other people, including neighbors, co-workers, and extended family members. This is especially true of political reconciliation. I propose that the key to robust political reconciliation involves the acceptance of the fact that most members of a society, even some members of the so-called victim group, are often complicit in genocide. People need to be aware of the need to guard against future complicity as a way to move a society toward long-term harmony.

My reasons for looking to the guarding against complicity as the key to reconciliation are complex having to do with a reading of history and of recent genocides and other mass atrocities across the globe. Think of the case of Australia. In my view it is not enough that the perpetrator group of whites of European ancestry apologize or that Aboriginal and Torres Strait Islander peoples forgive these whites, although this is a start. In addition, the members of society need to recognize their actual roles as bystanders to the atrocities that were committed. This is not "to blame the victim" but to recognize what each of us is capable of and to commit ourselves to thwart the causes of genocide in the future. At least one online dictionary, the *Free Dictionary by Farlex*, comes close to what I propose when it lists cooperation as the synonym of reconciliation and then defines cooperation as "joint operation or action...as in 'their cooperation with us was essential for the success of our mission.'"

The United Nations Commission on Human Rights lists truth telling and reparations as the key to reconciliation and then lists five things that are involved in reparation for gross violations of human rights: acknowledgment and apology, guarantees against repetition, measures of restitution, measures of rehabilitation, and monetary compensation.[29] It must be admitted, though, that as one reads widely about reconciliation there is very little consensus about the elements of reconciliation, not

[29] Quoted in *eMJA*, the Medical Journal of Australia, 1999, issue 170, pp. 437–40.

only about how it is to be defined. William Long and Peter Brecke give a different list than the UN Commission on Human Rights, namely, public truth telling, justice short of revenge, redefinition of the identities of former belligerents, and calls for a new relationship."[30]

Rajeev Bhargava, a political scientist, talks of reconciliation between victims and perpetrators and urges that in responsible societies, political reconciliation does not occur unless certain conditions are met. In his view "a victimized group can forgive former perpetrators if it owns up collectively to responsibility for wrongdoing and repents."[31] The law professor Ronald Slye, whose view comes closer to my own than Bhargava's, argues that for reconciliation there are two necessary conditions: first, "accountability" and, second, the "creation of a human rights culture (a culture that values human dignity and the rule of law)." In his view, more is needed than accountability, and this is what poses problems for criminal trials: "A society is not reconciled with its violent past unless it works toward the creation of respect for fundamental human rights."[32]

Reconciliation is generally a relative term. People may fight with each other and not speak. After reconciliation, people may stop fighting but still not speak. This may not be as much of a reconciliation as if they also now talked to each other, but in my view it is a reconciliation nonetheless. Similarly, we can speak of a mere end of hostilities as a reconciliation just as we can speak of a turn toward social harmony also as a reconciliation. Indeed, there is a sense in which nearly any significant betterment of social relations could be characterized as a reconciliation.

In my view, political reconciliation means the ending of current hostilities and the establishment of some of the conditions that would make it likely that harmonious relations will obtain in the future. Robust political reconciliation means the ending of current hostilities and the establishment of conditions that would make it *highly* likely that harmonious relations will obtain in the future. As I will argue, robust political reconciliation, in cases such as genocide, additionally involves the recognition that most members of society were bystanders and the resolve that they won't be in the future.

[30] William J. Long and Peter Brecke, *War and Reconciliation*, Cambridge, MA: MIT Press, 2003.
[31] Rajeev Bhargava, "Restoring Decency to Barbaric Societies," in *Truth v. Justice*, edited by Robert I. Rotberg and Dennis Thompson, Princeton: Princeton University Press, 2000, p. 60.
[32] Ronald Slye, "Amnesty, Truth, and Reconciliation: Reflections on the South African Amnesty Process," in *Truth v. Justice*, edited by Robert I. Rotberg and Dennis Thompson, Princeton: Princeton University Press, 2000, pp. 170–1.

Some philosophers have begun by employing the marital, two-person model, but then move somewhat away from that model of reconciliation. Trudy Govier has argued that we can begin to understand reconciliation by thinking about interpersonal situations such as that between husband and wife. Govier then defines political reconciliation as "the building or rebuilding of relationships characterized by attitudes of acceptance and nonhostility."[33] There is a sense in which marital reconciliation and political reconciliation are similar in that robust reconciliation in both cases involves a kind of moral repair that is facilitated by a change in attitudes so that the people involved come to trust each other and hence to establish or reestablish healthy relationships.

Janna Thompson is one of the few philosophers to approach reconciliation in the spirit that I support. She says: "reconciliation is achieved when the harm done by injustice to relations of respect and trust that ought to exist between individuals or nations has been repaired or compensated for by the perpetrator in such a way that this harm is no longer regarded as standing in the way of establishing or reestablishing these relations."[34] But it is not just the perpetrators that need to act, and in large group reconciliation, the perpetrators, victims, and bystanders are often from the same groups.[35]

The key to robust political reconciliation is that the underlying causes of violence and animosity are diminished significantly, and that some degree of trust is achieved that makes it possible for people to develop the capacity to handle continuing conflicts that will arise between group members in the future.[36] To achieve such reconciliation, people need to come to terms with past harms and future potential for repair.[37] Part of that task is to see that there are at least two sides to every story where the true account of a massive breakdown in harmony in a society such as occurs in genocide is portrayed as it is, namely, as highly complex and nuanced. In this respect there is an important role for criminal trials. The adversarial posing of stories and sides to a conflict can make all participants better able to see that the world is normally properly understood from multiple standpoints.

[33] Trudy Govier, *Taking Wrongs Seriously*, Amherst, New York: Humanity Books, 2006, p. 18.
[34] Jana Thompson, *Taking Responsibility for the Past*, Cambridge: Polity Press, 2002, p. 50.
[35] See Govier's treatment of this topic in chapter 2 of her book *Taking Wrongs Seriously*.
[36] Ibid., p. 21.
[37] See Margaret Walker, *Moral Repair: Reconstructing Moral Relations after Wrongdoing*, New York: Cambridge University Press, 2006.

Another way that criminal trials could achieve reconciliation is by a collective expression of condemnation of those people who are most responsible for the genocide. There is some sense in which trials lay the atrocity to rest and allow for people to attempt to regain some non-hostile feelings toward those who had attacked them. Some trials have this effect, despite the difficulties discussed in the previous section. But there is also a sense in which reconciliation of a more robust sort will rarely be achieved for generations after a genocide. Here more than scapegoating is required. People need to understand that it is not merely one or even a small number of people who are normally responsible for a genocide. Rather, it is often a large proportion of a society that is responsible. Criminal trials can sometimes promote reconciliation in this regard as well.

It is not merely that trials tell a certain kind of narrative but that the narrative achieves an authentication by the public. Such an idea requires that there is a coherent public that can in some sense authenticate the narratives told by the trial. Here we can begin to see how the goals of reconciliation and those of international criminal trials can converge in significant ways. As I said, trials are especially good at deterrence and retributive goals; but trials also can express the kind of condemnation of genocide that could help reconcile the parties to a genocide. There is thus a cautionary tale to be told about how trials for genocide and other horrible atrocities should be conducted. Pursuing deterrence and retribution must not be allowed to demonize the defendant – fairness must be maintained to all parties.[38]

Robust political reconciliation is best seen as a form of self-understanding, especially where every member of a society understands that each has equal status before the law. Equal status before the law does not mean loss of group identity and status, indeed, it enhances group identity. In addition, robust political reconciliation is also about self-understanding of the roles that people played in genocide, especially in a realization of complicity. Although reconciliation is also clearly about attitudes, knowledge and understanding are more important yet. In many situations of genocide, such understanding will involve the recognition that one is primarily a member of a society and not of a "victim" group or an "oppressor" group. A shift from hostility and mistrust to attitudes of trust and nonhostility needs to be grounded in some

---

[38] See Mark Freeman, *Truth Commissions and Procedural Fairness*, New York: Cambridge University Press, 2006.

kind of self-understanding if it is to be long lasting. And the behavioral changes that will indeed bring an end to violence and acrimony need to be grounded in such a recognition of one's own role in the genocide, whether that is as active or passive participant, as well as victim. Robust political reconciliation is not just about attitude change but also about reexamining one's place in society. Criminal trials can play a significant role in fostering that aspect of reconciliation.

IV. Bystanders and Shared Responsibility

One of the key problems often identified in criminal trials for atrocities such as genocide is that trials seemingly cannot deal with the crucial role that bystanders play in these atrocities, and hence these trials do not advance reconciliation. I began to discuss this issue above when I suggested that criminal trials might be bifurcated, with a sizeable portion devoted to the circumstances of the larger events than just those that the defendant contributed to. If trials can be set up in this way without significant loss of rights of the defendant, there can be some discussion at trial of the role of bystanders. Bystanders may be morally guilty, but it is very hard to show that they are legally guilty, and hence bystanders are rarely indicted in mass atrocity cases. Hence, it seems that criminal trials are simply not good vehicles for addressing the role of bystanders in a way that would lead to the kind of self-understanding on the part of members of the society where genocide has occurred that would lead to changes that would make atrocities less likely in the future. I will say much more about this issue in the current section of the chapter.

The term "bystander" admits of several meanings, at least three of which are initially obvious. Bystanders are those who do not directly cause the harm in question. But they could be those who indirectly cause such harm by facilitating it. Or they may allow it to occur by not stopping it. Or bystanders may be those who neither indirectly cause harm, nor who could have prevented it, but are merely those on the sidelines who are present when the harms occur. Bystanders rarely are mentioned by prosecutors in international criminal trials. Even those bystanders who are straightforwardly complicit, in that they facilitate these crimes, are not normally charged unless they are high-ranking members of the armed services, such as General Krstic, or high-profile members of the society, such as Jean-Bosco Barayagwiza, both cases discussed earlier. Those who played lesser roles, but were crucial for the perpetration of the crimes, are not considered to be indictable.

Laurel Fletcher has recently written on the role and responsibility of bystanders. She has identified several problems that need to be addressed, most importantly:

> International criminal convictions single out and stigmatize the accused, normalizing the behavior of bystanders and potentially creating a false moral innocence for the unindicted and their bystander supporters... [and] international criminal law constrains the doctrinal ability of international justice mechanisms to address more directly the role of bystanders in atrocities.[39]

Fletcher is right to think that courts cannot do a good job of "examining the [defendant's] behavior against that of the nonaccused – whether bystanders or other perpetrators."[40] But judges and prosecutors are not the only participants in trials.

Although the prosecutor often cannot be successful and focus attention on other perpetrators than those in the dock, this has historically been one of the main strategies of good defense attorneys. I agree with Fletcher that what is needed is for someone to discuss openly and in an aggressive way the "false moral innocence" of bystanders. Defense attorneys are well placed to do this. The legal guilt of the bystanders does not need to be established either for defense or ultimately for reconciliation. What needs to be established is that the defendant is not alone responsible, and hence cannot be a mere "scapegoat" for the larger atrocity, even if he or she did participate in the genocide.

There are other problems with international tribunals that are perhaps not so easy to address. Fletcher is right to note that the complicated and highly differentiated roles that bystanders play cannot easily be addressed at trial, and I would add that this is true even if we focus on defense counsel rather than prosecutors and judges. This is especially true in international trials if we continue to focus, as we should, on the big fish rather than the small fry. It remains a strong possibility that convicting the big fish will make it seem as if others, especially bystanders, didn't really do anything wrong after all. I want to say two things about this point. First, it may be possible, as I'll indicate in the final sections of this chapter, to have lesser localized trials that focus on the small fish, perhaps very many small fish and hence begin to address the roles of bystanders, at least those who were complicit. Second, the point of focusing on bystanders in terms of moral responsibility has to do not with

---

[39] Fletcher, "From Indifference to Engagement," pp. 1076–7.
[40] Ibid., p. 1078.

justice or with reconciliation directly, but with an intermediate idea, namely, shared responsibility.

In some of my earlier writings I focused on the idea that in mass violence what is crucial for change is that members of a community come to see how they shared responsibility for those atrocities.[41] Here legal complicity is not the issue, because a large basis of shared responsibility for atrocities comes from one's attitudes and omissions rather than from any direct harm that one caused. Yet it is still true that those who held attitudes similar to those of the direct perpetrators, or whose omissions played a causal role, can be viewed as having facilitated the atrocity. It may be that moral blame is not appropriate, even as it still might be said that moral shame or moral taint is assigned to all those who were complicit. Of course, there are no clear legal parallels to moral taint and moral shame, but reconciliation may be advanced by recognition of such categories.

The idea of bystander complicity certainly blurs the line between moral and legal responsibility. At least in part this is because of the idea that people who do not seem to play a major role, indeed, people who may appear to play no role at all, in a harm are nonetheless stained with taint as if they had played a major role in the harm. This idea surely goes back in time at least to Oedipus and calls forth a very ancient idea of the stain of taint.[42] Bystanders do not necessarily have dirty hands, but they are nonetheless often tainted by association with the harms and wrongs that they could have prevented or mitigated on their own, or where such things could have been accomplished if only these bystanders had organized. Those who are bystanders on a beach when someone is drowning in very choppy waters may not be able individually to swim out and save the drowning swimmer, but they may be able to save the swimmer by collective action. They are at very least tainted by not having done so.

In mass atrocity cases normally the victims are to a certain extent like the drowning swimmer – if only someone had stepped forward and acted, or organized other bystanders to take collective action, or refused to facilitate the actions of the perpetrators. As Mark Drumbl has said, "Part of the riddle of purposively responding to mass atrocity, and preventing it, is to assess how law can implicate the complicit and

[41] See May, *Sharing Responsibility*.

[42] See "Metaphysical Guilt and Moral Taint," ch. 8 of May, *Sharing Responsibility*. Also see Marina Oshana, "Moral Taint," in *Genocide's Aftermath,* edited by Claudia Card and Armen T. Marsoobian, Oxford: Blackwell Publishing, 2007, pp. 71–93.

acquiescent masses who are responsible even if not formally guilty."[43] And in figuring out what kind of response will be efficacious, responding to bystander complicity will be key. Drumbl says, "The deep complicity cascade plays a much more dynamic role in the commission of mass atrocity than it does in isolated, ordinary common crimes. Ignoring or denying the uniqueness of the criminality of mass atrocity stunts the development of effective methods to promote accountability for mass criminals."[44] Punishment can play a role here, but it is complicated by the different type of psychology that is involved in mass killing as opposed to isolated killing.[45]

Ervin Straub argues that bystanders have a potential to stop or diminish mass atrocity but are often so beaten down that they lack the psychological resources to act. He lists several ingredients in the psychological incapacity of bystanders. Straub points to the fact that "Severe, persistent difficulties of life" frustrate people and make them turn against one another.[46] In addition, he says that studies show that "Devaluation of individuals and groups, whatever its source, makes it easier to harm them."[47] And most significantly for bystanders, "Scapegoating protects a positive identity by reducing the feeling of responsibility for problems. ... It can unite people against the scapegoated other, thereby fulfilling the need for positive connection and support in difficult times."[48] Socialization toward obedience also plays a role.[49] As a result of these psychological factors, Straub concludes, "In the face of suffering of a subgroup of society, bystanders frequently remain silent, passive."[50] Indeed, Straub brings us to our main topic when he links these factors to why it is that external bystanders, including nations, become passive bystanders: "Rwanda presents a recent, disturbing, example of international passivity."[51]

---

[43] Drumbl, *Atrocity, Punishment, and International Law*, p. 26.
[44] Ibid., p. 32.
[45] See James Waller, *Becoming Evil: How Ordinary People Commit Genocide and Mass Killing*, New York: Oxford University Press, 2002. Also see Ervin Straub, "The Psychology of Bystanders, Perpetrators, and Heroic Helpers," in Leonard S. Newman and Ralph Erber, editors, *Understanding Genocide*, New York: Oxford University Press, 2002, pp. 11–42.
[46] Straub, "The Psychology of Bystanders, Perpetrators, and Heroic Helpers," p. 13.
[47] Ibid., p. 15.
[48] Ibid., p. 19.
[49] Ibid., p. 21.
[50] Ibid., p. 24.
[51] Ibid., p. 27.

Yet Straub is hopeful that bystanders can be motivated not to remain passive in the face of mass atrocity, despite the fact that "complicity by bystanders is likely to encourage perpetrators even more."[52] Bystanders can exert both negative and also positive influence on those who perpetrate an atrocity: "By speaking out and taking action, bystanders can elevate values prohibiting violence, which over time perpetrators had come to ignore in their treatment of the victim group. Most groups, but especially ideologically committed ones, have difficulty seeing themselves, having a perspective on their own actions and evolution. They need others as mirrors."[53]

Once bystanders start to act, they tend to do so more and more. "The research on rescuers of Jews and other information suggests that over time the range of concern for engaged helpers usually expands."[54] Straub offers this insight into how to get bystanders to act: "This will only happen if people – children, adults, whole societies – develop an awareness of their common humanity with other people, as well as of the psychological processes in themselves that turn them against others."[55] People can still have significant group identities even as they also see themselves as primarily part of a human community.

In my view, mass killing cannot normally take place in a region where people have the disposition to act to protect each other. And such dispositions are made more likely when population groups do not divide themselves up into "us and them" oppositions. Reconciliation involves the confrontation of conditions that foster such dispositions. Part of this task is to see oneself as tainted or shamed when one fails to act to prevent atrocities. To a certain extent, former Australian Prime Minister John Howard was right to say that the key to reconciliation is to see that there really are not two groups but one overarching society. Of course, talking in this way is not enough – and Howard's administration did not show much sensitivity toward the actions that also must accompany such statements. Indeed, that John Howard refused to repudiate, or apologize for, the harms to Aboriginals and Torres Strait Islanders is a sign that he was not serious about reconciliation. As Marina Oshana has argued, "the extent to which each of these persons remains tainted and their moral record darkened is a function of the person's refusal to repudiate the

[52] Ibid.
[53] Ibid., p. 29.
[54] Ibid., p. 35.
[55] Ibid.

wrong that has been done and to repair the circumstances" that could cause such harms.[56]

Let me mention another way that morality and legality can partially merge as a way to motivate bystanders. Thomas Hill has talked of second-order moral responsibilities most appropriate for bystanders. The responsibility that seems most apt is what Hill calls the "duty of moral self-scrutiny." Hill argues that bystanders generally do not have cognitive failings but rather have motivational failings. In particular, bystanders let their baser inclinations rule them "through self-deception, special pleading, and other ways of representing our motivations to ourselves as better than they are." One of the most serious of these motivational problems is that bystanders often do not see themselves as acting for bad reasons because they assume that their motives are good whatever those motives are.[57] If we combine this idea with the idea of moral taint, we get the idea that bystanders need to see themselves as tainted by their passivity and to see their passivity, even in the light of widespread commonality of behavior by others, as a failure of responsibility. Once again, this is also the underlying idea behind the "responsibility to protect" movement that was spawned by the United Nations General Assembly–sponsored conference in 2005.[58]

Paying attention to bystanders allows us to see how large-scale harm can occur in societies where there were so many people "standing around." One way to prevent such atrocities is for people to see themselves as capable of acting and as motivated to do so. As we will next see, the recognition of the fact of widespread complicity, and of one's role in it, is crucial for self-understanding and then also for providing an impetus for change in those societies. But there is no magic here – individual cases will differ, and pointing a finger at those who were complicit may further entrench mutual resentments. I have been speaking of only some of the factors that can advance reconciliation and that are not inconsistent with criminal trials. It is beyond the scope of this final chapter to address the other factors in the detail they deserve.

---

[56] Oshana, "Moral Taint," p. 85.
[57] Thomas Hill, "Moral Responsibilities of Bystanders," unpublished paper presented on a panel at the American Philosophical Association's Eastern Division meetings, December 2007, Baltimore, MD, copy in the possession of the author.
[58] See U.N. General Assembly World Outcome Document, paras. 138 and 139.

V. The *Gacaca* Process in Rwanda

In Rwanda there has been a serious attempt to deal with the desire for justice after genocide and the sometimes conflicting need to have reconciliation after such a horrific experience in a society. As we have seen, one of the main difficulties faced is that many members of Rwandan society either participated in the killings, directly or indirectly, or were passive bystanders who could have stopped the horror. Reconciliation is not merely a matter of getting the Tutsis and Hutus to stop harming each other and come to have some minimal respect for each other. Reconciliation will also involve the population coming to terms with the widespread complicity in the genocide, where the two ethnic group affiliations did not match up with victim and perpetrator groups in the society, for this is important to prevent future atrocities. Here is where criminal trials could, in my view, help in that reconciliation endeavor. In Germany, the continuing trials, after the main Nuremberg trial, of lower-level officials played a large role in postwar reconciliation.

Earlier I discussed the point often made by critics of international criminal trials that such trials can further inflame the passions of two sides to an ethnic or religious group dispute. Passions have been inflamed in the Balkans, where the trials in the Hague have often made ethnic Serbs even more suspicious and resentful of the other ethnic groups in the former Yugoslavia. But in Rwanda the trials of those responsible for the genocide have taken two forms: a small set of trials by the International Criminal Tribunal for Rwanda (the ICTR) sitting across the Rwandan border in Arusha, Tanzania, aimed at the main perpetrators, and a large set of local trials, the *gacaca*, that have looked at a wide array of those who were potentially complicit in the genocide. In these cases, despite their difficulties, both types of trial have aided in making it clear how extensive was the complicity in the genocide and how much shared responsibility there was for the atrocity, although members of only one ethnic group have been subject to these proceedings.

The *gacaca* have been trials rather than truth and reconciliation–style proceedings, although there is a bit of a mixture of both. The *gacaca* are "trials" in that proceedings are held and judges pass sentences. There is then an appellate level, where judges all apply the same substantive criminal law. But the local-level trials are presided over by elected elders rather than by trained lawyers, and the rules of evidence are partially relaxed in these proceedings, with the judges having more discretion than would be true in normal trials but with an attempt to protect the rights of the defendants nonetheless. The decentralized trials of the *gacaca* have been credited with helping the communities repair themselves, by bringing community and perpetrator together, although it is also true that the communities are not the same as they were before the genocide because so many people have become dislocated or have relocated themselves.[59]

Mark Drumbl raises the worry that the ICTR, sitting in Arusha, has put pressure on the *gacaca* process in the local regions of Rwanda, perhaps to the *gacaca*'s detriment.[60] There is pressure from the ICTR trickling down to the *gacaca* to look to retributive and deterrent goals of the punishments meted out by the *gacaca*, rather than the traditional restorative goals of the older versions of *gacaca*. And, indeed, other critics contend that deterrence and retribution, the traditional normative goals of criminal law, are largely inconsistent with reconciliation.[61] This is one of the reasons that the South African Truth and Reconciliation Commission (TRC) did not allow for criminal trials for atrocities at the same time that the TRC was operating, much to the dismay of many families of victims who sought something other than reconciliation, namely, justice.[62]

Political reconciliation is not primarily about individuals, and for this reason the normative goal of retribution can indeed conflict with reconciliation. Retribution is, in effect, one sided, not two sided or multisided as is reconciliation. The idea that there could be reconciliation where only one of two parties was satisfied with the result runs contrary to what the term "reconciliation" means. Retribution is not about two parties feeling satisfied, but only one, the party who has been aggrieved. Retribution, especially when it is the focus of a criminal trial, is concerned with the society and the victim. The perpetrator is a subject of the trial not as someone who is to achieve satisfaction but as someone generally who is about to become greatly dissatisfied if found guilty. For the victim and the society to achieve retribution, there must be some suffering on the part of the perpetrator, either

[59] See Drumbl's discussion of *gacaca* in *Atrocity, Punishment, and International Law*, ch. 4.
[60] Ibid.
[61] See Michael Scharf, "Swapping Amnesty for Peace: Was There a Duty to Prosecute International Crimes in Haiti?" *Texas International Law Journal*, vol. 31, 1996, pp. 1–38; and Leila Sadat, "Exile, Amnesty, and International Law, *Notre Dame Law Review*, vol. 81, no. 3, March 2006, pp. 955–1036.
[62] See the case of Steve Biko discussed in the final chapter of May, *Crimes Against Humanity*.

266 *Special Problems of Genocide*

monetary loss or incarceration. But the suffering need not involve long prison terms, especially if the participation by the defendant was not major.

The *gacaca* process in Rwanda has attempted to provide a modicum of retribution for the victims and their families, through meting out some punishments, as it has also sought to foster reconciliation among previously antagonistic social groups in the society, by the involvement of the community in the proceedings. In my view, this is best carried out when the community members look inside themselves and ask about their complicity, not merely when they look to those who are marked as perpetrators. It is true that achieving both retribution and reconciliation is a delicate balance, and if pressure is exerted to move the *gacaca* process more in line with standard trials, retribution tends to become dominant over reconciliation. But this is not to say that the balance between the two goals cannot be maintained – only that the delicacy of the balance needs to be protected from outside pressure that could disrupt that balance.

Those who take a defendant-oriented approach, as I do, will put pressure on international criminal trials not to focus exclusively on the victims but also to respect the accused perpetrators, as well as other possible perpetrators within the larger population. Such considerations make trials focus on goals that are not necessarily opposed to reconciliation. Take the recent trial of Saddam Hussein. If more consideration were given to preserving the dignity and rights of that defendant in the trial, and to those who still cared about Saddam, the trial and execution would not have risked worsening the long-term prospects of reconciliation in Iraq. The pressure that should have been placed on those conducting the trial to treat the defendant humanely could have easily aided in reconciling Shiites and Sunnis in this ravaged country. The pressure to have retribution, but to do it in a fair trial, is not inconsistent with the goals of reconciliation.

So the worries that some critics, such as Drumbl, have expressed about having trials that put pressure on other methods of reconciliation occurring at the same time as the trials is not an insurmountable problem. The problem does become acute if international criminal trials are seen as providing satisfaction only for the victims and their families. Indeed, this trivializes the retributive justice dimension of trials. But in my view, international criminal trials should pay as much attention to the rights and treatment of the alleged perpetrators, both those in the dock and those outside it, as to the victims and their families. If so, then international criminal trials will not necessarily work at cross-purposes to the goals of reconciliation.

There is one other problem that I will discuss in this section. For some of the members of the society in Rwanda, the *gacaca* have reinforced the government's attempt to blame "'outsiders' for creating divisions in Rwanda society."[63] This is an unfortunate result of the *gacaca* process, but not one that is necessarily linked to the process itself. It may very well be that the *gacaca* process could play quite a different role. By showing how many members of the Rwandan society were complicit, the *gacaca* can show that the problem was also very much one of what "insiders" did, including those who used the machetes to kill their neighbors, those who sold the machetes, and those who looked the other way. Most of those who were complicit in the Rwandan genocide were not mere "outsiders." In general there are reasons to think that some criminal trials could positively advance reconciliation in a society that has experienced genocide.

One of the problems discussed above is that focusing on just a few individuals makes it very hard indeed to understand what caused, and who is responsible for, the genocide. The more trials there are the more pieces of the puzzle will be exposed to the light of day. But if trials do indeed sweep to capture very low-ranking people whose role is minor, localized trials that stress healing as much as retribution may be the best proceedings. It is for this reason that I endorse the *gacaca* process in Rwanda, even as I remain worried about issues of procedural fairness.

VI. Taking Account of Complicity

As I have argued, robust political reconciliation is not merely a matter of getting the Tutsis and Hutus to stop harming each other. Reconciliation will also involve the population coming to terms with the widespread complicity in the genocide, where the two ethnic group affiliations did not match up with victim and perpetrator groups in the society. By complicity I mean the commissions and omissions that allow harm to occur but that are not necessarily causally efficacious in a straightforward way. What is crucial is to break down the "us-versus-them" mentality of ethnic conflict. Recognition of the fact that many people in a society, those from "oppressor" as well as "oppressed" groups, often share responsibility for an atrocity breaks down one of the most significant conceptual

---

[63] Clark, "Hybridity, Holism and "'Traditional' Justice," p. 48.

barriers that prevent reconciliation after mass atrocity. As I have argued throughout, criminal trials are not at odds with, and can advance, such an endeavor.

At least as importantly as getting us to rethink how trials should be conducted, focusing on genocide also helps us see how to rethink reconciliation as well. Here the most important consideration is that we somehow get the two groups, who see themselves in irreconcilable conflict, to realize, when the facts warrant it, that their group memberships do not necessarily match the victim and perpetrator groups. If people can come to see that in many atrocities victims and perpetrators typically come from both groups, then one of the chief obstacles to reconciliation can be overcome. One way to accomplish this is to guarantee a fair proceeding for the alleged perpetrators.[64] Criminal trials, when conducted fairly, often provide the facts that will make it clear that one person or group cannot easily be demonized, because the vigorous defense of the alleged perpetrators will often provide a more nuanced view of who were the responsible parties.

At this point let me say something brief about my empirical claim that in many genocides there is a blurring of victim and perpetrator groups. This claim is confined to genocides that have occurred since the Middle Ages, for before that time genocides were largely carried out by perpetrators who were in different societies from the victim group. Once genocides are largely carried out against victims that are in the same society as the perpetrators, the blurring of groups becomes nearly inevitable.[65] In many societies the victim group was so intertwined with the perpetrator group that quite elaborate mechanisms had to be developed to make it appear that victim and perpetrator groups were utterly different. Campaigns of demonization, common to many modern genocides, were aimed at separating these groups who had long been associated with each other.[66] This was also true in Bosnia where its most important city, Sarajevo, was well known for its multicultural society with widespread intermarriage between Serbs and Croats.[67] The ethnic group lines had already greatly blurred, and it took effort to make it appear that the groups were completely distinct from one another.

---

[64] See Freeman, *Truth Commissions and Procedural Fairness.*

[65] See Frank Chalk and Kurt Jonassohn, *The History and Sociology of Genocide,* New Haven, CT: Yale University Press, 1990.

[66] See Shimon Samuels, "Applying the Lessons of the Holocaust," in *Is the Holocaust Unique?* edited by Alan S. Rosenbaum, Boulder: Westview Press, 2001, pp. 209–20.

[67] See Michael Scharf, *Balkan Justice,* Durham, NC: Carolina Academic Press, 1997.

Although it is often said that truth and reconciliation approaches to genocide primarily concern the victims and their families, surely this cannot be right. Reconciliation involves both the group that has been the victim and the group from whom the perpetrators have come. In some cases perpetrators and victims come from the same ethnic or racial group. One of the keys to reconciliation is to break the silence about who was responsible for what.[68] Trials can be especially good at getting at who were the responsible parties in a mass atrocity such as genocide. A related issue is to break the silence about who was complicit in not acting during a mass atrocity such as genocide, as well as who would have stood by or is likely to stand by in the future when mass atrocity looms. I believe that having criminal trials can also aid in breaking this silence as well. But the full defense of this view will turn on the facts of whether trials do indeed have the kind of impact on reconciliation I have hypothesized.

The case of genocide trials teaches us that reconciliation is hard to achieve in war-ravaged States because it is often not clear what the sides to be reconciled are, and also not clear what some of those offenders of each side did wrong. Especially in cases of genocide, there is often widespread complicity, and even the victims' family members may be involved in the atrocity. Good criminal defense work in recent genocide trials illustrates that it is often hard to see just two sides that need to be reconciled. Robust political reconciliation is here not best seen on the model of two spouses getting back together again. Robust political reconciliation is about learning the ways that many members of a society participate in injustice, and how they can come to live together harmoniously by being motivated to act to prevent future atrocities by not being bystanders. Robust political reconciliation thus hinges on knowledge, indeed, self-knowledge, where people come to understand atrocities from various points of view and come to appreciate that often the "victim group" is not all good, and the "perpetrator group" is not all bad.

In her heralded study of genocide, Samantha Power says: "time and again, decent men and women chose to look away. We have all been bystanders to genocide. The crucial question is why."[69] And Desmond

---

[68] See Arman T. Marsoobian, "Epilogue: Reconciliation in the Aftermath of Genocide," in *Genocide's Aftermath*, edited by Claudia Card and Arman T. Marsoobian, Oxford: Blackwell, 2007, pp. 260–71.

[69] Power, *A Problem from Hell*, p. xvi.

Tutu has eloquently stated: "Reconciliation was the way out. It is a way to transform individuals and the whole society. It is a way to look at perpetrators of human rights abuses and see brothers and sisters. A way to look at the victim in oneself and see a survivor."[70]

Criminal trials, with all of their many faults, can be successfully enlisted to bring out this feature of genocide and hence advance rather than retard reconciliation. There is no incompatibility between achieving reconciliation in genocide-ravaged societies and holding trials for those who are responsible for the genocide. As we have seen throughout the book, international criminal trials for genocide can be successfully defended, but perhaps not as involving "the crime of crimes."

[70] Desmond Mpilo Tutu, "Foreword" to Erin Daly and Jeremy Sarkin, *Reconciliation in Divided Societies*, Philadelphia: University of Pennsylvania Press, 2007, pp. ix–x.

Bibliography

Application of the Convention on the Prevention and Punishment of the Crime of Genocide (Bosnia and Herzegovinia v. Yugoslavia (Serbia and Montenegro)), International Court of Justice, 13 September 1993, Judgment.

Arendt, Hannah. *Eichmann in Jerusalem*, New York: Viking Press, 1963.

Origins of Totalitarianism, New York: Harcourt, Brace and World, 1951, 2nd edition, 1966.

Aristotle, *Nicomachean Ethics*, Book III.

Ashworth, Andrew. *Principles of Criminal Law*, Oxford: Clarendon Press, 1995.

Bassiouni, M. Cherif, and Edward M. Wise. *Aut Dedere Aut Judicare: The Duty to Extradite or Prosecute in International Law*, Dordrecht: Martinus Nijhoff, 1995.

Bentham, Jeremy. *Introduction to the Principles of Morals and Legislation* (1789), edited by J. H. Burns and H. L. A. Hart, Oxford: Oxford University Press, 1970.

Bhargava, Rajeev. "Restoring Decency to Barbaric Societies," in *Truth v. Justice*, edited by Robert I. Rotberg and Dennis Thompson, Princeton: Princeton University Press, 2000, pp. 45–67.

Bolton, Martha. "Universals, Essences, and Abstract Entities," in *The Cambridge History of Seventeenth Century Philosophy*, edited by Daniel Garber and Michael Ayers, New York: Cambridge University Press, 1998, vol. I, pp. 178–211.

Card, Claudia. *The Atrocity Paradigm*, New York: Oxford University Press, 2002.

"Genocide and Social Death," *Hypatia*, vol. 18, no. 1, Winter 2003, pp. 63–79.

Case Concerning the Application of the Convention on the Prevention and Punishment of the Crime of Genocide (Bosnia and Herzegovinia v. Serbia and Montenegro), International Court of Justice, 26 February 2007, Judgment.

Chalk, Frank, and Kurt Jonassohn. *The History and Sociology of Genocide*, New Haven, CT: Yale University Press, 1990.

Charter of the International Military Tribunal at Nuremberg, Annex to the London Agreement (8 Aug. 1945).

Clark, Phil. "Hybridity, Holism and 'Traditional' Justice: The Case of the Gacaca Courts in Post-Genocide Rwanda," *George Washington University Law Review*, September 2007, pp. 1–68.

"When the Killers Come Home," *Dissent*, Summer 2005, pp. 14–21.

Clark, Roger S. "The Crime of Aggression," in Carsten Stahn and Goran Sluiter, editors, *The Emerging Practice of the International Criminal Court*, Leiden: Martinus Nijhoff, 2009, pp. 709–24.

Cohen, Stanley. *States of Denial: Knowing about Atrocities and Suffering*, Cambridge: Polity Press, 2001.

Convention on the Prevention, and Punishment of Genocide, adopted December 9, 1948; entered into force January 12, 1951, 78 U.N.T.S. 277.

Darcy, Shane. *Collective Responsibility and Accountability under International Law*, Leiden: Transnational Publishers, 2007.

Donnelly, Jack. *Universal Human Rights in Theory and Practice*, Ithaca, NY: Cornell University Press, 2nd edition, 2003.

Doris, John. *Lack of Character*, New York: Cambridge University Press, 2002.

Douglas, Lawrence. *The Memory of Judgment: Making Law and History in the Trials of the Holocaust*, New Haven, CT: Yale University Press, 2001.

Drumbl, Mark. *Atrocity, Punishment, and International Law*, New York: Cambridge University Press, 2007.

"Collective Violence and Individual Punishment: The Criminality of Mass Atrocity," *Northwestern University Law Review*, vol. 99, no. 2, Winter 2005, pp. 101–79.

"The Expressive Value of Prosecuting and Punishing Terrorists: *Hamdan*, The Geneva Conventions, and International Criminal Law," *George Washington Law Review*, vol. 75, no. 5/6, August 2007, pp. 1165–99.

Duff, Antony. *Criminal Attempts*, Oxford: Clarendon Press, 1996.

Dworkin, Ronald. *Taking Rights Seriously*, Cambridge, MA: Harvard University Press, 1977.

eMJA, the Medical Journal of Australia, 1999, issue 170, pp. 437–40.

Farer, Tom J. "Humanitarian Intervention before and after 9/11," in *Humanitarian Intervention: Ethical, Legal, and Political Dilemmas*, edited by J.L. Holzgrefe and Robert O. Keohane, New York: Cambridge University Press, 2003, pp. 53–89.

Feinberg, Joel. *Harm to Others*, Oxford: Oxford University Press, 1984.

Fletcher, Laurel. "From Indifference to Engagement: Bystanders and International Criminal Justice," *Michigan Journal of International Law*, vol. 26, Summer 2005, pp. 1013–95.

Freeman, Mark. *Truth Commissions and Procedural Fairness*, New York: Cambridge University Press, 2006.

Frost, Mervyn. "Constitutive Theory and Moral Accountability: Individuals, Institutions, and Dispersed Practices," in Toni Erskine, editor, *Can Institutions Have Responsibilities?* London: Palgrave/Macmillan, 2003, pp. 84–99.

Gilbert, Margaret. *On Social Facts*, London: Routledge, 1989.

Govier, Trudy. *Taking Wrongs Seriously*, Amherst, NY: Humanity Books, 2006.

Greenawalt, Alexander. "Rethinking Genocidal Intent: The Case for a Knowledge-Based Interpretation," *Columbia Law Review*, vol. 99, 1999, pp. 2259–94.

Grotius, Hugo. *De Jure Belli ac Pacis* (On the Law of War and Peace) (1625), translated by Francis W. Kelsey, Oxford: Clarendon Press, 1925.

Grunfeld, Fred, and Anke Huijboom. *The Failure to Prevent Genocide in Rwanda: The Role of Bystanders*, Leiden: Martinus Nijhoff, 2007.

Hart, H.L.A. "Negligence, Mens Rea, and Criminal Responsibility," in *Punishment and Responsibility*, Oxford: Oxford University Press, 1968, 2nd edition, 1973, pp. 136–57.

Hill, Thomas. "Moral Responsibilities of Bystanders," unpublished paper presented on a panel at the American Philosophical Association's Eastern Division meetings, December 2007, Baltimore, MD, copy in the possession of the author.

Hobbes, Thomas. *De Corpore*, part I, ch. 2, in *Body, Man , and Citizen*, edited by Richard S. Peters, New York: Collier Books, 1962.

Leviathan (1651), edited by Richard Tuck, New York: Cambridge University Press, 1996.

Horder, Jeremy. "Crimes of Ulterior Intent," in *Harm and Culpability*, edited by A.P. Simester and A.T.H. Smith, Oxford: Clarendon Press, 1996, pp. 153–68.

Keohane, Robert O. "Political Authority after Intervention," in *Humanitarian Intervention: Ethical, Legal, and Political Dilemmas*, edited by J.L. Holzgrefe and Robert O. Keohane, New York: Cambridge University Press, 2003, pp. 268–82.

Koskenniemi, Martti. "Between Impunity and Show Trials," *Max Planck Yearbook of United Nations Law*, vol. 6, 2002, pp. 1–35.

Kutz, Christopher. *Complicity*, New York: Cambridge University Press, 2000.

LaFave, Wayne R., and Austin W. Scott, Jr. *Handbook of Criminal Law*, St. Paul, MN: West Publishing, 1972.

Lang, Berel. *Act and Idea in the Nazi Genocide*, Chicago: University of Chicago Press, 1990.

Lemkin, Raphael. *Axis Rule in Occupied Europe, Laws of Occupation, Analysis of Government, Proposals for Redress*, Washington, DC: Carnegie Endowment for World Peace, 1944.

Long, William J., and Peter Brecke. *War and Reconciliation*, Cambridge, MA: MIT Press, 2003.

Luban, David. "Beyond Moral Minimalism," *Ethics & International Affairs*, vol. 20, no. 3, 2006, pp. 353–60.

"A Theory of Crimes against Humanity," *Yale Journal of International Law*, vol. 29, no. 1 (2004), pp. 85–140.

Marsoobian, Arman T. "Epilogue: Reconciliation in the Aftermath of Genocide," in *Genocide's Aftermath*, edited by Claudia Card and Arman T. Marsoobian, Oxford: Blackwell Publishers, 2007, pp. 260–71.

May, Larry, "Act and Circumstance in the Crime of Aggression," *Journal of Political Philosophy*, vol. 15, no. 2, 2007, pp. 169–86.

Aggression and Crimes Against Peace, New York: Cambridge University Press, 2008.

Crimes Against Humanity: A Normative Account, New York: Cambridge University Press, 2005.

"How Is Humanity Harmed by Genocide?" *International Legal Theory*, vol. 11, no. 1, Summer 2005, pp. 1–23.

"Humanity, International Crime, and the Rights of Defendants," *Ethics &* *International Affairs*, vol. 20, no. 3, 2006, pp. 373–82.
The Morality of Groups, Notre Dame, IN: University of Notre Dame Press, 1987.
Sharing Responsibility, Chicago: University of Chicago Press, 1992.
The Socially Responsive Self, Chicago: University of Chicago Press, 1996.
War Crimes and Just War, New York: Cambridge University Press, 2007.
McMahan, Jeff. "Just Cause for War," *Ethics & International Affairs*, vol. 19, no. 3, 2005, pp. 55–75.
Miller, Arthur G., Amy M. Buddie, and Jeffrey Kretschmar. "Explaining the Holocaust: Does Social Psychology Exonerate the Perpetrators?" in *Understanding Genocide*, edited by Leonard S. Newman and Ralph Erber, New York: Oxford University Press, 2002, pp. 301–24.
Minow, Martha. *Between Vengeance and Forgiveness*, Boston: Beacon Press, 1998.
Model Penal Code, sec. 2.02, Comment (Tentative Draft No. 4, 1955).
Moody, Ernest A. "William of Ockham," in *The Encyclopedia of Philosophy*, edited by Paul Edwards, New York: Macmillan, 1967, vol. 8, pp. 306–17.
Nagel, Thomas. "The Problem of Global Justice," *Philosophy & Public Affairs*, vol. 33, no. 2, Spring 2005, pp. 113–47.
Normore, Calvin G. "Ockham's Metaphysics of Parts," *Journal of Philosophy*, vol. 103, no. 12, December 2006, pp. 737–54.
Ockham, William of. *Ockham: Philosophical Writings*, translated and edited by Philotheus Boehner, O.F.M., London: Thomas Nelson and Sons, 1957.
Ockham's Theory of Terms (Part I of the *Summa Logicae*), translated by Michael J. Loux, South Bend, IN: St. Augustine's Press, 1998.
Oshana, Marina. "Moral Taint," in *Genocide's Aftermath*, edited by Claudia Card and Armen T. Marsoobian, Oxford: Blackwell, 2007, pp. 71–93.
Patterson, Orlando. *Slavery and Social Death*, Cambridge, MA: Harvard University Press, 1982.
Payne v. Tennessee, 501 U.S. 808 (1990).
Power, Samantha. *A Problem from Hell*, New York: Harper and Row, 2002.
Prosecutor v. Dusko Tadic, International Criminal Tribunal for the Former Yugoslavia, case no. IT-94-1-T, Trial Chamber Judgment, 7 May 1997.
Prosecutor v. Dusko Tadic, International Criminal Tribunal for the Former Yugoslavia, case no. IT-94-1-A, Appeals Chamber Judgment, 15 July 1999.
Prosecutor v. Ferdinand Nahimana, Jean-Bosco Barayagwiza, and Hassan Ngeze, International Criminal Tribunal for Rwanda, case no. ICTR-99-52-T, Trial Chamber Judgment, 3 December 2003.
Prosecutor v. Fernando Nahimana, Jean-Bosco Barayagwiza, and Hassan Ngeze, International Criminal Tribunal for Rwanda, case no. ICTR-99-52-A, Appeals Chamber Judgment, 28 November 2007.
Prosecutor v. Jean-Bosco Barayagwiza, International Criminal Tribunal for Rwanda, Amended Indictment, 4 April 2000.
Prosecutor v. Jean-Paul Akayesu, International Criminal Tribunal for Rwanda, case no. IT-96-4-T, Trial Chamber Judgment, 2 September 1998.
Prosecutor v. Jean-Paul Akayesu, International Criminal Tribunal for Rwanda, case no. IT-96-4-A, Appeals Chamber Judgment, 1 June 2001.

Prosecutor v. Mirjan Kupreskic et al., International Criminal Tribunal for the Former Yugoslavia, IT-95-16-T, Trial Chamber Judgment, 14 January 2000.

Prosecutor v. Radislav Krstic, International Criminal Tribunal for the Former Yugoslavia, case No. IT-98-33-T, Trial Chamber Judgment, 2 August 2001.

Prosecutor v. Radislav Krstic, International Tribunal for the Former Yugoslavia, case no. IT-98-33-A, Appeals Chamber Judgment, 19 April 2004.

Quillet, Jeannine. "Community, Counsel, and Representation," in *The Cambridge History of Medieval Thought*, edited by J. H. Burns, New York: Cambridge University Press, 1988, pp. 520–72.

R v. Coney (1882) 8 QBD 534.

Rademaker, Stephen. "Unwitting Party to Genocide: The International Criminal Court Is Complicating Efforts to Save Darfur," *Washington Post*, January 11, 2007, p. A25.

Ratner, Steven R., and Jason S. Abrams, *Accountability for Human Rights Atrocities in International Law*, Oxford: Oxford University Press, 1997.

Report of the International Commission of Inquiry for Darfur to the United Nations Secretary-General, Pursuant to Security Council Resolution 1564 of 18 September 2004, Geneva, 25 January 2005.

Robinson, Nehemiah. "The Genocide Convention: Its Origins and Interpretation," 1949, reprinted in *Case Western Reserve Journal of International Law*, vol. 40, nos. 1 and 2, 2007–8, appendix, pp. 1–75.

Rome Statute of the International Criminal Court, July 17, 1998, Article 6.

Rosenbaum, Alan S., editor. *Is the Holocaust Unique?* Boulder: Westview Press, 2001.

Rotberg, Robert I., and Dennis Thompson, editors. *Truth v. Justice*, Princeton: Princeton University Press, 2000.

Sadat, Leila. "Exile, Amnesty, and International Law, *Notre Dame Law Review*, vol. 81, no. 3, March 2006, pp. 955–1036.

Samuels, Shimon. "Applying the Lessons of the Holocaust," in *Is the Holocaust Unique?* edited by Alan S. Rosenbaum, Boulder: Westview Press, 2001, pp. 209–20.

Schabas, William. *Genocide in International Law*, New York: Cambridge University Press, 2000, 2nd edition, 2009.

The UN International Criminal Tribunals, New York: Cambridge University Press, 2006.

Scharf, Michael. *Balkan Justice*, Durham, NC: Carolina Academic Press, 1997.

"Swapping Amnesty for Peace: Was There a Duty to Prosecute International Crimes in Haiti? *Texas International Law Journal*, vol. 31, 1996, pp. 1–38.

Scheffer, David. "Atrocity Crimes Framing the Responsibility to Protect," *Case Western Reserve Journal of International Law*, vol. 40, nos. 1 & 2, 2007–8, pp. 111–35.

Searle, John. *The Construction of Social Reality*, New York: Free Press, 1995.

Shue, Henry. "Bombing to Rescue: NATO'S 1999 Bombing of Serbia," in *Ethics and Foreign Intervention*, edited by Dean Chatterjee and Don Sheid, New York: Cambridge University Press, 2003, pp. 97–117.

"Torture," *Philosophy & Public Affairs*, vol. 7 no. 2, Winter 1978, pp. 124–43.

Simester, A.P., and A.T.H. Smith. *Harm and Culpability*, Oxford: Oxford University Press, 1996.

Skinner, Quentin. "Hobbes and the Purely Artificial Person of the State," *Journal of Political Philosophy*, vol. 7, no. 1, 1999, pp. 1–29.

Slye, Ronald. "Amnesty, Truth, and Reconciliation: Reflections on the South African Amnesty Process," in *Truth v. Justice*, Princeton: Princeton University Press, 2000, pp. 170–88.

Smith, K.J.M. *A Modern Treatise on the Law of Criminal Complicity*, Oxford: Oxford University Press, 1991.

State v. Kudangirana 1976(3) SA 565 AT 566 PER Macdonald JP (AD).

Straub, Ervin. "The Psychology of Bystanders, Perpetrators, and Heroic Helpers," in Leonard S. Newman and Ralph Erber, editors, *Understanding Genocide*, New York: Oxford University Press, 2002, pp. 11–42.

Stromseth, Jane. "Rethinking Humanitarian Intervention," in *Humanitarian Intervention: Ethical, Legal, and Political Dilemmas*, edited by J.L. Holzgrefe and Robert O. Keohane, New York: Cambridge University Press, 2003, pp. 232–72.

Sumner, L. Wayne. "Incitement and the Regulation of Hate Speech," 2008, unpublished manuscript in the possession of the author.

Teson, Fernando. "The Liberal Case for Humanitarian Intervention," in *Humanitarian Intervention: Ethical, Legal, and Political Dilemmas*, edited by J.L. Holzgrefe and Robert O. Keohane, New York: Cambridge University Press, 2003, pp. 93–129.

Thompson, Jana. *Taking Responsibility for the Past*, Cambridge: Polity Press, 2002.

Thompson, Warren K. "Ethics, Evil, and the Final Solution," in *Echoes from the Holocaust*, edited by Alan Rosenberg and Gerald E. Myers, Philadelphia: Temple University Press, 1988, pp. 181–222.

The Trial of the Major War Criminals before the International Military Commission, Secretariat of the Tribunal, Nuremberg, 1948.

Tuomela, Raimo. *The Philosophy of Sociality: The Shared Point of View*, New York: Oxford University Press, 2007.

A Theory of Social Action, Dordrecht: D. Reidel, 1984.

Tutu, Desmond Mpilo. "Foreword" to Erin Daly and Jeremy Sarkin, *Reconciliation in Divided Societies*, Philadelphia: University of Pennsylvania Press, 2007, pp. ix–x.

United Nations General Assembly World Outcome Document, G.A. Res. A/RES/60/1, para. 139, U.N. Doc. A/RES/60/1 (Oct. 24, 2005).

Universal Declaration of Human Rights, U.N. G.A. Res. 217A, 3 U.N. GAOR, U.N. Doc. A/810, at 71 (1948).

Vattel, Emer de. *Le Droit des Gens, ou Principes de la Loi Naturelle* (The Laws of Nations or the Principles of Natural Law; 1758), Washington, DC: Carnegie Institute, 1916.

Vetlesen, Arne Johan. "Genocide: A Case for the Responsibility of Bystanders," in *Ethics, Nationalism, and Just War*, edited by Henrik Syse and Gregory M. Reichberg, Washington, DC: Catholic University of America Press, 2007, pp. 352–71.

Walker, Margaret. *Moral Repair: Reconstructing Moral Relations after Wrongdoing,* New York: Cambridge University Press, 2006.

Waller, James. *Becoming Evil: How Ordinary People Commit Genocide and Mass Killing,* New York: Oxford University Press, 2002.

Walzer, Michael. "The Moral Standing of States: A Response to Four Critics," *Philosophy & Public Affairs,* 1980, pp. 209–29.

Williams, Paul R., and Meghan E. Stewart. "Humanitarian Intervention: The New Missing Link in the Fight to Prevent Crimes against Humanity and Genocide?" *Case Western Reserve Journal of International Law,* vol. 40, nos. 1 & 2, 2007–8, pp. 97–110.

Index